ROUTLEDGE LIBRARY EDITIONS: PERCY SHELLEY

Volume 4

SHELLEY'S MUSIC

SHELLEY'S MUSIC
Fantasy, Authority, and the Object Voice

PAUL A. VATALARO

Routledge
Taylor & Francis Group
LONDON AND NEW YORK

First published in 2009 by Ashgate Publishing Limited

This edition first published in 2016
by Routledge
2 Park Square, Milton Park, Abingdon, Oxon OX14 4RN

and by Routledge
711 Third Avenue, New York, NY 10017

Routledge is an imprint of the Taylor & Francis Group, an informa business

© 2009 Paul A. Vatalaro

All rights reserved. No part of this book may be reprinted or reproduced or utilised in any form or by any electronic, mechanical, or other means, now known or hereafter invented, including photocopying and recording, or in any information storage or retrieval system, without permission in writing from the publishers.

Trademark notice: Product or corporate names may be trademarks or registered trademarks, and are used only for identification and explanation without intent to infringe.

British Library Cataloguing in Publication Data
A catalogue record for this book is available from the British Library

ISBN: 978-1-138-65476-1 (Set)
ISBN: 978-1-315-62261-3 (Set) (ebk)
ISBN: 978-1-138-64587-5 (Volume 4) (hbk)
ISBN: 978-1-138-64588-2 (Volume 4) (pbk)
ISBN: 978-1-315-62785-4 (Volume 4) (ebk)

Publisher's Note
The publisher has gone to great lengths to ensure the quality of this reprint but points out that some imperfections in the original copies may be apparent.

Disclaimer
The publisher has made every effort to trace copyright holders and would welcome correspondence from those they have been unable to trace.

Shelley's Music
Fantasy, Authority, and the Object Voice

PAUL A. VATALARO
Merrimack College, USA

ASHGATE

© Paul A. Vatalaro 2009

All rights reserved. No part of this publication may be reproduced, stored in a retrieval system or transmitted in any form or by any means, electronic, mechanical, photocopying, recording or otherwise without the prior permission of the publisher.

Paul A. Vatalaro has asserted his right under the Copyright, Designs and Patents Act, 1988, to be identified as the author of this work.

Published by
Ashgate Publishing Limited
Wey Court East
Union Road
Farnham
Surrey, GU9 7PT
England

Ashgate Publishing Company
Suite 420
101 Cherry Street
Burlington
VT 05401-4405
USA

www.ashgate.com

British Library Cataloguing in Publication Data
Vatalaro, Paul A.
　Shelley's music: fantasy, authority, and the object voice.
　1. Shelley, Percy Bysshe, 1792–1822 – Criticism and interpretation. 2. Music in literature. 3. Self in literature.
　I. Title
　821.7–dc22

Library of Congress Cataloging-in-Publication Data
Vatalaro, Paul A.
　Shelley's music: fantasy, authority, and the object voice / Paul A. Vatalaro.
　　p. cm.
　Includes bibliographical references and index.
　ISBN 978-0-7546-6233-4 (alk. paper)
　1. Shelley, Percy Bysshe, 1792–1822 – Criticism and interpretation. I. Title.
　PR5438.V28 2009
　821'.7–dc22

2009013491

ISBN 978-0-7546-6233-4
EISBN 978-0-7546-9459-5

Printed and bound in Great Britain by
TJ International Ltd, Padstow, Cornwall

Contents

List of Abbreviations   *vii*
Acknowledgements   *ix*

Introduction   1

1   Subjectivity and the Self-Present Voice   21

2   Poetic Authority and "Interpassivity"   43

3   Sounding the "Real"   95

4   Power, Desire and Poetics   147

Conclusion: Fantasy and Renunciation   187

Bibliography   *191*
Index   *197*

List of Abbreviations

CWWH	*The Complete Works of William Hazlitt*. Ed. P. P. Howe. 21 vols. New York: AMS P, 1967.
JMS	*The Journals of Mary Shelley: 1814–1844*. Ed. Paula R. Feldman and Diana Scott-Kilvert. Baltimore and London: The Johns Hopkins UP, 1987.
MWSL	*The Letters of Mary Wollstonecraft Shelley*. Ed. Betty T. Bennett. 3 vols. Baltimore and London: The Johns Hopkins UP, 1980–8.
MYR	*The Manuscripts of the Younger Romantics. Percy Bysshe Shelley. Fair Copy Manuscripts of Shelley's Poems in European and American Libraries*. Vol. 8. New York and London: Garland Publishing, 1997.
PBSL	*The Letters of Percy Bysshe Shelley*. Ed. Frederick L. Jones. 2 vols. Oxford: Clarendon P, 1964.
SPP	*Shelley's Poetry and Prose*. Ed. Donald H. Reiman and Neil Fraistat. New York and London: W. W. Norton & Company, 2002.
SPW	*Shelley's Poetical Works*. Ed. Thomas Hutchinson. Corr. G. M. Mathews. Oxford and New York: Oxford UP, 1970.

Acknowledgements

I would like to thank Marilyn Gaull and Adam Potkay for their valuable advice early on, and I remain grateful to William Keach, whose response to an early iteration of this project proved helpful right to the end. I am greatly indebted to Ann Donahue, my commissioning editor at Ashgate, for her unwavering support and to my anonymous reader at Ashgate, who reviewed my manuscript and pointed me in the right direction. Finally, I would like to thank Steven Scherwatzky, my friend and colleague at Merrimack, who has shepherded this project right from the very beginning.

Introduction

Music signals a fundamental division within Shelley's collective fantasy regarding the nature and purpose of human relationships and the nature and purpose of poetry. Often, music promises or confirms the formation of intimacy; regularly, however, it provokes the recognition of loss and of lacking; it accompanies moments of emptiness. In the "Hymn to Intellectual Beauty," for example, Shelley likens the unpredictable visitations of "unseen Power" to the "memory of music fled" (*SPP* 1, 10), but compares the sacred "light" offered by the "Spirit of BEAUTY" to animating "music by the night wind sent / Through strings of some still instrument" (*SPP* 13, 32–4). The "Hymn" expresses Shelley's frustration with this "Spirit's" inconstancy and with its apparent abandonment of intimacies he shared with it when he was "yet a boy" (*SPP* 49). In *Alastor*, the appearance of a "veiled maid" in the Poet's dream tantalizes him with the prospect of extraordinary fulfillment. The poem's narrator records that the maid speaks to the Poet in "low solemn tones, / Her voice ... like the voice of his own soul / ... its music long" (*SPP* 152–4). The sounds of her harp serenade him with a "strange symphony" of longing, and her sudden disappearance leaves him with a "vacant brain," surrounded by "vacant woods," as "His wan eyes / Gaze on the empty scene as vacantly / As ocean's moon looks on the moon in heaven" (*SPP* 191–202). The maid's overpowering psychosomatic effect on him resembles Laone's enchantment of Laon in *The Revolt of Islam*.

Addressing "restless multitudes" from atop her pyramidal altar, Laone bathes Laon's soul with a voice that is "like music of some minstrel heavenly gifted," filling it with calm and joy, but also with uneasiness; he confesses not wanting Laone's "veil to be uplifted" (*SPW* 2125–7). Though Laon doesn't identify the reason motivating his reaction, it seems likely he cannot accept the idea that his former protégée now wields the power of revolutionary expression to which he may no longer lay claim. To cite one additional example, in the essay "On Love" Shelley says that "when we are surrounded by human beings and they sympathise not with us," we turn to Nature and find "eloquence in the tongueless wind and a melody in the flowing of brooks and the rustling of the reeds beside them which by their inconceivable relation to something within the soul awaken the spirits to a dance of breathless rapture, and bring tears of mysterious tenderness to the eyes" (*SPP* 504). Unfortunately, however, Nature's ministries only remind us of something, some human treasure, lost but still desired: "the enthusiasm of patriotic success or the voice of one beloved singing to you alone" (*SPP* 504).

As these examples suggest, music images, allusions to music, and women who have musical gifts or qualities proliferate in Shelley's writing. This book sets out to identify and explore the fantasy construct that provides this textual feature of

Shelley's writing with collective purpose. Once exposed that fantasy will suggest that Shelley's fascination with music is symptomatic of a more deeply rooted issue, specifically the fear of estrangement from his own poetic voice. Ultimately, two things troubled him: first, that a man's poetic utterance, in stark contrast to a woman's singing performance, proceeds from vacancy rather than presence; second, that inscription remains silent and mortal, and that, in the end, written words do no more than constitute a non-speaking subject.

Scholars who initiated consideration of music's significance in Shelley's poetry took a mostly biographical approach to the issue. Neville Rogers, for example, writes that the Great Marlow period of 1817 represented a watershed moment in Shelley's development with respect to music's influence on him. During that time the Shelley household bustled with artistic activity. Percy, Mary, Claire and their children spent musical evenings with the Hunts and Novellos singing to the accompaniment of a new piano they had purchased. Leigh Hunt was an accomplished singer and became an important reviewer of the London opera, and Vincent Novello was one of the founding members of the London Philharmonic Society. At this time, Claire's singing voice filled the Shelley home, as she received voice instruction. The Shelleys attended the London opera with Peacock, who introduced them to Mozart, among other composers. In Rogers's estimation, these experiences, especially listening to Claire practice her scales and perform, eventually found expression in *Prometheus Unbound*.[1]

In an essay devoted to musical themes in Shelley's mature poetry, Jean L. De Palacio amplifies the claims made by Rogers, asserting that Shelley's personal circumstances of 1817 not only encouraged him to associate music with spiritual matters, but to forge a link between it and woman. "In Shelley's poetry," Palacio writes, "music always is the intimation of something beyond. As woman is more than her flesh and blood appearance, so Music outdoes the strings which tingle it out, and the song is more than the lips that tell it ... His ideas on music remained much the same throughout his life."[2] Palacio's essay supports Rogers's belief that witnessing Claire's singing performances affected Shelley profoundly.

Full-length studies of Romantic poets by Erland Anderson and Lawrence Kramer extend the inquiry initiated by Rogers and Palacio to include the influence of nineteenth-century aesthetics. Anderson's book argues that Shelley's philosophical interest in music as a metaphor of ideal love and visionary experience wound up surfacing structurally and stylistically in his poetry. It contends that Shelley came to view music as a medium capable of capturing but also representing intense feeling and fluid sensation, particularly when stimuli overload them.[3] Perhaps frequenting

---

[1] Neville Rogers, "More Music at Marlow," *Keats-Shelley Memorial Bulletin* 5 (1953): 24.

[2] Jean L. De Palacio, "Music and Musical Themes in Shelley's Poetry," *Modern Language Review* 59 (1964): 357.

[3] Erland Anderson, *Harmonious Madness: A Study of Musical Metaphors in the Poetry of Coleridge, Shelley and Keats* (Salzburg: Institut fur Sprache und Literatur, U of

the opera fostered the formation of this perspective in Shelley's mind. Anderson and Theodore Fenner each write that during the early part of the nineteenth century, the prima donna dominated the London opera scene.[4] Performances by the day's star singers might have reinforced what Shelley had witnessed in the more intimate setting of his own home whenever Claire sang.

Kramer's study places Shelley's philosophical fascination with music's apparent transcendent qualities within an effort by nineteenth-century writers and composers to explore the longstanding perception that music and poetry are the most closely related of all the arts. Kramer observes that some artists working in each medium gravitated toward the idea that subjects and objects remain fluid and transitive in time rather than fixed and static, making them capable of intermingling. Because of their temporal nature, poetry and music emerge as perfect metaphors and transmitters of this process. When one listens to a melody or audits a poem, writes Kramer, that person recognizes that "what I hear, unlike what I see or touch, is not set over against me; it is set *into* my consciousness, mixed into my reflexive awareness of my own presence."[5] Kramer believes Shelley was particularly struck by this notion of "transitivity," so much so that it surfaces throughout his work:

> Shelley regards the transit of identity as intrinsically musical, and he consistently gives it musical representation, from the early lyric "To Constantia, Singing," to the group of poems written to Jane Williams at the end of his life. A basic role of music in his work—probably the primary role—is to provide a concrete middle term between an identity disrupted and an identity revived.[6]

Ronald Tetreault and Jessica Quillin narrow the conversation by elucidating parallels between *Prometheus Unbound* and the opera of Mozart and Rossini. Tetreault connects Shelley's interest in the transformative properties of music to "the growing opinion in revolutionary Europe that awakening a sensitivity to beauty might open an avenue to moral receptivity and so pave the way for political liberty."[7] Consequently, the structure and dramatic development of action Shelley conceived for *Prometheus Unbound*, says Tetreault, owes more to Mozart than it does Greek tragedy:

> Though dramatic in structure, it is lyrical in its communication of the inward life of the human spirit. Since Shelley's play depicts an inner drama of spiritual transformation, it is best understood as unfolding not by means of legitimate

---

Salzburg, 1975).

[4] Theodore Fenner, *Leigh Hunt and Opera Criticism* (Lawrence: UP of Kansas, 1972).

[5] Lawrence Kramer, *Music and Poetry: The Nineteenth Century and After* (Berkeley: U of California P, 1984) 98.

[6] Kramer 118.

[7] Ronald Tetreault, "Shelley at the Opera," *ELH* 48 (1981): 145.

drama but according to the conventions of opera, in which, not action, but the quality of an action, the intensity of the moment, is elaborated musically.[8]

Tetreault's approach moves the discussion of Shelley's music away from its prior concentration on trope and theme to music as a structural and stylistic feature of his writing. Quillin sharpens the resolution even more by looking closely at the opera buffa tradition. She notes the traditional split between recitative and lyrical/ musical forms of expression and contends that Shelley structured his lyrical drama along these lines, with recitative and lyric alternating within Act I and Act II and between Acts III and IV. Resonant with Tetreault's, her point is that in opera Shelley saw the opportunity to use music to push beyond the limits of language in order to represent the true revolutionary nature of the kind of cosmic transformation he had in mind. Music in opera does not always advance dramatic action. Often, music deepens the action and it deepens character. "Ultimately," Quillin says,

> the poetic form of Shelley's *Prometheus Unbound* demonstrates the poet's ability to combine music and poetry to create a mental drama that is nonetheless radically performative. Utilizing music as a dramatic tool, Shelley's operatic employment of discursive and lyrical language and his opera-like methods of characterization all coalesce in a project that strains the limits of poetic form into the realm of musical drama.[9]

Another article by Quillin argues for taking a historicized approach to the significance of music in the personal lyrics Shelley wrote during the Great Marlow period. She claims that all the Romantic poets would have been familiar with the writings of Rousseau, Monboddo and others who insisted that music and speech—hence "sung poetry"—formed the earliest roots of language. Shelley, she says, linked poetry to music, emotion, imagination and love.[10] Echoing Kramer's discussion of the confluence of music and poetry in the nineteenth century, Quillin posits that Shelley, as other poets of his period, "depends upon a fictionalized historical account of music. I define this account as 'pseudo-historical' and show that it is appropriated from an aesthetics in which music and poetry are functionally and ideologically interdependent."[11]

---

[8] Tetreault 152.

[9] Jessica K. Quillin, "'An Assiduous Frequenter of the Italian Opera:' Shelley's *Prometheus Unbound* and the Opera Buffa." Opera and Romanticism-Praxis Series. *Romantic Circles*, www.re.umd.edu/praxis/opera/quillin/quillin.htm: 12.

[10] Jessica K. Quillin, "Shelleyan Lyricism and the Romantic Historicization of Musical Aesthetics," *Keats-Shelley Journal* 54 (2005): 139. For an earlier discussion of Monboddo's influence on Shelley, see Stuart Peterfreund, "Shelley, Monboddo, Vico, and the Language of Poetry," *Style* 15 (1981): 382–400.

[11] Quillin, "Shelleyan Lyricism" 134.

Broadening the definition of music leads to an offshoot of this line of inquiry. It involves the substance and operation of Shelley's lyricism, or what might be called the "music" of his style. This subsidiary approach consists largely of phonological analyses of his poetic language, examining the rhetorical effects of meter, rhyme and other sonic elements of Shelley's writing. Chris Foss, for example, argues that Shelley's dissatisfaction with the constitution of the third, originally final, act of *Prometheus Unbound* led Shelley to conceive of a dramatic supplement that would enact, rather than reduce to narrative, Shelley's vision of the rejuvenated cosmos. According to Foss, Shelley came to realize that the decision to represent his vision in conventional terms would only consolidate the binding power of the very interpretive conventions he wished to puncture, therefore undermining his revolutionary aims. To mitigate the impact of Act III, Shelley composed a radically different conclusion for the play—a fourth act—that successfully deploys phonic and stylistic features capable of disrupting conventional syntax and grammar and reaching readers along non-cognitive channels.[12] "It is possible, then," Foss points out, "to see *Prometheus* as a poetic expression of Shelley's position in 'On Life' and the *Defence*, of how poetry (with its attunement to processes which reveal the arbitrariness of thought-constructions) can liberate humankind from the error of denotative certainty and open people instead to the freedom of possibility."[13]

Susan Wolfson explores what she believes constitutes Shelley's intuitive awareness of the poet's ultimate inability to shape the social reception of his own work, whether he "projects" a public or private audience. She writes:

> Thus, while his defense of poetry deems it "vitally metaphorical" in the way it "marks" previously "unapprehended relations," his practice as poet senses that its forms cannot ultimately legislate reading by their marks, and that other self-devitalizing relations, unapprehended in the poet's conception, may evolve in the convergence of text and reader that brings a poet's work into existence.[14]

---

[12] Chris Foss, "Shelley's Revolution in Poetic Language," *European Romantic Review* 9 (1998): 501–18. Foss's interpretation builds on the work of Barbara Gelpi, who approaches *Prometheus Unbound* from the perspective that a culturally induced "mother-centeredness" drove Shelley to reject the language of patriarchy and search for the "core point" of the "mother's immanence in language." Gelpi's reading of Act IV includes an examination of Shelley's manipulation of phonics as a way of pushing beyond the limitations imposed by masculine language structures. See *Shelley's Goddess* (New York and Oxford: Oxford UP, 1992).

[13] Foss 504.

[14] Susan Wolfson, *Formal Charges: The Shaping of Poetry in British Romanticism* (Stanford: Stanford UP, 1997) 195. Wolfson's study amplifies work done earlier by her colleague William Keach, who also focuses on the rhetorically charged aspects of Shelley's final poems, in which words converge with deeds. For Keach's reading of the Jane Williams lyrics, see *Shelley's Style* (New York and London: Methuen, 1984).

Wolfson singles out the personal lyrics Shelley devoted to Jane Williams as, paradoxically, "the most intensely social of Shelley's poems" and draws attention to the performative qualities of Shelley's lyrical language, through which he endeavors to manage a socially and rhetorically unstable situation, establishing self-possession while unleashing desire through poetry.[15] In Wolfson's view, Shelley counted on the poems being read to Jane (chiefly by her husband, Edward, whose voice Shelley's stylistic choices would control) or by Jane. Jane's recitation of the poems would marry her voice to the words, rhythm and rhymes Shelley chose for her. She notes, for example, that many of the lyrics employ hard *a* rhymes, chiming out by implication Jane's name, even when she is not directly mentioned. Effects such as this one create what Wolfson calls a "phonic field."[16] Viewed from this perspective, it would appear that these poems mark Shelley's struggle to exert his will and his vision through the sounds of his words, especially when they take shape in the mouths of others.

A conceptual link emerges between this strain of criticism, which concentrates, generally speaking, on Shelley's interest in manipulating the reception of his words by conducting the voices of his readers, and another strain of scholarship that explores issues concerning vocal authority and voice management. Two of these studies adopt a feminist critical perspective.[17] Laura Claridge, for example, includes Shelley in her study of canonical male Romantic writers. These poets, she contends, prefer the Lacanian "imaginary" to the Lacanian "real," because the imaginary "represents the realm of that illusory fullness of the primal union with the mother."[18] Moreover, they share one "key to desire," that is, "the radical and humanly unsatisfiable yearning of the infant for the lost Eden of a unified self, before the advent of symbolic organization."[19] Claridge believes that Shelley and his contemporaries were drawn to questions involving originality and issues concerning self-creation through poetry. Self-construction, after all, depends on a medium, language, that preexists and necessarily dictates, therefore, individuality. Construction of self through writing, in other words, necessitates "borrowing another's tongue."[20] This agenda projects their work into the realm of paradox, since they end up attempting the impossible: "to transcend the medium of words

---

[15] Wolfson 206, 226.

[16] Wolfson 209.

[17] Though I am singling out studies that focus primarily on the nature and potency of voice, more general approaches to the politics governing the relationship between masculine and feminine expression can be found in Anne K. Mellor, *Romanticism and Gender* (New York and London: Routledge, 1993); Anne K. Mellor, ed., *Romanticism and Feminism* (Bloomington: Indiana UP, 1988); Margaret Homans, *Women Writers and Poetic Identity* (Princeton: Princeton UP, 1980).

[18] Laura Claridge, *Romantic Potency: The Paradox of Desire* (Ithaca and London: Cornell UP, 1992) 8.

[19] Claridge 3.

[20] Claridge 3.

and reach that original paradise of silence—but with their voices intact. The poets desire more than they can speak, but their 'impotence,' their inability to escape language, ensures the life and infinity—the potency—of their art."[21] With regard to Shelley in particular, she says, the idea that he

> wants to locate thought anterior to language is, in fact, the desire that I find motivating his poetry. The pleasure he occasionally takes in exposing logocentrism results from the boon to poetry if an originary truth cannot be unveiled: desire can then never be fully articulated, and thus "all high poetry" will be ensured infinite life.[22]

In her essay on *Alastor*, Susan Fischman claims that Shelley consciously harbored misgivings about the potential power of feminine modes of expression. She underscores the importance of reading the poem as a reworking of the Narcissus and Echo myth, arguing that Shelley saw in Ovid's story a vehicle for exploring his own ambivalence toward the power of the female voice. Fischman proposes that the veiled maid should be regarded as a "dreamt poet," because she not only serves as a projection of the wandering Poet's mind, but she becomes a foreign and dangerous poetic agent in her own right.[23] The maid's appearance in the Poet's dream parallels Echo's appearance before Narcissus, except that the maid, herself a poet, initiates the exchange. This feature, asserts Fischman, reflects Shelley's wish to spellbind a captive audience. While speaking in the voice of the Poet's own soul, however, the maid's discourse graduates to a point at which it no longer echoes his but articulates her own aural range and agenda. The poem's narrator counters the threat by reducing the dreamt poet to natural phenomena, thereby locking her in between the realms of nature and culture (a fate that recalls Echo's dissolution in the Ovid story) and maintaining Shelley's interests at a safe distance in the form of the poem's narrative frame.[24] *Alastor* presents a dichotomy, therefore, in which the female voice and female vocal initiative is marveled over as much as it is feared. Fischman concludes: "if the narrator has succeeded in presenting a 'didactic' tale, a story whose mission is to warn its audience of the dangers inherent in women speaking, and in man listening to her, he has also succeeded ... in celebrating the powers of man's speech."[25]

Finally, I would like to include under this same subcategory Andrew Bennett's *Romantic Poets and the Culture of Posterity*, even though it is not about music or voice per se. The book deals primarily with issues involving the Romantic poet's effort to preserve his identity. His discussion of this agenda, however, indirectly

---

[21] Claridge 2.
[22] Claridge 26.
[23] Susan Fischman, "'Like the Sound of His Own Voice': Gender, Audition, and Echo in *Alastor*," *Keats Shelley Journal* 43 (1994): 144–5.
[24] Fischman 146–7.
[25] Fischman 167.

concerns the constitution of authority and the poet's imposition of his voice—traditionally, that most basic expression of identity—on his passive auditor. Though Bennett looks at what distinguishes male from female Romantic writers with respect to this issue, his study stands apart from those conducted by Claridge and Fischman, because he shifts the point of concentration away from gender politics. Bennett examines the cultural shift that took place in the early nineteenth century with regard to the poet's conception of reputation, identity and audience, arguing that eighteenth-century writers believed great literature would survive beyond a given historical moment and would preserve indefinitely the writer's genius. An important shift in perspective occurred, though, when Romantic writers developed what Bennett calls a "culture of posterity."[26]

The phrase refers to the Romantic writer's belief that the poetic genius and his work must be neglected in their own time. Compensation comes by way of the survival of the writer's identity through his words in the future, a self-inscription in which the poet lives not just through words on the page but within the minds of his readers, his words occupying the reader's consciousness. In this way, according to Bennett, the culture of posterity for the Romantic poet involves the composition of identity through writing, but also the dissolution of that identity by way of a text that will live on into the future. Different from earlier periods when poets valued posthumous reception and recognition, the Romantics were interested in the survival of the identity of the writer himself, implicitly speaking through the poet's agential reader. Applying this interpretation to Shelley, Bennett avers that "the fiction of posthumous writing" takes the form of a haunting, a ghostliness, a constantly "deferred reception" in which the writer's identity and consciousness are delivered by way of his words and measures and come back to life in the minds and bodies of readers, the poet haunting that reader as a ghostly presence—there, but also not there.[27]

Though the approaches in this body of scholarship range from biographical and historical to feminist and psychoanalytic, the majority of the treatments assume that Shelley's fascination with the substance and power of music resulted from conscious efforts to bring his aesthetic and social agendas to fruition. All of the studies focusing specifically on music or on musical style, furthermore, attribute these phenomena to the social, philosophical, aesthetic and political atmospheres in which Shelley composed. Two considerations of Shelley's struggles with issues involving vocal authority, those done by Claridge and Fischman, underscore the function of gender politics in his aesthetic agenda. My aim is to draw all three critical strands into closer proximity with one another, conceiving of voice and music as correlative components of a fantasy narrative that consistently recycles itself throughout Shelley's writing, and assuming that Shelley's fascination with voice and music interacts with a larger cultural fantasy that sexualizes human

---

[26] Andrew Bennett, *Romantic Poets and the Culture of Posterity* (Cambridge: Cambridge UP, 1999).

[27] Bennett 169.

expression. Though Shelley might have recognized the more prominent contours of this fantasy profile along the horizon of his awareness, it is unlikely that he understood that profile in detail and, from a Lacanian perspective, it might make no difference even if he had achieved that level of awareness.

Chapter 1 provides a detailed discussion of the Lacanian concepts on which I have grounded this study, but for the purposes of introduction I would like to provide here a brief overview of them, particularly the idea of fantasy. By and large, tradition regards fantasy as a wish for something forbidden or made impossible to acquire under normal circumstances—a hallucinatory indulgence of desires prohibited by law. Zizek tells us, however, that fantasy supports and sets the coordinates for the ordinary, symbolic state of existence. It serves as "the primordial form of *narrative*, which serves to occult some original deadlock."[28] In the case of Shelley's fascination with music, vocality and feminine expression, the deadlock becomes an ontological one, because it involves the possibility that no poet, that no subject for that matter, achieves self-presence through writing. In addition, it involves the possibility that the human voice fails to reflect self-presence, though it paradoxically constitutes the Lacanian subject as an object in which the subject sees, or in this case hears, and, therefore, defines itself. Finally, the fantasy that surfaces in Shelley's writing traces its lineage to a cultural deadlock, manifest in metaphysical tradition, that has divorced masculine and feminine expression, associating the former with logos and the word, the latter with voice, music and *jouissance*.[29] Though the fantasy inherent to metaphysical tradition for the most part insists on the separation as a way of preserving masculine power, Shelley transforms that metaphysical model into a medium for integrating voice, music and *jouissance* with word and logos, in the end conflating living presence with language.

Anamorphically, this approach to Shelley's music supplements existing explanations as to why Shelley consistently associates music with woman. Additionally, it provides an explanation regarding why he links music to loss, absence, vacancy and even death. Bereft of its object voice, the subject fails to achieve meaningful articulation or inscription. According to Zizek, "fantasy, at its most elementary, is inaccessible to the subject and it is this inaccessibility which makes the subject 'empty.'"[30] If fantasy were accessible, in other words, the subject would soon have to face the possibility that nothing exists inside; fantasy comforts the subject by convincing him or her that negation itself is an illusion. Zizek indicates that it is impossible for the subject to see through, to "traverse," the fantasies that channel his or her desires and imbricate them within the symbolic framework of which reality consists.

---

[28] Slavoj Zizek, *The Plague of Fantasies* (London and New York: Verso, 1997) 10.

[29] Mladen Dolar, "The Object Voice," *Gaze and Voice as Love Objects*, ed. Renata Salecl and Slavoj Zizek (Durham and London: Duke UP, 1996) 7–31

[30] Zizek, *Plague* 122.

To illustrate his point, Zizek refers to an advertising campaign for suntan lotion "depicting a series of well-tanned women's behinds in tight bathing suits, accompanied by the slogan 'Each has her own factor.'"[31] The slogan implies, he says, that each woman has her own unique sexual catalyst and can be had by the man who discovers it: "The Freudian point regarding fundamental fantasy would be that each subject, female or male, possesses such a 'factor' which regulates her or his desire."[32] He concludes, however, that even if the subject were to discover this fact about him or herself, "such awareness can never be subjectivized; it is uncanny—even horrifying—since it somehow 'dispossesses' the subject, reducing her or him to a puppet-like level 'beyond dignity and freedom.'"[33] If music, particularly that which inheres within feminine expression and is related to the irrecoverable lost voice, constitutes Shelley's "factor," Zizek's comment suggests that it would have done Shelley little good to have recognized its hold over him. This interpretation might explain why, moreover, the "phantasmic," or fantasy, pattern repeats itself regardless of genre or year composed, and why Shelley never achieved his goal.

Other than Jessica Quillin's work, no other new studies of Shelley's music have appeared. Furthermore, Ghislaine McDayter is the only recent scholar to have approached Shelley's writing from a Lacanian perspective. McDayter examines Shelley's iteration of unification fantasies in which the desiring poet or poetic speaker seeks to fill the void within himself, eliminating loss by uniting with a feminine other—what contemporary feminist critical readings regard as a colonization or appropriation of the feminine. McDayter argues, however, that Shelley's poetry, specifically *Epipsychidion* (with groundwork laid in *Alastor*), expresses not a desire for unification, for blissful, paradisiacal oneness, but for a reenactment, or retrieval, of the moment of castration, because that is the moment that makes subjectivity and desire possible in the first place. To become one with Emily means to suffer a loss of subjectivity in fluid oneness and no longer to desire. It also means an end to authority over language. The real fantasy for Shelley, according to McDayter, then, involves suspension at the very moment of castration, the point at which a person experiences subjectivity and desire. "Far from indulging in fantasies of a return to a maternal, unfallen, and undivided state," as Gelpi and, to some extent, Claridge maintain, "Shelley recognized that 'the fall' and division from such a realm was essential for the birth of desire and thus for creation itself,"[34] writes McDayter. She concludes, "Shelley's poetic fantasy is thus rather more complex than the critical tradition has imagined. If *Epipsychidion*

---

[31] Zizek, *Plague* 7.
[32] Zizek, *Plague* 8.
[33] Zizek, *Plague* 8.
[34] Ghislaine McDayter, "'O'er Leaping the Bounds': The Sexing of the Creative Soul in Shelley's *Epipsychidion*," *Keats-Shelley Journal* 52 (2003): 26.

establishes the *mise en scene* of an Edenic union as the site of its fantasy, it does so only to repeatedly re-enact a fall or descent from its harmonious bliss."[35]

The strength of McDayter's approach is that it does not reduce the particular Shelleyan fantasy it identifies to the level of personal pathology. Zizek's reading of the composer Schumann's relationship with his beloved Clara employs a similar perspective and serves as a model for interpreting Shelley's relationship with all forms of feminine expression and expressive females. Schumann's correspondence with Clara, observes Zizek, reveals that he wanted her close to him, while at the same time that he "dreaded" her:

> this split in Schumann, this radical oscillation between attraction and repulsion, between longing for the distant beloved and feeling estranged and repelled by her proximity, by no means exposes a "pathological" imbalance within his psyche: such an oscillation is constitutive of human desire, so that the true enigma is, rather, how a "normal" subject succeeds in covering it up and negotiating a fragile balance between the sublime image of the beloved and her real presence, so that the flesh-and-blood person can continue to occupy the sublime place and avoid the sad fate of turning into a repulsive excrement.[36]

The same ambivalence appears in Shelley's writing, whether the relationship portrayed is fictional, as in the case of Lionel and Helen, as one example, or actual, as in the case of Shelley and Jane Williams, as another. In addition, Shelley faced the same outcome with regard to his own subjectivity. If the voice he heard inside his head was not the self-present manifestation of identity common sense claimed it was, that same voice, then, would become a lost and foreign object and the subject poet it nonetheless constituted would emerge as "repulsive excrement."

Psychoanalytic interpretations of Shelley's writing have become rare, however. The bulk of the most recent scholarship devoted to Shelley is overwhelmingly historicist in its orientation. Terence Hoagwood's review of three recent books supports this observation, claiming that critics now focus on the "political Shelley of historical fact."[37] Contemporary treatments may be subdivided into three categories: historicist readings that examine the intertextual dialogue between Shelley's poetry and other forms of expression from the eighteenth and nineteenth centuries; historicist readings that elucidate the intertextual dialogue between Shelley's poems and those written by his contemporaries, as well as those composed by previous generations; historicist readings that illuminate the dialogue between Shelley's poetry and the political, religious, philosophical, aesthetic and material conditions of his age.

---

[35] McDayter 32.
[36] Zizek, *Plague* 67.
[37] Terence Hoagwood, rev. of Colbert *Shelley's Eye*, by Benjamin Colbert; *Shelley and the Revolutionary Sublime*; by Cian Duffy; *Shelley and Vitality*, by Sharon Ruston, *The Wordsworth Circle* 37 (Autumn 2006): 252.

Examples from the first category include studies by Colbert, Duffy, Peterfreund, Brzezinski Potkay, Clarke and Harrison.[38] Colbert explores Shelley's engagement with contemporary travel writings and his inclination toward problematizing the function of reflexivity—that is, the traveler's eye seeing itself in its observations—"by considering the ways in which perception and expression are implicated in the cultural conditioning of the age as well as the ways in which a truly authentic and revolutionary aesthetic might be forged to fit the needs of post-revolutionary Europe."[39] Duffy challenges the longstanding assumption that Shelley would have been familiar with Kant's philosophy of the transcendental ideal through Kant's writing, arguing "that the connection between the sublime and the revolutionary in Shelley's work is the product of a lifelong, skeptical engagement with the eighteenth-century British discourse on the natural sublime."[40]

Peterfreund situates Shelley's theory of language within eighteenth-century language theory and the two traditions that intersected within it: the discourse of rhetoric from Plato onward and the ideas of seventeenth-century "New Philology."[41] According to Peterfreund, Shelley believed that poetic language is originary and metaphorical, that it comes before prose and metonym, and that, when it inevitably devolves to lesser forms, it requires renewal. Peterfreund claims that Shelley's skepticism underwrites his language theory not simply in the post-structuralist sense that all writing is somehow self-referential, self-conscious of itself and about itself, but in the sense that Shelley remains aware of the mind's tendency to metonymize, to elide the distinction between a perception of a divine harmony and a belief that what the poet has perceived constitutes divine harmony.

The three essays by Brzezinski Potkay, Clarke and Colbert focus on the intertextuality of *The Cenci*. Brzezinski Potkay concentrates on Shelley's adaptation of images, themes and structures from the Bible, The Nicene Creed and the poetry of Dante and Milton in order to transmit an anti-Christian message in the play. Shelley, she points out, burlesques some of Christianity's most fundamental concepts, such as the idea of the trinity, though he does so from inside rather than outside the faith, relying on his own Christian orientation. Clarke observes that elements of *The Cenci* resonate with female slave narratives that were beginning to

---

[38] Benjamin Colbert, *Shelley's Eye: Travel Writing and Aesthetic Vision* (Aldershot: Ashgate, 2005); Cian Duffy, *Shelley and the Revolutionary Sublime* (Cambridge: Cambridge UP, 2005); Stuart Peterfreund, *Shelley Among Others* (Baltimore and London: The Johns Hopkins UP, 2002); Monica Brzezinski Potkay, "Incest as Theology in Shelley's *The Cenci*," *The Wordsworth Circle* 35 (Spring 2004): 57–65; George Elliott Clarke, "Racing Shelley, or Reading *The Cenci* as a Gothic Slave Narrative," *European Romantic Review* 11 (Spring 2000): 168–85; Margot Harrison, "No Way for a Victim to Act? Beatrice Cenci and the Dilemma of Romantic Performance," *Studies in Romanticism* 39 (Summer 2000): 187–211.

[39] Colbert 9.

[40] Duffy, *Shelley and the Revolutionary Sublime* 7.

[41] Peterfreund 17.

emerge "in the early nineteenth-century Black Atlantic world," and he asserts that the play's "ideational content" raises the issue of whether or not "the oppressed may employ violence virtuously—to oppress their oppressors."[42] Finally, Harrison examines ways in which *The Cenci* expresses Shelley's ambivalence with regard to the nature of acting, participating, therefore, in a debate fuelled by Diderot, Godwin and others.

The second subdivision, which explores Shelley's engagement with the work of other poets and other poems, even his own, includes treatments by O'Neill, Hubbell, Schmid, Roussetzki, Randel and Ferber.[43] O'Neill illuminates dialogic connections between *Adonais*, Coleridge's "The Aeolian Harp," Arnold's "The Scholar Gypsy," and aspects of Byron's *Childe Harold's Pilgrimage*. The achievement of Shelley's poem, O'Neill concludes, is in its presentation of the expressive imagination's struggle to transfigure the world without resorting to despotism. Randel also sees an intertextual link between Shelley, Coleridge and Dante, suggesting that Shelley remodeled the work of other poets in order to advocate political change by conveying poetic truths. With regard to Coleridge, who Shelley saw as a representative of high culture and traditionalism, for example, Shelley in *Lines written among the Euganean Hills* responds to *The Rime of the Ancient Mariner* by articulating "a perspective of radical traditionalism, which extracts 'new fires from antique light.'"[44]

Hubbell reads *Laon and Cythna* as a response to Wordsworth's *The Excursion*, disputing the traditional assumption that Wordsworth and Shelley represented successive literary generations. He suggests that the issue of how to break free of post-Revolutionary conditions, in which one form of failure and oppression quickly replaced another, perplexed both poets. Roussetzki's discussion of *The Cenci* shifts attention away from Shelley's interaction with sociopolitical and aesthetic discourse, the points of emphasis for Brzezinski Potkay, Clarke and Harrison, and explores Shelley's departure in the play from the Elizabethan tradition of tragedy in which the hero wears the signs of physical and spiritual corruption visibly on stage and his implementation of a theater of anxiety, in which the outward form of

---

[42] Clarke 174.

[43] Michael O'Neill, "*Adonais* and Poetic Power," *The Wordsworth Circle* 35 (Spring 2004): 50–7; Andrew J. Hubbell, "*Laon and Cythna*: A Vision of Regency Romanticism," *Keats-Shelley Journal* 51 (2002): 174–97; Thomas Schmid, "'England Yet Sleeps': Intertextuality, Nationalism, and Risorgimento in Percy Bysshe Shelley's *Swellfoot the Tyrant*," *Keats-Shelley Journal* 53 (2004): 61–84; Remy Roussetzki, "Aggravating Shakespeare: Endless Violence in Shelley's and in Musset's Theater of Anxiety," *European Romantic Review* 15 (2004): 493–510; Fred V. Randel, "Shelley's Revision of Coleridgean Traditionalism in *Lines Written Among the Euganean Hills*," *Keats-Shelley Journal* 52 (2003): 50–76; Michael Ferber, "Shelley and the Disastrous Fame of Conquerors," *Keats-Shelley Journal* 51 (2002): 145–73.

[44] Randel 52.

the Romantic hero remains seemingly untouched, invulnerably beautiful, on the outside, but tortured and torn unspeakably within.

Schmid makes a case for reading "Ode to Naples," "Ode to Liberty" and *Swellfoot the Tyrant* as Shelley's "intertextually related" response to the "declaration of constitutionality in Spain," the resistances in Naples and Sicily, and the emergence of slim hope for constitutional reform in England. Shelley worried that the Queen Caroline affair, in which "Caroline Brunswick returned to England to claim her rights as Queen (only to be tried for adultery by her duplicitous husband)" was suffocating that hope.[45] Schmid maintains that Shelley uses images of sleeping and waking to represent responsive recognition of Liberty's success at various locations in Europe and suggests that Shelley believed the Caroline scandal had lulled England to sleep, distracting its citizens from the real struggles for liberty and reform in Naples, Spain and Sicily. Finally, Ferber investigates Shelley's ambivalence toward the concept of glory. He shows that Shelley clung to the ideals of republican reform and endorsed the virtues of Christian pacifism in his own war against tyranny's perversion of a true glory based on love, liberty and justice. However, as much as Shelley embraced the idea of reform and wished to celebrate the sacrifices of fallen heroes and martyrs, the tendency among many of the great poets in Western culture to glorify violence troubled him.

Historicist readings that highlight Shelley's interaction with the political, religious, philosophical, aesthetic and material currents of his age are too numerous for me to summarize here. Studies published by Ruston, Molinari, Fraistat, Keach and Chandler, however, might provide an adequate sampling of what this body of scholarship offers.[46] I would add to this group an article by Gillen D'Arcy Wood that focuses on opera and the Hunt Circle, because the discussion provides such a fine portrait of the politics behind the London opera scene and therefore bears,

---

[45] Schmid 63.

[46] Sharon Ruston, *Shelley and Vitality* (Basingstoke: Palgrave Macmillan, 2005); Lori Molinari, "Revising the Revolution: the Festival of Unity and Shelley's 'Beau Ideal.'" *Keats-Shelley Journal* 53 (2004): 97–126; Neil Fraistat, "The Material Shelley: Who Gets the Finger in *Queen Mab*?" *The Wordsworth Circle* 33 (Winter 2002): 33–6; William Keach, *Arbitrary Power: Romanticism, Language, Politics* (Princeton: Princeton UP, 2004); James Chandler, *England in 1819: The Politics of Literary Culture and the Case of Romantic Historicism* (Chicago: U of Chicago P, 1998). Other works representing this critical approach include the following: Eric Glenn Wilson, "Shelley and the Poetics of Glaciers," *The Wordsworth Circle* 36 (Spring 2005): 53–6; Nancy Goslee, "Shelley's Cosmopolitan 'Discourse': Ancient Greek Manners and Modern Liberty," *The Wordsworth Circle* 36 (Winter 2005): 2–5; Mark Lussier, "Shelley's Poetics, Wave Dynamics, and the Telling Rhythm of Complementarity," *The Wordsworth Circle* 34 (Spring 2003): 91–5; Andrew M. Stouffer, "Celestial Temper: Shelley and the Masks of Anger," *Keats-Shelley Journal* 49 (2000): 138–61.

though indirectly, on the subject of Shelley's experience of attending Mozart performances and socializing with Hunt's friends and colleagues.[47]

Ruston establishes Shelley's friendship with the physician David Lawrence and his membership in a circle of skeptics who opposed Abernathy's claims in the vitality debate that life is superadded to the body. Lawrence and his supporters argued that life, while remaining a mystery, derives from a combination of physiological functions all working together. According to Ruston, Shelley not only followed the vitality debate, but he knew it intimately and used some of its language in his poetry. She contends that much of Shelley's writing should be read in the context of the vitality debate, noting that, while its features clearly inform his writing, his writing also contributes to the conversation.

Molinari's article "Revising the Revolution" searches out sources for the Canto V festival that appears in *Laon and Cythna*. It concludes that the French festival called the Reunion, which occurred on August 10, 1793, emerges as the most likely source for Shelley's poem. Molinari examines Shelley's adaptation of the fete's iconography to demonstrate that Shelley altered the historical images to convey his own idea of the ideal revolution and to convey where the French model went wrong. Fraistat's "The Material Shelley" investigates Shelley's relationship to the materiality of his texts, specifically the eight indicator hands that appear, facing away from the text, in the margins of the notes to *Queen Mab*. Fraistat opens this critical line in the context of evidence suggesting that Shelley had taken an interest in typesetting and might have installed the marks to suggest a collaborator for the incendiary philosophical and politically charged notes to the poem. Fraistat uses Zizek's *The Plague of Fantasies* to raise the possibility that the indicator hands might be read as indicative of Shelley's development as a poet, initially representing the paranoid distance of the subversive, but ultimately confirming Shelley's entrapment by the very cultural apparatus he has no power to overturn.

In *Arbitrary Power*, William Keach focuses on the relationship between language and power that arose during the eighteenth and nineteenth centuries and continues to resonate in contemporary theory. Keach's opening chapter, for example, observes that discourse concerning the word "arbitrary" turns out to be two discourses that remain at odds with one another, but nonetheless overlap. One discourse involved the despotic, or "arbitrary," exercise of absolute power over one's subjects; the other involved the capricious and unpredictable status of words in their relationship with ideas and with things. Summarizing the overlap that occurs and its significance, Keach says:

> What I want to insist on here is that in both political and linguistic frames of reference it is not only the doubleness of the *arbitrary* ... that characterizes the problematic I am attempting to define. It is also the interaction between the terms of doubleness—the historical and social processes through which what is

---

[47] Gillen D'Arcy Wood, "Cockney Mozart: The Hunt Circle, the King's Theatre, and *Don Giovanni*," *Studies in Romanticism* 44 (2005): 367–97.

initially random and contingent becomes absolute, or conversely through which absolute will and authority give way to the random and contingent.[48]

With regard to Shelley, Keach illuminates elements of dividedness within Shelley's theory of language and within his radical revolutionary politics. These conflicts often involve the incongruity between Shelley's republican sympathies and his upper-class heritage. Evidence of "doubleness" emerges in *A Defence of Poetry* when Shelley identifies the capacity of the imagination to produce language arbitrarily, that is, freely and beyond restraint, with an "imperial faculty" seated upon a hidden throne, implicitly occupying the position of a despot.

Chandler's book explores issues surrounding the pedagogical and/or critical decision to date a literary work or focus on a literary period, and he makes the case that literary artists and journalists writing at the time of the "Peterloo" massacre were self-consciously aware of their historical moment and of the prospect that they were nation-building, composing history with the knowledge that such efforts are at least in part determined. Shelley, Byron and others, Chandler claims, were aware that "human beings make their own history," in other words, "but not just as they please."[49] Shelley was cognizant of this concept, particularly with regard to language and the possibility of using an established medium to enact change. Chandler notes that, in the *Defence*, Shelley primarily uses the term "power" to refer to the spirit of the age that speaks through the poet whether the poet wills it or not, but that Shelley also manipulates this concept to empower the poet. Just as God made the poet to make God to make the poet, writes Chandler, so the spirit of the age makes the poet to make the spirit of the age to make the poet, and so forth. This arrangement places the poet on equal footing with those agencies that influence him or her. Chandler provides provocative discussions of Shelley's writing from 1819, including the sonnet problematically bearing that date as its title, *The Cenci* and the "Ode to the West Wind."

Wood's "Cockney Mozart" is not about Shelley so much as it is about Hunt's circle of friends and colleagues, who saw themselves as England's "tastemakers," and their public advocacy for Mozartian opera. However, the article provides us with a useful profile of Shelley's social atmosphere and gives us some indication of the views concerning the politics of opera to which Shelley might have been exposed. The group opposed what was then regarded as the "anti-Mozart cabal," which consisted of aristocrats who preferred a brand of opera that privileged bravura performances by the day's elite prima donnas. The Hunt circle regarded this predilection as indicative of the lust for power that corrupted the upper class.[50] Opposing birth with taste, middle-class reformers regarded the opera house as a battleground where class interests clashed. Wood writes:

---

[48] Keach, *Arbitrary Power* 4.
[49] Chandler 554.
[50] Wood 367–9.

> *The Examiner's* campaign for reform of the Italian Opera House thus harmonized closely with its larger reformist goals. Diva culture at the King's Theatre, and its anti-Mozartian "cabal," echoed the corruption and retrogressions of Regency culture itself ... Mozart's operas did not merely symbolize change for Hunt and *The Examiner*. Their aesthetic content suggested the longed-for democratic order itself. On the most basic level of plot, both *Don Giovanni* and *Le Nozzi di Figaro* delivered a decisive come-uppance to licentious noblemen.[51]

Given what Keach observes regarding the dividedness that contoured Shelley's loyalties, his reformist aspirations and his writing, Shelley might have found himself sympathetic to the position represented by the Hunt circle, but might also have harbored sympathies with the other side.

The Lacanian orientation of *Shelley's Music* classifies it as a psychoanalytic approach to Shelley's writing and moves it alongside McDayter's interrogation of unification fantasies in *Epipsychidion*. Adopting a Lacanian reading angle enables her to illuminate Shelley's confrontation with the possibility that achieving unification means sacrificing subjectivity. McDayter insightfully points out that "Shelley's poetic fantasy is thus rather more complex than the critical tradition has imagined;" however, the scope of Shelley's fantasy might be even wider and more complex than she contends. Her concentration on Shelley's desire to recycle the moment of castration (when subjectivity asserts itself, a repetition Lacan refers to as a "pulsation"),[52] does not take into account the role of the object voice in that castration moment, its relevance to the music that characterizes the island paradise Shelley wishes to inhabit with Emily, or the specific significance of the symbolic heterosexual model that becomes the main vehicle for Shelley's fantasy.

Though the agenda informing *Shelley's Music* differs significantly from the one informing Wolfson's *Formal Charges*, her exploration of Shelley's interest in conditioning readers and in conducting the reception of his writing resonates with my sense of Shelley's desire to remain eternally present, and therefore effectual and potent, in his poetry. While my reading of the Jane Williams lyrics builds upon those performed by Wolfson and Keach in *Shelley's Style*, it applies a psychoanalytic model to the lyrics Shelley wrote for Jane. Keach's analysis of *The Revolt of Islam* in *Arbitrary Power* focuses on Shelley's "representations of woman's discursive and political authority" and aims at elucidating some of the problems with Shelley's linguistic empowerment of Cythna.[53] Keach argues that Cythna's creation of a "'subtler language within language' through which she reclaims her access to earthly struggle and renewal" represents

---

[51] Wood 384.

[52] Jacques Lacan, *The Four Fundamental Concepts of Psychoanalysis*, ed. Jacques-Alain Miller, trans. Alan Sheridan (New York and London: W. W. Norton & Company, 1981) 43.

[53] Keach, *Arbitrary Power* 95.

the core of Shelley's revolutionary re-vision, the key to his attempt, two years after Waterloo, to produce a poem that might restore the belief in the unrealized political potential of the French Revolution. It is politically and poetically momentous that he gives this vision to a woman in the process of discovering ... her own imaginative, linguistic, and political power. We can recognize these dimensions of Shelley's poetic agenda without disabling ourselves from thinking seriously about the problems and limitations in Shelley's, or in any male writer's, effort to give voice to or project a woman's self-liberation.[54]

Keach's discussion of Cythna—a "rethinking simultaneously of Wollstonecraft's key interventions in the political debates of the early 1790's, and of Joan of Arc's relation to the voices of visionary prophecy in Southey's epic"[55]—illuminates Shelley's attraction to the idea that revolutionary political authority should be represented in the figure of a woman. Keach's reading agrees with mine to the extent that it highlights Shelley's interest in the potential of a woman's expression. Whereas Keach situates that interest within the historical context formed by Shelley's awareness of unsatisfactory models created by Wollstonecraft and Southey, my study situates Shelley's interest within a contemporary psychoanalytic model, and it attributes the dividedness evident within Shelley's perspective on feminine expression not to the complexity of Shelley's historical position, but to the nature of fantasy.

The limits of an exclusively historicist approach to the relevant topics of voice and music in Shelley's writing involve its inability to regard *jouissance*, that force constantly at odds with the symbolic because it gestures in the direction of the Real, as non-historical. The metaphysical tradition, according to Dolar, had divorced word from voice and music, thereby sexualizing human expression.[56] It did so because it sought to maintain the privileged status of logos and perhaps because it feared what Lacan considers to be the "'undecideable,'" "'free-floating'" nature of *jouissance*.[57] It was exactly this amorphous vitality that Shelley sought to integrate, or more appropriately reintegrate, into the masculine poetic word in order to consolidate masculine poetic authority. Ideally, the achievement of this goal would insure recovery of the lost voice, which would establish self-presence and guarantee the living vitality of his poetry. In pointing out that neither historicist nor metaphysical interpretations of phenomena, including human behavior, have the right to claim ultimate authority, Zizek writes

> In short, what the historicists accept as primordially given, as the "nature of things" ("in social life, everything results from the process of contingent construction"), is that which is at stake in a difficult uphill struggle; it has to

---

[54] Keach, *Arbitrary Power* 102.
[55] Keach, *Arbitrary Power* 96–7.
[56] Dolar 22.
[57] Zizek, *Plague* 50.

be (re)gained by a continuous struggle; it never fully succeeds ... Therein resides the key point: historicity is not the zero-level state of things secondarily obfuscated by ideological fixations and naturalizing misrecognitions; historicity itself, the space of contingent discursive constructions, must be sustained through an effort, assumed, regained again and again ... This non-historical kernel of *jouissance* is not something accessible only in "metaphysical" or "mystical" limit-experiences; it permeates our daily lives—one only needs eyes to see it.[58]

Following Zizek's lead, it might prove productive to view Shelley's fantasy as an expression of something other than a symptom of a personal pathology.[59] Furthermore, it might be regarded as something other than an individualized historical expression. The alternative would be to see Shelley's fantasy as his endeavor to resolve the fundamental deadlock confronting each one of us. The particular watermark of that fantasy which finds expression in Shelley's writing should be recognized, then, as the "factor" he could do nothing about.

---

[58] Zizek, *Plague* 53.

[59] In addition to Barbara Gelpi's *Shelley's Goddess*, to which I have long been indebted, other provocative feminist psychoanalytical studies of Shelley include: Barbara Schapiro, *The Romantic Mother: Narcissistic Patterns in Romantic Poetry* (Baltimore and London: The Johns Hopkins UP, 1983); Teddi Chichester Bonca, *Shelley's Mirrors of Love: Narcissism, Sacrifice and Sorority* (Albany: The State U of New York P, 1999); Christine Gallant, *Shelley's Ambivalence* (New York: St. Martin's, 1989). Schapiro's Object-relations approach to Shelley claims that he suffered from a split ego, which derived from an unresolved ambivalence toward the mother image. Schapiro's chapter on Shelley focuses on his images of women. Bonca isolates Harriet Grove's rejection of Shelley as the traumatic event responsible for encouraging him to rid himself of masculinity as the necessary means for establishing his eligibility for sorority. Gallant blends Jungian with Object-relations models to discuss the relevance of archetypal images to the quest for emotional healing evident in Shelley's poetry.

Chapter 1
Subjectivity and the Self-Present Voice

Shelley's writing consistently reveals a fascination with the music of feminine expression. In all cases this fascination occurs within a phantasmic, or fantasy, structure[1] involving heterosexual coupling and heteroerotic correspondence. This dominant fantasy corresponds in some ways with the longstanding Western metaphysical tradition of separating the word, which it has associated with masculinity, from voice and music, which it has associated with femininity,[2] and it represents an attempt to fuse the two forms of expression in order to consolidate masculine poetic authority. Ultimately, Shelley's fascination with feminine expression reveals his desire to become the ideal male poet who finds a way to remain eternally present in his own words and whose unbridled, immortal voice spellbinds multitudes as it challenges the establishment. A number of faultlines crisscross this phantasmic structure, however, the most devastating of which proves to be the possibility that vocal self-presence and vocal self-preservation become no more than fantasy constructs.

Though vocal potency represents the key issue for Shelley, the root issue remains the formation of subjectivity. Lacan's conception of this dynamic, open-ended process suggests that the human subject is by definition "split," or "decentered."[3] To use Lacan's most notable example, when the subject sees the image of itself looking back at him or her from a mirror, the conventional way to interpret the experience would be to say that a sovereign, self-present individual sees the image of itself that the world sees, a person with his or her own distinct personality traits, distinct values and convictions. From Lacan's perspective, however, the experience of seeing oneself seeing oneself serves as a mutilation of sorts in which the subject is constituted not by virtue of the being looking into the mirror but by virtue of the image, always at one remove, always estranged, always cut off, permanently castrated, staring back.[4] In Lacan's schema, the "you" looking back in the form of the mirror image is the object, or objectified subject, that goes about its business living its everyday reality, not the empty "you" that gazes into the mirror. To illustrate this difficult concept, Lacan references the story of Freud's

---

[1] Slavoj Zizek, *The Plague of Fantasies* (London and New York: Verso, 1997).
[2] Mladen Dolar, "The Object Voice," *Gaze and Voice as Love Objects*, ed. Renata Salecl and Slavoj Zizek (Durham and London: Duke UP, 1996) 7–31.
[3] Zizek.
[4] Jacques Lacan, *The Four Fundamental Concepts of Psychoanalysis*, trans. Alan Sheridan, ed. Jacques-Alain Miller (New York and London: W. W. Norton & Company, 1981) 80.

grandson playing the "fort-da" game, in which the boy tossed and retrieved a reel of cotton, after his mother had left the room:

> This reel is not the mother reduced to a little ball by some magical game ... it is a small part of the subject that detaches itself from him while still remaining his, still retained. This is the place to say, in imitation of Aristotle, that man thinks with his object ... If it is true that the signifier is the first mark of the subject, how can we fail to recognize here ... that it is in the object to which the opposition is applied in act, the reel, that we must designate the subject. To this object we will later give the name it bears in the Lacanian algebra—the *petit a*.[5]

It is important to emphasize here that the reel of cotton functions not as a metaphoric stand-in for the mother, but as a metaphor of the boy's subjectivity, formed by this object to which he remains attached and dependent, but alienated from at the same time.

To this object that becomes and is the subject, Lacan gives the name *petit a*, or small other, and to it he assigns the role of figuring forth the subject's symbolic castration. Elsewhere he states: "The *objet a* is something from which the subject, in order to constitute itself, has separated itself off as organ. This serves as s symbol of lack, that is to say, of the phallus, not as such, but in so far it is lacking."[6] Under this same heading the human voice belongs.[7] Lacan identifies voice as suited to the *objet petit a* label, because it operates in the same way as an image in the mirror or, to cite another illustration, as the Cartesian *cogito*.[8] Just as the experience of seeing oneself seeing oneself creates the fantasy of the sovereign individual seeing him or herself in the mirror, so do the experiences of hearing oneself hearing oneself and, in the Cartesian formula, thinking oneself thinking oneself into being. All of these arrangements involve distance. The subject creates himself by splitting off into a signifier, the "I" in the Cartesian "I think," by which means an inversion takes place in which the duplicate determines the subject, who "sees himself as constituted by the reflected, momentary, precarious image of mastery, imagines himself to be a man merely by virtue of the fact that he imagines himself."[9]

The point is that each of these occurrences results in subject formation, which, by Lacanian definition, involves "decenterment." Voice, in fact, has long been regarded in Western tradition as the initial and the superior signature of self-presence, because the ability to hear oneself speak precedes the ability to recognize oneself in the mirror. Performing the function of "acoustic mirror," voice appears to maintain each of us, "auto-affectively,"[10] in his or her own interiority, guaranteeing

---

[5] Lacan 62.
[6] Lacan 103.
[7] Lacan 104, 200.
[8] Lacan 35–7, 43–4.
[9] Lacan 142.
[10] Dolar 12–13.

that at the foundation of each individual resides a little "man" in charge, what Lacan refers to as the "homunculus," authoring our actions.[11] Natural and intuitive though these experiences seem, they emerge, in Lacan's view, as the unavoidable and necessary operations of fantasy.

Subject formation intertwines with fantasy and the narrative structure that derives from it, and it also creates desire. The object through which the subject articulates himself becomes something that can never be retrieved, reintegrated or "subjectivized," though the subject throughout his experience fantasizes that the capture is possible.[12] What is more, this unassimilable object of desire emerges as the keystone to the subject's sense of his own value; he regards it as a "'secret treasure'"[13] of sorts that makes him desirable to others. In other words, "The *objet petit a*, as the object of fantasy," therefore, is that "something in me more than myself" on account of which I perceive myself as "worthy of the Other's desire."[14] Zizek writes:

> For late Lacan, the object is precisely that which is "in the subject more than the subject itself," that which I fantasize the Other (fascinated by me) sees in me ... It is the Other's desire itself which serves as the mediator between the "barred" subject ($) and the lost object that the subject "is",—that provides the minimum of phantasmic identity to the subject.[15]

The subject is "'barred'" in the sense that it is not free to merge with its object, but remains trapped in a dynamic that motivates the subject to pursue continually a merger, in part because the subject believes the object confers value upon it. The subject "traverses the fantasy" only if circumstances were to allow him or her to approach "the fact that *there is no secret treasure in me*, that the support of me (the subject) is purely phantasmic."[16]

Theoretically, voice represents a universal iteration of the *petit a*, because common sense informs each of us that expression registers the conceptual, emotional and spiritual substance of the individual enunciating himself or herself into consciousness and into the world. The prospect that subjectivity exists within the object-voice challenges the concept of expression, of a person pressing the self out, and suggests instead that voice signifies a void. With regard to the relationship between subject and voice, Dolar emphasizes:

> In itself [the subject] is without foundation and without a substance; it is a lack, an empty space necessarily implied by the nature of the signifier ... So the voice

---

[11] Lacan 129.
[12] Zizek.
[13] Zizek 8.
[14] Zizek 8.
[15] Zizek 9–10.
[16] Zizek 10.

seems to endow this empty and negative entity with a counterpart, its "missing half," so to speak, a "supplement" that would enable this negative being to acquire some hold in positivity, a "substance," a relationship to presence.[17]

The prospect proves particularly deleterious for the literary artist, who has chosen to communicate a personal vision via the word as a way of speaking to present and future generations, someone who endeavors, that is, to survive as a voice of inspiration reaching across time. An acute sensitivity to this fantasy prevails throughout Shelley's writing, surfacing in his poetry and in his poetics; however, we need to recognize that, while a susceptibility to fantasy often qualifies as pathological within the traditional view of human behavior, the product, that is, of a "sick" mind unable to cope with the demands of "reality," within the Lacanian view of the human universe, fantasy serves, rather, as the vital support upon which the entire symbolic structure (which makes subjectivity possible) relies.[18] If fantasy serves as the construct which enables the subject to constitute and sustain himself, Shelley's fascination with voice and correlative attraction to the phantasmic narrative supporting it reveals not only the desire for self-presence we all share, but also his desire to sustain himself as a vocal force within his own words.

Lacan writes that "man's desire is the desire of the other" and Zizek amplifies the idea by stating, "at its most fundamental, fantasy tells me what I am to my others."[19] The poetic voice, which hypothetically could become an eternally seductive and transformative articulation of truth, justice and beauty, represented for Shelley that "secret treasure" he believed made him desirable to his Other—in this case, the poetry reading audience and mainstream establishment he hoped to reach—but also to the other sex. Zizek points out that a tendency to expose the very thing it seeks to conceal, that is, the "horror of the Real," inheres to all phantasmic structures and he cites the example of airline crash pamphlets, which make disaster appear to be orderly and survivable, but which, nonetheless, confirm the possibility of death by air travel.[20] Fantasy, therefore, "constitutes our desire, provides its co-ordinates; that is, it literally 'teaches us how to desire' ... It provides a 'schema' according to which certain positive objects in reality can function as objects of desire, filling in the empty places opened up by the formal symbolic structure."[21] The fantasy involving the substance and staying power of voice we find in Shelley's writing, what might be regarded as his personal signature within the larger phantasmic structure involving the mythic substance of voice, conceals the possibility that voice, in either its personal or poetic modes, can neither be recaptured nor reassumed. It should be noted, furthermore, that even if Shelley had been aware of his desire for vocal permanence, making it a prominent feature in

---

[17] Dolar 11.
[18] Zizek 67–9.
[19] Lacan 9.
[20] Zizek 7.
[21] Zizek 7.

his agenda as a writer, the nature of fantasy would insure that the more devastating implications of his desire would remain concealed. Zizek tells us that "such awareness can never be subjectivized," "depossessing" the subject to a zero point at which he or she experiences the horror of losing all "'dignity and freedom.'"[22]

Shelley's writing indicates that Western metaphysical tradition, itself a fantasy narrative, supplied a solution to the problem of harnessing elusive vocal power. At its most fundamental, the solution amounts to conjoining with a woman. Dolar reminds us that Western metaphysical tradition has divorced word from voice, logos from wild pleasure, what Lacan refers to as *jouissance*, in order to privilege masculine expression, associated with the former, over feminine, associated with the latter, but not without plaguing itself with inconsistency.[23] The tradition assumes that the word draws humans closer to the divine creative order, while the voice, most dangerous when it escalates into music, paves the way to chaos and disruption, prized by evil. Instabilities within the fantasy emerge by way of countercurrents that raise the possibility that voice and music capture and elevate the spirit beyond the mundane concerns of material existence and therefore create a trajectory toward God. The word, conversely, tethers the human being to earth and mortality. Despite these contradictions, philosophers and theologians have managed to establish and maintain gender specificity for each of the two forms of expression.

Shelley's writing fits within this phantasmic frame, because it appoints men as the authors and governors of words, and it envisions women as the custodians of voice and music, often typing them as prima donnas who can dominate auditor and moment by means of performance. This traditional dichotomy provides Shelley with an apparatus that promises to fulfill his desire of recapturing the object voice, the *objet petit a* dominating his consciousness. The bipolar male–female, word–voice, logos–*jouissance* structure evidently presented itself to his mind as a metaphoric representation of both the problem and the solution to that problem. The attempt to bridge the metaphysical and ontological gaps emerges as one of the most dominant features of Shelley's writing. His poems and essays consistently focus on the constellation of the male subject with some female or feminine musical agent, such as Nature, in order to produce the complete, auto-affective, ever self-present poet whose verse disrupts the established authority of the "big Other," spectrally manifest in the law,[24] and inflates the souls of its auditors by way of captivating music.

"In order to be operative," Zizek remarks, "fantasy has to remain 'implicit,' it has to maintain a distance towards the explicit symbolic texture sustained by it, and to function as its inherent transgression."[25] Adultery, for example, serves as the implicit alternative to monogamous marriage, a transgression that, while

---

[22] Zizek 7–8.
[23] Dolar 22–3.
[24] Zizek.
[25] Zizek 18.

it promises "true" sexual intimacy, ultimately supports the thing it means to undermine through a process called "desublimation."[26] "Desublimation" occurs when the subject achieves his or her transgressive goal and realizes that it has failed to pay off as promised, that it falls well short of the ideal. This circumstance motivates the subject to stop short of consummating with his or her adulterous partner and to retreat to the safe, though stultifying, haven of marriage. Shelley's complex fantasy regarding vocal authority and the music of feminine expression exhibits all of the features of this arrangement.

First of all, Shelley's fascination with the power of feminine expression, concretized in rhythmic somatic movement and in emotionally charged song, diminishes the historical authority of the word. Furthermore, in promising to bridge the gap between word on the one hand and voice/music on the other, between, that is, masculine and feminine expression, Shelley's fantasy strays from the dichotomy Western philosophy had established. At the same time, however, the phantasmic outlook Shelley espoused in the end only winds up supporting the very structure it purports to transgress in the specific sense that poetry, Shelley's chosen medium, fails to regenerate his voice, consisting exclusively of silent words and measures which at best require performance by the voice of a reader. Poetry composed and performed extempore, in the style, perhaps, of a prima donna showing off her vocal range at the London opera houses,[27] remains confined to the temporal and must be experienced immediately. Once it is recorded, such a poetic moment becomes by definition a graphic inscription; it enters the world of the signifier, the place where subjectivity exists, but paradoxically fails to refer back to the subject, only to other signifiers.[28] In this regard, voice functions as the object constituting Shelley's subjectivity, his desire, and textuality itself. Written text promotes the fantasy of self-present expression, but ultimately it represents an ever-elusive acoustic mirror of every poet's subjectivity. Feminine expression mirrored back to him the vacancy behind his own silent expression.

To counteract the "horror" of this ineradicable phantasmic feature, Shelley's writing suggests that he paradoxically sheltered himself in language and the tradition of male authority, opting to use poetry as the means to record, conduct, program, and thereby control the music of feminine expression. According to Dolar, the Western metaphysical tradition of privileging word over voice and music extended to a preference for string over wind instruments. String instruments don't physically restrict the voice, but act as a collective governor for vocalized expression. Wind instruments, though they eliminate the performance of voice,

---

[26] Slavoj Zizek, "There Is No Sexual Relationship," *Gaze and Voice as Love Objects*, ed. Renata Salecl and Slavoj Zizek (Durham and London: Duke UP, 1996) 211.

[27] See Theodore Fenner, *Leigh Hunt and Opera Criticism: The Examiner Years, 1808-1821* (Lawrence: U of Kansas P, 1972) for a discussion of the prima donna's liberties. See also Gillen D'Arcy Wood, "Cockney Mozart: The Hunt Circle, The King's Theater, and *Don Giovanni*," *Studies in Romanticism* 44 (Fall 2005): 367–97.

[28] Lacan.

serve as an amplified extension of it, increasing its range, volume and reach. Shelley's presentation of erotic exchanges indicates his support for this mode. He grounds women's singing performances in a variety of ways: by bridling them to scripts composed by men; by joining them to string accompaniments; by subordinating them to male conductorship; by reprogramming them within his own measures. Moreover, he represents heterosexual and heteroerotic exchanges by way of string instrument metaphors, relegating all intercourse between the two sexualized poles of expression to the realm of the trope. When masculine and feminine harps harmonize, they do so ultimately within the field of words Shelley has composed. These strategies protect Shelley from the onslaught of "desublimation." They maintain the fantasy that the *jouissance* of a woman's music can be integrated into male authority. Furthermore, they preserve the fantasy of "treasured" status for Shelley's male poetic voice.

Shelley customized his fantasy narrative to include a cluster of images that links musical and vocal expression to feminine agency, air and fluid. The operation of this image pattern in his writing illustrates Lacan's contention that

> The *objet petit a* is not what we desire, what we are after, but, rather, that which sets our desire in motion, in the sense of the formal frame which confers consistency on our desire: desire is, of course, metonymical; it shifts from one object to another; through all these displacements, however, desire none the less retains a minimum of formal consistency, a set of phantasmic features which, when they are encountered in a positive object, make us desire this object—*objet petit a* as the cause of desire is nothing other than this formal frame of consistency.[29]

Shelley's desire achieves consistent and metonymical expression, because voice incorporates air, fluid and music. Voice consists of air in the sense that exhalation serves as the vehicle for speech; it consists of fluid in the sense that respiratory moisture accompanies enunciation; finally, it consists of music in two ways: the voice box vibrates before words form in the mouth, and melody and rhythm accompany spoken words.

Woman, particularly one who possessed a gifted singing voice, became Shelley's "positive object" within the symbolic structure all subjects regard as reality. Her voice and even her physical movements summoned his desire, as his imagination made her the tangible repository of the self-present voice from which the early moments of subject formation had stripped him. As Lacan says, "the interest the subject takes in his own split is bound with that which determines it—namely, a privileged object, which has emerged from some primal separation, from some self-mutilation."[30] This phantasmic current runs beneath the more general surface fantasy in Shelley's writing that made closing the gap between

---

[29] Zizek, *Plague* 39.
[30] Lacan 83.

the masculine word and the feminine voice a priority. Given the nature of the phantasmic construct, however, the most Shelley could have achieved would have been a state of "'extimacy,'"[31] not intimacy, for at least two reasons: first, because couplings usually result in "desublimation;" second, because masculine poetic values subordinate speech and its physical accompaniments; air, fluid and music. To fantasize about having it both ways is not identical to having it both ways.

Shelley's essay "On Love" provides us with a schematic for his fantasies. At its core lies the prospect of an Aristophanic coupling of complementary halves that, if it were to be achieved, would produce music. Many elements of Lacan's description of the human universe underwrite Shelley's fantasy of the prototype–antitype merger, which, for example, turns on the idea that lacking and vacancy characterize individual experience. Shelley postulates:

> We are born into the world and there is something within us which from the instant that we live and move thirsts after its likeness. It is probably in correspondence with this law that the infant drains milk from the bosom of its mother. This propensity develops itself with the development of our nature. (*SPP* 504)

Yet love for Shelley amounts to more than just a search for likeness; it is more a matter of coping with the "chasm of an insufficient void," dating back to our earliest moments, which experience reveals cannot be filled. To overcome one's lacking, Shelley's individual conceptualizes a perfect "miniature as it were of our entire self ... deprived of all that we condemn or despise" (*SPP* 504). In Shelley's language, this "ideal prototype" acts as a "mirror whose surface reflects on the forms of purity and brightness: a soul within our soul that describes a circle around its proper Paradise which pain and sorrow and evil dare not overleap" (*SPP* 504). In Lacan's terms, it amounts to "secret treasure," that internal commodity the subject believes makes him or her desirable to the other. Shelley's use of the mirror trope confirms that the prototype represents a constitutional signifier, to which the subject remains both estranged and related.

Shelley's enlistment of "thirst" as a metaphor of motivation might initially indicate that love can be satisfied only temporarily, placing his outlook on love within the field of drive—which can be satisfied—rather than within the field of desire—which cannot. However, his selection of music metaphor and his emphasis on voice and vibration as consequences of the erotic goal achieved (when, that is, a prototype finds its corresponding antitype), place the fantasy in the realm of desire and identify the object of that desire as Lacan's *petit a*. In terms that are characteristic for Shelley, he describes the engagement as a musical performance:

> The discovery of its antitype: the meeting with an understanding capable of clearly estimating the deductions of our own, an imagination which should enter into and seize upon the subtle and delicate peculiarities, which we have delighted

---

[31] Dolar 27.

to cherish and unfold in secret, with a frame whose nerves, like the chords of two exquisite lyres strung to the accompaniment of one delightful voice, vibrate with the vibrations of our own; and of a combination of all of these in such proportion as the type within demands: this is the invisible and unattainable point to which Love tends; and to attain which it urges forth the powers of man to arrest the faintest shadow of that without the possession of which there is no rest or respite to the heart over which it rules. (*SPP* 504)

The impossible coupling of prototype with antitype represents an ontological ideal, because it confers wholeness and sovereignty to the subject, who reintegrates the voice and music that had been taken from it. The achievement represents a Western metaphysical ideal, furthermore, because it serves as a model for sublime communication. Shelley, the essay's author, confesses in the second paragraph that he has consistently "found [his] language misunderstood like one in a distant and savage land" whenever he has endeavored to communicate with others. The union of prototype with antitype forecloses on this malfunction by marrying voice to string music, creating a balance, therefore, between spiritual and intellectual communion.

The engagement about which Shelley fantasizes in the essay "On Love" is, admittedly, only implicitly heterosexual, especially when he stipulates that what each of us seeks is his or her own likeness. Though the ambiguous formation of the antitype—specifically, the "nerves" of its "frame" resemble the music produced by not one but by "two exquisite lyres strung to the accompaniment of one delightful voice"—makes it difficult to determine its substance, Shelley's alignment of the entity first with nonverbal, musical expression (in the form of vibrations) and then with a verbal "singing voice" would seem to confirm its gender as feminine. This implication becomes even more noticeable later in the essay, especially given Shelley's personal history with Claire Clairmont, Sophia Stacey and Jane Williams, when he compares the joy one experiences as a result of correspondence with nature to the "enthusiasm" one feels when listening to "the voice of one beloved singing to you alone" (*SPP* 504).

One turns toward nature, Shelley says, when the search for the antitype fails, or when one cannot successfully garner the sympathy of others. Nature responds to the individual's needs heteroerotically through a broad range of transmissions:

> In the motion of the very leaves of spring in the blue air there is then found a secret correspondence with our heart. There is eloquence in the tongueless wind and a melody in the flowing of brooks and the rustling of the reeds beside them which by their inconceivable relation to something within the soul awaken the spirits to a dance of breathless rapture, and bring tears of mysterious tenderness to the eyes. (*SPP* 504)

"Tongueless," though still capable of "eloquence," nature is ostensibly wordless and by implication, therefore, feminine. Communion with her remains fundamentally spiritual and elicits a psychosomatic response (awakened spirits dancing in a state of "breathless rapture") that combines music with performance. Nature "speaks" by means of the "tongueless wind," by the "motion of the very leaves ... in the blue air," and by "melody" caused by the "flowing of brooks and the rustling of the reeds beside them." She reaches the solitary soul, in other words, by means of wordless vibrations and melodies. Her method of communication, though non-linguistic, is metonymically vocal, since it involves expression to which fluid and air inhere. The essay's troping of the correspondence generated when human lyres conjoin suggests that the union belongs on the same non-linguistic spiritual and emotional scale. It consists of an instrumental duet in which two nervous systems respond to one another by means of sympathetic vibrations which signal mutual rapture.

Fluid and air also figure into Shelley's conceptualization of fantasy heterosexual relationships in the essay "On Love." References to these elements don't always stand in directly for vocal or musical expression, though they do metonymically represent the fantasy status of the secret treasure others desire, and they reinforce the constitutional function of the *petit a* within Shelley's phantasmic field. The equation of love with thirst, for example, suggests that love amounts ultimately to an unquenchable desire for oral satisfaction. The infant, Shelley says, "in correspondence with this law ... drains milk from the bosom of its mother" (*SPP* 504). The analogy suggests that the mother articulates her love for the child through her breasts—that she does her talking, in other words, through the medium of fluid, in the same way, perhaps, that nature creates "melody" out of "flowing brooks." Though removed during the weaning process in a way not parallel to the loss of the object voice, the breast, as locus of maternal expression, nonetheless serves as a metaphor within the symbolic field that retrospectively signifies those other losses, manifest most especially through voice and gaze, that constitute subjectivity.[32]

This emphasis on fluid oral communication also appears earlier in the essay. Shelley's depiction of the state of mind engendered by "powerful attraction" indicates that "lips of motionless ice should not reply to lips quivering and burning with the heart's best blood" (*SPP* 504). The metaphor allows for two possibilities: that lips convey words and that lips communicate non-linguistically via kisses. Shelley's image is especially interesting in light of Lacan's contention that the body's orifices function in the same way as the unconscious, delivering momentary pulsations of desire. The rim of each orifice, which in this case would be the lips,

---

[32] Object-relations psychology regards the maternal breast as representative object introjected by the infant and then split into good and bad categories, the good breast manifesting constant care and fulfillment, the bad breast manifesting neglect and alienation. While the breast's psychological function involves an element of loss and figures into ego formation, it fails to constitute subjectivity in the way Lacan theorizes. Object-relations theory contends that the infant possesses an ego, though that ego relies on relationships to complete its formation.

becomes the trigger point of that "pulsation."[33] For Shelley, desire, or the icy lack of it, finds mouth-to-mouth expression by means of fluid. Under ideal conditions, hot blood would melt and animate "motionless ice." The image's specular pedigree incorporates a measure of instability, furthermore, because it suggests that the substance of the other's desire is elementarily alien to the subject's. The ostensibly feminine other Shelley has in mind, in other words, speaks a foreign language of ice to his language of fire. Each pulsation releases her *jouissance*, which might be regarded as a "tic," an element of the "real," threatening to tear the envelope of perfection in which her masculine counterpart has placed her.[34]

Within this same depiction of desire, Shelley transfigures lips into watery gaze. Gaze emerges as an additional manifestation of the *petit a*, because it mirrors and therefore constitutes the subject scopically in the same way that voice mirrors the subject acoustically.[35] Following the "motionless ice" metaphor, Shelley elaborates that the incomplete, loving individual fantasizes "that the beams of [the potential lover's] eyes should kindle at once and mix and melt into our own" (*SPP* 503). The metaphor underscores further the importance of specular correspondence in Shelley's fantasy of heterosexual intimacy, as it conveys his desire to commune through a medium superior to the desiccated lifelessness of words. The confluence resulting from this erotic meltdown, moreover, would fulfill the fantasy of reintegrating the lost object. The problem, of course, is that one's subjectivity—one's identifiable stature in the symbolic world of everyday—gets lost in the process, in the same way that ice loses shape and contour once it melts. If the icy lips of the object-other melt, the subject whose meaning and integrity they constitute melts along with them.

Personal circumstances must have intensified Shelley's fascination with music and they must have consequently fuelled the complex of fantasies involving feminine expression, masculine self-presence and subjectivity that informs his writing. Shelley's residence at Great Marlow in 1817 was filled with musical activity and friends who loved music. It was at Marlow that Shelley had consistent exposure to singing performances by Hunt and Claire. Hunt was not only a good singer, but he was proficient on the piano and on the flute.[36] The experience of hearing Hunt sing and perform within the intimacy of his own home must have formed a counterpoint to the experience of hearing Claire, and the former might have served as an example for Shelley of what the masculine voice, even when confined within a temporal framework, might be capable of accomplishing.

Mary's letters and journal entries testify to the centrality of music in their lives at this time period. On Saturday, February 1, for example, she reveals, "in the evening ... H. Mrs. H. and I go to the opera—Figaro—I am very much pleased" (*JMS* 161). On Tuesday, February 4, and on Thursday, February 6, she records

---

[33] Lacan 154, 178.
[34] Zizek, *Plague* 49.
[35] Lacan 73–83.
[36] Fenner 28.

that she listened to Hunt's music and on the ninth of the same month writes, "walk with S. and Hunt to Brougham's in the morning—after dinner read the arcadia. Several of Hunt's acquaintances come in the evening—music" (*JMS* 162–3). In a letter to Shelley, dated October 5, 1817, she tells her husband, "I have written to Hunt but tell him over & above that our piano is in tune and that I wish he would come down by Monday's coach to play me a few tunes—he will think I jest but it would really give me the greatest pleasure" (*MWSL* 52–4). Earlier, on March 5, 1817, she had asked Hunt to learn the "Rantz des Vaches and the Marcellois hymn with the French words which Claire will teach you to pronou[nce] if necessary" (*MWSL* 32–3). While at Marlow, the Shelleys purchased a piano from Joseph Kirkman with the help of Vincent Novello,[37] and Shelley evidently shared with him a love of Mozart. According to Tetreault, Shelley "almost certainly shared Peacock's judgment that 'there is nothing perfect in this world except Mozart's music.'"[38] Once they departed from England, Percy and Mary maintained their passion for opera, attending "five performances at La Scala, as well as taking in various productions at Turin, Rome, Naples, and Pisa as their bases changed over the succeeding years."[39]

During the eighteenth century, the Italian opera became very popular in London, particularly among the aristocracy. The aria became its trademark, and it came to signal the achievement of "a kind of emotional plateau, which projected the dominant mood of the character at strategic points of the drama."[40] Consequently, the Italian opera, or opera seria, emerged as the "singer's opera."[41] "The da capo aria, especially, which repeats itself," writes Fenner, "permitted the prima donna unlimited possibilities for demonstrating the vocal dexterity of her coloratura; in the reprise she was expected to add such improvised embellishments as her agility and artistry could command."[42] According to Fenner, even though the Italian and English operas were at their nadirs during Shelley's final years in England, interest in female vocal performances remained a commonplace at the noisy London opera houses, where male and female members of the audience would pause from playing cards or from socializing just long enough to hear a favorite singer perform. Erland Anderson agrees with Fenner's assessment, adding that adoration of the prima donna approached almost cult status among opera-going middle and upper class males, prompting many composers to tailor their music for a popular female singer. Prima donnas regularly took liberties

---

[37] Erland Anderson, *Harmonious Madness: A Study of Musical Metaphors in the Poetry of Coleridge, Shelley and Keats* (Salzburg: Institut fur Sprache und Literatur: University of Salzburg, 1975) 31.

[38] Ronald Tetreault, "Shelley at the Opera," *ELH* 48 (1981): 147.

[39] Tetreault 147.

[40] Fenner 4–5.

[41] Fenner 4–5.

[42] Fenner 4–5.

with the composer's text, as they sought to demonstrate the range and power of their voices.[43]

Trips by Shelley to the opera house no doubt reinforced what he had witnessed in his own home, as Claire practiced her scales and sang by the piano. She had virtually been a constant presence in Shelley's life from the time of his elopement with Mary and he became accustomed to taking her into his confidence when tensions arose between him and Mary. But their relationship might have been even more complex than that. Michael O'Neill believes the two were probably intimate.[44] Given what Shelley's poems and essays reveal about the allure of musically gifted women, Claire's singing voice, which one musical instructor compared to a "chain of pearls,"[45] likely became an early focal point of his desire. She studied voice while living with the Shelleys and at one point Percy was paying for her voice lessons. The lyric "To Constantia," which Shelley composed at Marlow, illustrates the phantasmic character of Shelley's attraction to musical females. Discussed in Chapter 3, the poem reveals the speaker's efforts to harness Constantia's expression of *jouissance* while at the same time corresponding with her on a level approaching the Lacanian "Real."

First-hand accounts of the power wielded by the prima donna can be found in opera reviews written by Leigh Hunt and William Hazlitt, and, given that the Hunts and the Shelleys were friends, it seems reasonable to assume that the topic had been discussed among them. Hazlitt, who wrote a number of opera reviews for Hunt's *Examiner* (a publication Mary and Percy frequently read), consistently applauds actresses who sing from the heart and with genuine feeling. He condemns those who perform their numbers mechanically and without feeling. Hunt, who pioneered a new standard for opera criticism in England,[46] held a view similar to Hazlitt's. Hunt also identified sincerity of expression and true passion to be the marks of a great performance. His recollection of Mrs Billington's singing abilities, for example, was that she "appeared to have more brilliancy of execution than depth of feeling."[47] On the other hand, he fondly recalled the genius of Madame Pasta, who "was a great tragic actress; and her singing in point of force, tenderness, and expression, was equal to her acting. All noble passions belonged to her … In every respect, perfect truth, graced by idealism, was the secret of Pasta's greatness. She put truth first always."[48]

---

[43] Anderson 35–7.

[44] Donald H. Reiman and Michael O'Neill, eds, *The Manuscripts of the Younger Romantics. Percy Bysshe Shelley. Fair-Copy Manuscripts of Shelley's Poems in European and American Libraries*, vol. 8 (New York and London: Garland Publishing, 1997) 277.

[45] Neville Rogers, "More Music at Marlow," *Keats-Shelley Memorial Bulletin* 5 (1953): 20.

[46] See Fenner, Chapter 2, "Leigh Hunt and the *Examiner*: Musical Developments."

[47] Leigh Hunt, *The Autobiography of Leigh Hunt* (Oxford: Oxford UP, 1928) 125.

[48] Hunt 127.

Hazlitt's favorite seems to have been Miss Stephens. Reviewing her performance of Mandane in *Artaxerxes* for *The Morning Chronicle* (appearing October 18, 1813), he states that "her singing is delicious," that "a voice more sweet, varied, and flexible, was perhaps never heard," and that "notes seemed to fall from her lips like the liquid drops from the bending flower … her voice fluttered and died away with the expiring conflict of passion in her bosom" (*CWWH* vol. 5, 192–3). By comparison, Miss Hughes, playing the role of Mandane two years later (review appearing in *The Examiner*, October 1, 1815), proved herself to be "a very accomplished singer, with a fine flexible voice, with considerable knowledge and execution," but her singing leaves the listener dissatisfied. "But where," muses Hazlitt,

> is the sweetness, the simplicity, the melting soul of music? There was a voluptuous delicacy, a naivete in Miss Stephens's singing, which we have never heard before nor since, and of which we should be loth to be deprived. Her songs in Mandane lingered on the ear like an involuntary echo to the music—as if the sentiment were blended with and trembled on her voice. (*CWWH* vol. 5, 248)

Hazlitt's reviews consistently emphasize the need for the female singer's voice to embody sweetness and they regularly compare the genuinely expressive prima donna's musical notes to "liquid drops" that satiate her listeners. His review of *Don Juan* (appearing in *The Examiner*, April 20, 1817), a production the Shelleys would see Friday, May 23, in which Madame Fodor performed, serves as a good illustration. Commenting on Fodor's singing of the number "La ci darem," he says,

> We could listen to the air for ever—with certain intervals: the first notes give a throb of expectation to the heart, the last linger on the sense. We encore it greedily, with a sort of childish impatience for new delight, and drink in the ethereal sounds, like draughts of earthly nectar … There is a clear, firm, silvery tone in her voice, like the reverberation of a tight-strung instrument. (*CWWH* vol. 5, 364)

Hazlitt's description of his experience, drinking Fodor's voice as though it were a delightful "draught," resonates with Shelley's description in the essay "On Love" of love as, essentially, a thirst for music. The reference to his "childish impatience," furthermore, places Fodor within a domestic economy, subordinating her to the role of mother or nursemaid. The description also bears close resemblance to a passage from Spenser Samuel Johnson had chosen to illustrate the word "musick" in his *Dictionary*. Johnson defines music first as "the science of harmonical sounds" and second as "instrumental or vocal harmony." He then draws an example from the *Faerie Queen*:

> When she spake
> Sweet words, like dropping honey, she did shed;

And 'twixt the pearls and rubies softly brake
A silver sound, that heavenly music seemed to make.[49]

It seems clear that some of the imagery Shelley associated with a woman's music, particularly its fluid properties, came from common stock, originating in the phantasmic narrative that supported Western culture's stake in keeping feminine expression separate from the masculine word, but that also underscored the potent allure of that music. From Hazlitt's perspective, the female voice evidently represented a powerful curiosity that should be experienced from a safe distance within a structured format and then subjected to masculine aesthetic judgment. It was a commodity the male auditor was entitled to devour for his own pleasure. From Shelley's perspective, though, the female voice proved to be far more promising and problematical, as it seemed to embody what he most desired: commanding self-presence and the prospect of becoming the living word.

All elements of Shelley's fantasy sit on the same shallow footings, however. Theoretically, the poet achieves immortality through his words in the specific sense that the images, rhythms and phonics of a poetic text enter and potentially dominate a person's consciousness during the reading process. This assumption informs the "culture of posterity" generally evident in the work of many Romantic poets.[50] At the moment of intersection, the reader hears the poet's voice speaking from the inside and in this way the reader occupies a position similar to the one occupied by someone attending a Mozart performance or a poetry reading. The experience would be immediate and potentially moving, though by definition temporary. Should the reader choose to recite or memorize the poem, measures devised by the poet might exercise command over the reader's heart and respiratory rates. Shelley seems to have this arrangement in mind when he pleads with the West Wind to "make me thy lyre, even as the forest is" (*SPP* 57). The auditor of the Wind's prophecies in this case becomes the Wind's instrument, in the same way that the reader becomes instrumental to the poet. Even the lyre metaphor Shelley uses to reveal the spiritual music that results when prototype and antitype in the essay "On Love" evokes the same idea. He characterizes the expression of the antitype's nervous system as two lyres "strung to the accompaniment of one delightful voice." Intercourse between complementary types, in other words, evidently involves the transit of one voice into the consciousness of the other.[51]

---

[49] *A Dictionary of the English Language*, 2 vols (London, 1755).

[50] Andrew Bennett, *Romantic Poets and the Culture of Posterity* (Cambridge: Cambridge UP, 1999).

[51] This portion of my discussion is indebted to William Ulmer's *Shelleyan Eros: The Rhetoric of Romantic Love* (Princeton: Princeton UP, 1990). Ulmer argues that Shelley's concept of poet–reader correspondence, a relationship based on what Ulmer calls "psychic coincidence," correlates with the "self/antitype paradigm" Shelley lays out in the essay "On Love." In the same way that the antitype serves as the necessary other and mirror image of the self that conceives it, the reader whom the writer conceives becomes the writer's

The *petit a* antitype coalesces with the prototype, speaking musically through and with him and in the process making him complete.

The idea that the poet needs the reader, or the antitype, to complete him undermines this phantasmic principle, however. The poet who writes, as opposed to the poet who performs, cannot escape the ontological "Real" of lacking. Poetic inscription functions as the *petit a*, in that it constitutes the poet's subjectivity, but its poignancy as a signifier of the poet's subjectivity deepens, because it reflects back to the poet only silence and vacancy. Furthermore, it demonstrates graphically that its reference point is not the poet who composed it, but other poems, other signifiers and collections of signifiers.[52] The process of writing, then, constitutes a castration in which the subject reproduces not his poetic vision, as it might appear, but his split status, necessarily estranged from his own voice in order to signify that he is a meaningful entity.

It might appear that the reader is capable of breaking this deadlock by serving as the instrument completing the open-ended transaction of the poem. Without this person, the text would remain lifeless on the page. While it is reasonable to assume that the poet's voice survives in the reader, it is equally reasonable to argue that the poet needs the reader to complete him. Poems read, recited and/or committed to memory become the property of the reader. His or her voice takes up residence in the poet's text and remains at liberty to exercise his or her own will with regard to the poem's aural character. The reader might choose to elide certain syllables, or customize by way of vocal emphasis choice phonic features. In many ways, in fact, the reader's ontological stature mirrors the poet's exactly. When reading a poem, one hears one's own voice registering itself inside, in the case of a poem read silently, or outside, in the case of a poem read aloud. Both acts confirm the poet's absence and, therefore, the poem's lacking; both acts also confirm the reader's absence, rather than presence, and the reader's lacking. Perhaps more unsettling than all of these hypotheses is the prospect that words spoken or written become nothing more than the spectral medium of Lacan's "big Other"—tradition, convention, language and the law—through which writers and readers constitute themselves.[53] In this way, language paradoxically underpins the fantasy of self-presence.

The nature of *jouissance* poses an even greater challenge to the fantasy of self-presence, though. Dolar observes that Lacan "didn't have to invent the ambiguity

---

offspring—the custom made sounding board for that particular author. According to Ulmer, "Shelley intended his texts to transmit resemblances by which the reader's consciousness would be linguistically reshaped to accord with the poet's consciousness, to reflect the poet's emotions and values as mirrored in turn by the words of his poems. Poets and readers are lovers in Shelley" (19). In such an arrangement, poets and readers come to share one voice and construct a cooperative meaning, perhaps in a way similar to that of a mother and a young child. My point, of course, is that, though Shelley might have conceived of the relationship as an ideal, it still would have been subject to the liabilities of fantasy.

[52] Lacan 198–9.
[53] Zizek, *Plague* 110.

of the voice and its perilous reverse side," citing examples beginning with the writings of the Chinese emperor Chun and ending with documents written during the French Revolution that struggled with the dual nature of music, particularly vocalized music. The crux of the matter involved the uncontrollable element of "feminine *jouissance*."[54] The problem for Catholic scholars, for example, was that the very thing, that is, music, which has the capacity to raise our souls to God leads to the possibility that God cannot be distinguished from the devil: "Music may well be the element of spiritual elevation beyond worldliness and representation, but it also introduces, for that very reason, the indomitable and senseless *jouissance* beyond the more tractable sensual pleasures."[55] The function of the "shofar," a hollow bull's horn from Judeo-Christian tradition one blows through on ritualistic occasions, says Dolar, illuminates the most disturbing aspects of the ambiguity inherent to voice and, by extension, to music.

The sound of the horn was meant to serve as an official validation of some decree, making a distant and mysterious divinity present to his people. The shofar stands totemically in for Him in the same way that the bull served one time as an object of worship and sacrifice. If the shofar represents the voice of God, it also represents, however, the object voice, a sound signifying God's absence, His death and His "decenteredness" as the original subject, or self-acting agent, of the universe. Underwriting God's law inscribed on the tablets Moses delivered from Mount Sinai and thereby establishing the presence of His will, for example, the sound of the shofar paradoxically announces itself as split off from the language of the law. In this regard, it occupies the same place as the nonsense of feminine *jouissance* Christian scholars in particular had feared, announcing not a definite presence, but an absence and a lacking. The word shofar, notes Dolar, translates in English as "trumpet," and its "object voice bears witness to the rest of that presupposed and terrible Father's *jouissance*, which couldn't be absorbed by the Law, that reverse side of the Father that Lacan calls *le-pere-la-jouissance*, his ultimate deadly cry that accompanies the instituted law."[56] Dolar's conclusion bears directly on the very substance of Shelley's fantasy:

> Ultimately, we don't have the battle of "logos" against the voice, but *the voice against the voice*. Yet, is that inaudible voice pertaining to logos something entirely different from the anathemized voice bringing unbounded *jouissance* and decay? Is the *jouissance* that the Law persecutes as its radical alterity other than the aspect of *jouissance* pertaining to the Law itself? Is the voice of the Father an altogether different species from the feminine voice? ... The secret is maybe that they are both the same; that there are not two voices, but only one object voice, which cleaves and bars the Other in an ineradicable "extimacy" ... Masculine and feminine positions are then two ways of tackling the same

---

[54] Dolar 22–3.
[55] Dolar 23.
[56] Dolar 27.

impossibility; they arise from the same predicament as two internally linked versions of the same voice, which retains an ineradicable ambiguity.[57]

The divine capacity to speak eternally through words serves as a root metaphor in Western culture, and it traditionally informs our understanding of the poet's function. That metaphor underpins Shelley's assertion in *A Defence of Poetry* that the work of great poets often takes generations to gain a foothold in the collective consciousness of a people. The premise that not even recitation succeeds in establishing contemporaneity, with voice always functioning as the subject's constitutive object, however, jeopardizes the hypothesis that the Judeo-Christian God and the poet achieve self-presence and ultimate authority. Furthermore, though the notion that the aggressively wild delights and energies of *jouissance* transcend gender and should, therefore, empower masculine as well as feminine expression, the same notion also assails the traditional empowerments to which Shelley clung. To acknowledge that there is only one voice is to relinquish one's claim to distinction; it means entering a realm outside the symbolic, where there is no subjectivity. The male poet's decision to take shelter in language creates a deadlock, though, because it means channeling the expression of life energy that comes from *jouissance*. In such an arrangement, feminine expression—because of its spontaneity, unfettered range, fluid melody and respiratory immediacy—ends up subordinating its masculine counterpart. Shelley's awareness of this rupture in his fantasy likely fuelled his efforts to manage feminine expression by scripting, reprogramming and conducting it, but, as is always the case with fantasy, awareness fails to make the subject his own master.

Genre and purpose adjust the timbre of Shelley's fantasy. Narrative and dramatic works such as *Alastor*, *The Revolt of Islam*, *Prometheus Unbound* and *Rosalind and Helen* feature heterosexual couplings between male poets and musically fluent females.[58] These females serve as positive objects who initialize male desire and mirror back to their respective poets what those poets conceive collectively to be their secret treasure, that is, what all auditors desire of them: vocal potency. In addition, the female characters who appear in these works embody the *petit a*, the fluid, airborne voice which beckons the male poet by promising to fulfill his longing, to complete him. Shelley achieves degrees of success within this phantasmic construct, but not without creating paradox and instability. The most distinct paradox involves the "interpassive" character of the relationships he imagines.[59]

---

[57] Dolar 27–8.

[58] Though perhaps more lyric than narrative, I will be including a discussion of *Epipsychidion* with my reading of these poems, primarily because it bears the imprint of "interpassivity," but also because the poem shares more in common with these works overall than it does with the personal lyrics Shelley wrote for Claire Clairmont, Jane Williams and Sophia Stacey.

[59] Zizek, *Plague* 116–18.

"Interpassivity" refers to the process in which the "decentered" subject defers enjoyment or suffering to some other in order to sustain the fantasy of activity. The subject becomes passive through his other in order to conceive of himself as active, dumping all inertia and inactivity into the object. While the maneuver constitutes the subject, it also registers as false activity. The subject, "living" in the place of the passive other, is himself passive; he reduces himself to the embarrassing kernel of passivity, since to be a subject means to exist not in yourself but in your others. Zizek illustrates this point by drawing on the function of a sitcom laugh-track: auditors other than the subject watching television laugh for him, yet he enjoys the experience as though he himself were laughing. Zizek elaborates:

> Crucial here is the reflective reversal of "the Other does it for me, instead of me, in my place," into "I myself am doing it through the Other": this reversal expresses the minimal condition of subjectivity—that is to say, the attitude which constitutes subjectivity is not "I am the active autonomous agent who is doing it," but "when another is doing it for me, I myself am doing it through him" (a woman who is doing it through her man etc.).[60]

Functioning as acoustic mirrors, Shelley's heroines act in place of his poet-protagonists in narrative and dramatic works that feature heterosexual unions. Male poets see themselves as composers and identify themselves with the first word, but fail to recognize that they speak through their female mates and protégées. In terms of Shelley's overall phantasmic narrative, the female counterpart serves as the male poet's instrument; however, it is also true that without her his expression has no medium and remains void. Among the more unsettling implications of this arrangement for the male poet is the possibility that the "original subjective gesture" is feminine—in the sense that women in Western culture have typically filled their lives with meaning and satisfaction by living through their men, that is, by "proxy."[61] The male authority Shelley seeks to consolidate in his narrative and dramatic poems collapses ultimately, because it paradoxically establishes the feminine posture of all poetic activity. The written text "interpassively" speaks for the ever-silent poet who lives by proxy through his poems, in the same way that Prometheus, Lionel, the Poet of *Alastor*, Laon and the Shelleyan narrator who addresses Emily in *Epipsychidion* live by proxy through their respective female complements. Narrative and dramatic elements and modes provide the author Shelley with a certain measure of protection against these instabilities, in that he dismisses himself from his own phantasmic storyline, yet he cannot escape the ontological implications of his own creations. Mirrored back to him is not acoustic richness and vivacity, but absence and silence. No living voice supports the poem the reader holds in his or her hands. Theoretically, Shelley becomes passive, not active, through his passive auditor.

---

[60] Zizek, *Plague* 117.
[61] Zizek, *Plague* 118.

Fantasy couplings in the lyrics Shelley wrote for musically gifted or, in Shelley's eyes, musically substantial women fail to offer the same structural safeguards as their narrative and dramatic counterparts (though they maintain narrative elements) and they place him in situations in which he cannot escape personal involvement. Social constraints force the submergence of Shelley's phantasmic agenda. Specifically, poems to Jane Williams, Sophia Stacey and Claire Clairmont indicate that correspondence between Shelley and his musically fluent female other happens primarily along somatically expressive wavelengths—at times, by means of cardio-respiratory transmission, at others by means of bodily gesture and movement. To a certain extent, the body's music, its various somatic rhythms and cyclical reprises, occur beyond the reach of legal and symbolic strictures. Shelley's strategy in these poems involves projecting these relationships into the realm Lacan identifies as the "real," which lies outside symbolic and imaginary registers and exists, theoretically, as a raw state of existence not formed by signifiers.[62]

One problem with this maneuver, namely the way in which this fantasy creates the horror it simultaneously works to conceal, is that Shelley chooses poetry to construct this ideal. Poetry remains a symbolic construct. Another problem, according to Lacan, would be that the "real" cannot be approached, which also means that the subject cannot achieve meaningful coupling outside the symbolic. Shelley's fantasy, therefore, becomes reliant upon but also bound by his art. A third problem concerns the nature of the somatic rhythms Shelley hopes to contact. Because they manifest *jouissance*, something which is conventionally inexpressible and also threatens to "desublimate" the woman Shelley desires by forcing him to face qualities of her that shatter the image he has created, these rhythms can neither be unambiguously embraced nor controlled.

Finally, the same phantasmic narrative of recapturing through woman the elusive object voice and achieving thereby the capacity to maintain presence in his words informs Shelley's poetics. Correspondence in this case involves the exchange between the poet's receptive mind and the inconstant movements of Power, which represents the *objet petit a*, the secret treasure that transforms an otherwise ordinary human being into a poet, whose voice reaches across space and time. Though not explicitly identified as feminine in *A Defence of Poetry* or poems Shelley devoted to the subject of the poet's substance and mission, Power by association assumes a feminine character, since it enters the world primarily as music and since it seems coexistent with *jouissance* in the sense that its full expression remains inexpressible by even the most poetic human mind. Within the phantasmic frame Shelley constructs, Power represents the elusive secret treasure that makes the poet desirable to his others, that is, to his auditors. When Power returns in the forms of truth and inspiration to the poet's consciousness, it thwarts his attempts to integrate it permanently into his subjectivity. When Power departs, it leaves the now metaphorically castrated poet with a fading record of itself, reducing him once again to a state of lacking: he lacks the ability to be a

---

[62] Zizek, *Plague* 175.

poet without it; in addition, he lacks the ability to draw the desire of his readers, a fate Shelley knew all too well.

Shelley's fantasy compensates for these factors by insisting that Power needs the Poet in order to enter the symbolic, so that its substance might incarnate itself through voice, music and words. This hypothesis places Power in the position of "decentered" subject and the poet in the position of the desired *objet petit a*, feeding Power's desire for self-presence, but in the end conferring no more than linguistic absence. The relationship binding the poet to Power cannot rid itself of instability, no matter how one turns it. Additional compensation would seem to adhere to the second half of the aesthetic transaction, however, the exchange between Power and the poet serving as the first. In the originary role of author, the poet occupies the position normally filled by Power, performing the role of *petit a*, that is, the voice of truth, inspiration and spiritual elevation the reader desires but has lost. If it is true that Power operates within the human mind as it does in all elements of creation, poetry, its perfect incarnation, would seem to possess the ability to reintroduce the reader to some crucial part of him or herself—the secret treasure—the reader believes he or she has lost. A poem, therefore, would constitute the reader. As is the case with the poet, however, the reader's constitution would be no more self-present than the poet's: both rely on silent, non-self-referential signifiers for their symbolic substance.

The economy characterizing Shelley's exchanges with Power consistently establish his instrumentality. In *A Defence*, the "Ode to the West Wind," and "To a Skylark," for example, he envisions himself as both auditor and "shofar," regarding the poet as Power's subject, as the West Wind's "trumpet of a prophecy," and as the skylark's protégée. Each of the three agents triggers desire without delivering satisfaction, leaving the poet writing but still lacking. Furthermore, each scenario places the *jouissance* of true, unfettered expression frustratingly but also necessarily outside of the poet's symbolic reach. If he were to integrate successfully their collective substance, his symbolic status, his subjectivity, would disappear. Moreover, Shelley's commitment to composing written text makes the phantasmic prospect of serving as the West Wind's trumpet and as Power's instrument theoretically impossible. The deadlock tightens, because, even though the shofar attends and also represents the divine word, it signals the incompatibility between itself and that word. In addition, as the non-linguistic "remainder" of language, sound produced by the shofar embodies *jouissance*, a phenomenon no poet can signify. In other words, to write poetically is not to speak of *jouissance*. And, if Dolar's proposition that *jouissance* exceeds all gender distinctions is sound, Shelley's fantasy of regaining vocal potency through heterosexual confluence, even when that confluence is figurative, emerges as fundamentally flawed.

Though stress fractures compromise Shelley's fantasy regarding voice, music and subjectivity, those weak points fail to diminish the vitality, importance or integrity of that fantasy. Fantasy, Zizek reminds us, is necessary first because it structures desire and second because it safeguards all subjects "against the direct intrusion of the Real."[63] For Shelley, having to face the possibility that the sound of his own voice, though constituting his subjectivity, resisted all claims to ownership and self-presence would have proved traumatic. The sexualized split of word from voice and music developed within the metaphysical tradition provided him with a preexistent narrative for resolving this antagonism. This model shaped his desire to master the full range of human expression, to consolidate his own authority as a poet, and to erase all vestiges of self-mutilation. For Shelley, fantasy served, as for each subject it continues to serve, not as a creative strategy meant to liberate him from "reality," but as the very structure that creates and continues to maintain that "reality," so that the non-symbolic "real" remains locked away.

---

[63] Zizek, *Plague* 65.

Chapter 2
Poetic Authority and "Interpassivity"

The concept of "interpassivity" applies to the process of composition, because in order for a writer to establish his or her authority, that writer articulates himself or herself by means of a textual other. Viewed conventionally, the transaction establishes the writer as active and the text as passive, as an object through which the author speaks. Viewed psychoanalytically, however, the transaction elucidates the paradox of subjectivity formation: because the textual other constitutes its subject author, that author becomes passive. Even more problematically, though the text retains stature and presence in the realm of the symbolic, it consists of silent language and remains void of living vocality; it too is passive. The text operates in the same fetishistic fashion as the object voice, in the sense that it leaves something to be desired and paradoxically forecloses on its writer's claim to authority. Writers struggle to compose themselves, to make themselves present in their own iterations, yet their desires remain unfulfilled. Before we say that all writers suffer from extraordinary psychic clamor, however, we should remind ourselves that "interpassivity" is not an "excessive phenomenon which occurs only in extreme 'pathological' situations," but the "feature which defines the most elementary level, the necessary minimum of subjectivity."[1] This proposition suggests that Shelley shared the same fantasy with all writers and that composition itself replays the necessary horror of castration, for without it there would be no poets, as without castration there would be no subjects.

A complex version of "interpassivity" inheres to those narrative and dramatic poems Shelley wrote that hinge on heterosexual coupling as the means to realizing the fantasy of achieving immortal self-presence in writing. To begin with, the fictional nature of *Alastor*, *The Revolt of Islam*, *Rosalind and Helen* and *Prometheus Unbound* creates the illusion of Shelley's absence from the narrative while paradoxically establishing his active role in creating and then governing that textual universe. Without an authorial presence underwriting and providing with legitimacy words, characters and storylines, these elements remain passive objects lacking a requisite voice. Challenging this convention, however, is the possibility that the poet is the one lacking. Composition renders him a speaker of words but a speaker, nonetheless, without a living, enduring voice, and the poem he creates acoustically mirrors this condition. *Epipsychidion*, which I include in this narrative and dramatic group, would seem to qualify as an exception to this pattern, since it features the unfinished story of Shelley's erotic frustrations and the prospect of eternal communion with Emily; however, though she and the poem serve as the

---
[1] Slavoj Zizek, *The Plague of Fantasies* (London and New York: Verso, 1997) 115–16.

instruments of Shelley's expression, they also undermine his status as active agent at the same time. While it might be true that the seemingly passive text remains vacant and silent—a closed book sitting on a shelf—it might also be true that the subject-author suffers the same fate, existing beyond all correspondence, the offspring of his own silent language. The inert poem on the page reflects not its author's vitality, but his inertia.

Serving as dynamic metaphors, the heterosexual couplings Shelley conceives for these poems deepen the operation of "interpassivity." On the surface, the "veiled maid" (*SPP* 151), Cythna, Helen, Asia and Emily would seem to fill adjunct roles, serving their male poet counterparts variously as muse, protégée, or instrument. Though it might be argued that Asia and Cythna, in particular, overtake the men to whom they remain devoted, in both cases those men set them in motion. Asia and Cythna emerge as transmitters, or amplifiers or even as texts whose substance has been shaped, respectively, by Prometheus and Laon. A slight shift in perspective reveals that each of the five expressive females becomes not only a metaphor of the object voice, but also a representative of *jouissance*, from which the male poet has become alienated.

Anamorphically, these women mirror back the inertia characterizing the male poets who have established them. In addition, they paradoxically maintain the musical and vocal energy to compromise the symbolic—generating a revolutionary potency of which male poets are theoretically no longer capable within the ordinary compositional schema. In the sense that they are active, they perform as free agents: prima donna-like, the "veiled maid" inflames the Poet's soul with a serenade he can imagine but not vocalize; Cythna escapes capture by way of vocal and musical persuasion and supplants Laon, to become Laone, the voice of revolution; Helen's musical performance surpasses Lionel's orchestration of that performance; Asia's musical vale and not Prometheus's verbal crag becomes the flashpoint for cosmic harmony, and Emily becomes the living embodiment of the musical paradise that promises to revitalize Shelley's spirit. In each poem, Shelley installs counteractive measures; however, they only enhance the resolution of fault lines in each narrative.

Ultimately, these problems surface because Shelley cannot escape the cultural sexualization of expression. By delegating vocal and musical spontaneity, hence *jouissance*, to the female other, the male poet confirms the absence of those elements in his own writing and ultimately the absence of a secret treasure within himself. The poetic authority celebrated in the text which takes the form of the poet-protagonist's ability to conceive a language of change—an ability spectrally manifest in Shelley's creative performance as author of the narrative or dramatic poem—ends up folding back in on itself, confirming its own phantasmic underpinnings. The most inspired inscription of visionary truth and beauty fails to transcend its status as object and as other, and as these things constitute the male poetic genius, they reveal that the substance of that vision, the expression of that genius, cannot be integrated into the poet's subjectivity.

The Poet of *Alastor* inhabits a world characterized by silent inscription, a world of words and signs.[2] The poem's narrator reveals that the Poet possesses a "sweet voice" (*SPP* 80) but little evidence of its character or its power appears in the narrator's account of the Poet's wanderings. When the Poet does speak, as he does to the swan that flees at the Poet's approach, he engages in monologue not dialogue, a characteristic indicating the private nature of his vocal expression and its lack of potency. The narrator makes clear the Poet's orientation in the masculine world of silent symbols.[3] Like his forefathers, who "Hang their mute thoughts on the mute walls around" (*SPP* 120), he is a reader and a writer, not a speaker. He is evidently accustomed to "gazing" on and drawing inspiration from "speechless shapes" (*SPP* 123–7).

His relationship with the "Arab maiden" (*SPP* 129), who longingly tends his steps and supplies him with food from her father's tent, confirms the Poet's vocal impotence and his lacking. She is her father's daughter. Viewed as the Poet's constitutive object, the maiden establishes his lack of voice. She is afraid to "speak her love" (*SPP* 134) and mirrors his desire. As he once gazed knowingly at "wild images" carved by "dead men" on the walls of "ruined temples"(*SPP* 116–19), she now gazes on his inexpressive "lips" while he slumbers, yet he utters no comforting words, forcing her to return home "Wildered, and wan, and panting" (*SPP* 139).

---

[2] With regard to how heavily music figured into Shelley's philosophy at this point, see Jean L. De Palacio, "Music and Musical Themes in Shelley's Poetry," *Modern Language Review* 59 (1964): 345–59 and Erland Anderson, *Harmonious Madness: A Study of Music Metaphors in the Poetry of Coleridge, Shelley, and Keats* (Salzburg: Institut fur Sprache und Literatur, 1975). Both critics agree that music eventually became a crucial component of Shelley's artistic vision, but Palacio asserts that, if anything, *Alastor* "may be termed a visual and olfactive poem far more than musical" (347). Anderson points to the Poet's relationship with the veiled maid as an early sign of the Shelley's interest in regarding music as a metaphor of visionary experience.

[3] The issue of the Poet's relation to the narrator lies at the heart of most of the scholarship that has been written about *Alastor*. Most readings of the poem point out that Shelley evaluates his own epistemology and aesthetics against those of William Wordsworth. Consequently, such readers as Wasserman, Steinman and Thurston regard the narrator, Poet (and in Thurston's case the Preface writer) as allegorical representatives of competing philosophical outlooks Shelley wished to interrogate. See Earl Wasserman, *Shelley: A Critical Reading* (Baltimore: The Johns Hopkins UP, 1971); Lisa Steinman, "Shelley's Skepticism," *ELH* 45 (1978): 255–69; Norman Thurston, "Author, Narrator and Hero in Shelley's *Alastor*," *Studies in Romanticism* 14 (1975): 119–31. Others, such as Keach, Kirchoff and Linkin see a far less distinct separation between the narrator, the Poet and Shelley. They believe that portions of the poem's identities manifest Shelley's sympathies, impulses and predilections, suggesting that Shelley is not as emotionally or intellectually distant as Wasserman, for example, indicates. See William Keach, *Shelley's Style* (New York: Methuen, 1984), Frederick Kirchoff, "Shelley's *Alastor*," *Keats-Shelley Journal* 32 (1983): 108–22; Harriet Linkin, "Shelley's Power as Perceiver," *European Romantic Review* 4 (1994): 151–62.

The secret treasure she had hoped to find, that which makes him desirable, remains buried in the world of his "innocent dreams" (*SPP* 137). In the end, she proves not to be the object voice, the positive object capable of producing vocal expression, he desires. The Poet's entire quest, his reason for leaving behind "his cold fireside and alienated home" (*SPP* 76), in fact, might be regarded as the consequence of subject formation and by necessity, therefore, of castration. Inscriptions left by "dead men" inspire, but they fail to satisfy. Obviously, the Poet searches for something else and that something might be his own public, dialogical voice.

The "veiled maid" he encounters in slumbering dream promises to satisfy that desire. She represents the object voice as well as the desiring other who seems to understand his secret treasure, holding "his inmost sense suspended in the web" (*SPP* 155) of her musical voice. Unlike the Arab maiden, whose pants of disappointment lack vocal accompaniment, the veiled maid draws body, music and desire into the same circle. Her disappearance at the conclusion of her performance, at the very moment when she embraces the Poet "in her dissolving arms" (*SPP* 187), repeats the Poet's initial castration, and it amplifies the lacking which has made him a desiring, wandering subject. The narrator's description of the maid establishes her as the Poet's specular other, as a metaphor of the vocal expressiveness he desires and as a medium of *jouissance*:

> He dreamed a veiled maid
> Sate near him, talking in low solemn tones.
> Her voice was like the voice of his own soul
> Heard in the calm of thought; its music long,
> Like woven sounds of streams and breezes, held
> His inmost sense suspended in its web
> Of many-coloured woof and shifting hues ...
> Soon the solemn mood
> Of her pure mind kindled through all her frame
> A permeating fire: wild numbers then
> She raised, with voice stifled in tremulous sobs
> Subdued by its own pathos: her fair hands
> Were bare alone, sweeping from some strange harp
> Strange symphony, and in their branching veins
> The eloquent blood told an ineffable tale.
> The beating of her heart was heard to fill
> The pauses of her music, and her breath
> Tumultuously accorded with those fits
> Of intermitted song. (*SPP* 151–7, 161–72)

Though the maid "talks," she apparently expresses herself not by way of words, but by means of "tones," "music long," "woven sounds," "wild numbers," "tremulous sobs" and the movement of her "eloquent blood." Captivating and perhaps taboo, the "tale" she tells is "ineffable." Her body functions as an instrument that conveys *jouissance,* a wild passion the Poet, at least in the context of his dream, seems to understand perfectly. The narrator's account of the maid's abilities connects the music she generates to fluid and air, "streams and breezes," suggesting paradoxically that this figment of the Poet's imagination is also a creature of nature, originating from a realm beyond the mute iterations of "dead men," whose carvings line the walls of "ruined temples," silent symbolic structures. More than this, the maid's affiliation with fluid and air confirms that her pedigree includes the object voice, which the subject cannot integrate into himself without jeopardizing his status as a subject. The idea that her departure from the Poet leaves him with a "vacant brain" (*SPP* 191) reinforces the notion that at the core of subjectivity lies emptiness, and, in this regard, the Poet serves as a self-reflexive figure: as are all written poems, this Poet is void of presence.

The maid's performance dramatizes the Poet's impotence. She sings to the accompaniment of her harp while he audits passively. While it might be argued, however, that this fantasy girl is no more than a passive performer and that it is the Poet's active imagination that conceives and then animates her, the concept of "interpassivity" suggests that the Poet's activity is hollow. He commands no vocal authority of his own and the illusory veiled maid becomes the passive embodiment of his inertia; surplus suffering and joy have been deposited within her, which explains why she utters during the same outpouring of expression "tremulous sobs" and "irresistible joy" (*SPP* 185). He, on the other hand, finds himself reduced to a "passive gaze impotently gaping at the object."[4] Impotence lingers after the dream, as the Poet awakes still gazing over "the empty scene, as vacantly / As ocean's moon looks on the moon in heaven" (*SPP* 201–2). He becomes the moon's image reflected by the ocean's surface; this reflected object, the *petit a* he has lost in the form of the veiled maid, constitutes him in his subjectivity, though the transaction paradoxically renders him a failed poet. A lament by the narrator, "Lost, lost, for ever lost, / In the wide pathless desart of dim sleep / That beautiful shape" (*SPP* 209–11), figures the Poet's ontological and vocational states: no fruitful self-presence, no capacity for social service.

The Poet's dream includes a fail-safe feature designed, perhaps, to counteract the effects of the maid's overpowering performance. The narrator reveals that her bare hands swept from "some strange harp / Strange symphony" and compounds the image by conveying that her "beating heart" filled the "pauses of her music," as though it were a percussion instrument punctuating the tale told by her "eloquent blood." By placing the maid's song within the context of a string instrument performance, the narrator employs convention as the means to structuring, harnessing and, therefore, limiting the "maid's" vocal expression. The construct implies, in other words, that instrumental accompaniment will keep the performing maid and her Poet-auditor grounded. The problem, though, is that the maid's body performs as though it were a wind instrument. Her "tremulous sobs," "gasping breath," which fuels "those fits / Of intermitted song," and

---

[4] Zizek 115.

"panting bosom" (*SPP* 183, 184), suggest that passion and spontaneity inform the "wild numbers" of her "voice" and that they cannot be successfully contained. Though she is clearly a product of dream, the veiled maid composes, performs and conducts her own expression, despite measures taken by the narrator and the Poet to channel her music.

The Poet's dream vision renders him more dead than alive. However, one wonders how we should regard his status, given that the maid's removal from him recalls the very transaction that makes subjectivity possible. He keeps "mute conference / With his still soul" (*SPP* 223–4) and travels among "the desolated tombs / Of Parthian kings" (*SPP* 242–3). The narrator records that the Poet lived "day after day, a weary waste of hours" (*SPP* 245) and that

> And now his limbs were lean; his scattered hair
> Sered by the autumn of strange suffering
> Sung dirges in the wind; his listless hand
> Hung like dead bone within its withered skin;
> Life, and the luster that consumed it, shone
> As in a furnace burning secretly
> From his dark eyes alone. (*SPP* 248–54)

As the last image in the series indicates, the Poet's orientation remains visual and by and large the memory of the veiled maid's "beloved eyes" (*SPP* 333), appearing later in the poem as "two eyes, / Two starry eyes" (*SPP* 489–90), is what motivates him to keep going. The image suggests that the Poet is at once the subject and the object of "gaze,"[5] an additional sign that something he perceives as vital to his makeup, the *petit a* belonging to the same category as voice, remains both relative but also estranged from him. Scopically, the maid's alluring gaze functions in the same way as the cotton reel Freud's grandson tossed and then retrieved. Both objects constitute subjectivity.

Once the Poet reaches his final resting place, however, that gaze becomes the object voice, fuelling his desire. On the narrative surface, at least, the genetics of that voice would seem to be equivocal; does it belong to the Poet or the maid? Perhaps it is an echo from his dream? As the Poet enters the bower, the narrator says

> One human step alone, has ever broken
> The stillness of its solitude:—one voice
> Alone inspired its echoes:—even that voice
> Which hither came, floating among the winds,
> And led the loveliest among human forms
> To make their wild haunts the depository

---

[5] Jacques Lacan, *The Four Fundamental Concepts of Psychoanalysis*, ed. Jacques-Alain Miller, trans. Alan Sheridan (New York and London: W. W. Norton & Company, 1981) 73–80.

Of all the grace and beauty that endued
Its motions, render up its majesty,
Scatter its music on the unfeeling storm .... (*SPP* 588-97)

The account suggests that the beckoning voice belongs both to the Poet and to the veiled maid. As living voice, she serves as the *objet petit a* evading the Poet, and her music constitutes him. The duality of that voice emphasizes that it both is and is not the Poet's and that to acquire it results in lost subjectivity, that is, in death. In typical elegiac fashion, the narrator laments the world's loss of a lovely spirit and he observes that the "breath of heaven" continued to blow through the "harmonious strings" of the deceased Poet's Adamic "frame," which has become a "fragile lute" (*SPP* 665-8). The image reveals the narrator's and, therefore, Shelley's phantasmic commitment not to the maid's unbridled expression, her ability to produce *jouissance*, but to the string instrument convention, regarding the Poet as, finally, someone capable of balanced expression.

The Poet's death-in-life existence once the maid divorces him qualifies as a life committed to death. The horror of the "real" haunting the Poet—that is, that *something* which resists symbolic articulation—stems not just from the fact that, lacking voice, he lacks something vital. Even more horrific is the possibility that lacking represents the price of subjectivity. To experience a symbolic life means leading a life of deprivation. Applying this same concept to the vocation of composing poetry suggests that following the poet's calling entails subjecting oneself to empty, voiceless language. Once the Poet leaves behind the symbolic realm of dead men, dead kings and the monuments they have constructed, he loses all sign of support. As for the narrator, he distances himself from the Poet and draws strength and security from his role as the Poet's elegist. However, the Poet's post-mortem status, serving as the divine wind's instrument, mirrors the narrator's.

By his own admission, the narrator hangs "moveless, as a long-forgotten lyre / Suspended in the solitary dome / Of some mysterious and deserted fane" (*SPP* 42-4). He "waits" to have the "breath" of his "Great Parent" (*SPP* 45) bestowed upon him, and the image suggests that until that happens, like Adam, he remains lifeless clay. In this respect, he and the Poet share the same ontological stature, the narrator remaining an instrument void of a self-present voice of his own. Shelley's traditional orientation (and perhaps his anxiety brought on by the horror of the "real") surfaces in the trope itself, however, which maintains the narrator's commitment to the world of the word. The lyre metaphor reveals the narrator's discomfort with his Mother's unpredictable and non-referential mode of expression via "hollow sighs," "voluptuous pantings," "tingling silentness" and "sweet kisses" (*SPP* 7-12). Whenever he employed those means in the past, mixing "awful talk and asking looks" and "breathless kisses," either Nature ignored him, refusing to "render up [her] charge" and unveil her "inmost sanctuary" (*SPP* 33-8), or his offerings failed to register. The entreaty to Nature serving as prelude to the Poet's story consists not of these things, not nearly of "awful talk and asking looks," but of conventional blank verse narrative. Metaphorically speaking, the narrator becomes the instrument of the Poet's story, not outlet to the "Mother of this unfathomable world" (*SPP* 18)

The narrator's split from Nature and his "beloved brotherhood" (*SPP* 1) classifies him with the Poet, his ontological brother, whose orientation is logos. Nature's elements communicate non-linguistically and this articulation of *jouissance*, of music in the metonymic form of "voluptuous pantings" and "sweet kisses," serves as the inaccessible lost object. The resultant deadlock accounts perhaps for the erotic and incestuous nature of the images he chooses, regarding his "Great Parent" (*SPP* 45) as a tease who refuses to satisfy him. The relationship qualifies as incestuous, because the narrator's Mother evidently both possesses something that belongs to her son and exists, in the form of his lost voice, as his offspring. In this respect, the same genetic constitution identifies her with the veiled maid.

An additional element of castration characterizes the narrator's relationship with the Poet, who might also serve as a vehicle for the narrator's lost object voice. In the narrator's eyes, the Poet credentials himself by becoming a lost soul who perhaps foolishly sacrifices all, including human companionship in the form of the Arab maiden, to pursue "strange truths" and "the thrilling secrets of the birth of time" (*SPP* 77, 128). His life, in other words, qualifies as a tragic composition, though apparently no one, except the narrator, recognizes or acknowledges its existence. The narrator's estimation of the Poet's abilities might be more important than the Poet's actual accomplishments (which, aside from wandering and exploring, never take written form), however. The narrator believes the Poet possessed a gift for expression, observing that "Strangers have wept to hear his passionate notes," and that "Silence, too enamoured of that voice, / Locks it mute music in her rugged cell" (*SPP* 61, 65–6). He recalls the Poet inquiring of the fleeing swan:

> "And what am I that I should linger here,
> With voice far sweeter than thy dying notes,
> Spirit more vast than thine, frame more attuned
> To beauty, wasting these surpassing powers
> In the deaf air, to the blind earth, and heaven
> That echoes not my thoughts?" (*SPP* 285–90)

Apparently, the Poet's ideal voice exceeds all but the narrator's capacity to appreciate it. The idea that no other writer "Breathed o'er his dark fate one melodious sigh" (*SPP* 59) suggests that the narrator alone detects a secret treasure in the Poet. In specular fashion, it also indicates that the Poet serves as the narrator's secret treasure. His exploits, after all, inspire the narrator to compose poetry. The narrator's desire—to fulfill his own fantasy of becoming the Poet by capturing the poet's life story—enables him to accomplish what the Poet cannot: he produces a narrative poem. Paradoxically, then, while the narrator serves as the Poet's vocal other, the Poet serves as the narrator's lost object, and each functions additionally as the object desired by his other. The arrangement fails to achieve phantasmic success for two reasons, though: neither writer manages to integrate *jouissance* into his chosen form of expression, written or living narrative; furthermore, neither poet manages to become enduringly self-present through composition. The narrator is a fictional character, who ostensibly speaks for Shelley, who himself exists outside of the text, and the Poet performs the same role in relation to the narrator. Furthermore, narrator and Poet channel expression and desire, and they become manifestations of the object voice Shelley fails to capture. The entire narrative arrangement forecloses, therefore, on Shelley's attempt to marry voice and music to his words. The veiled maid remains lost to the Poet, as both remain lost to the narrator; all three remain lost to the author.

Shelley's fantasy of achieving immortal self-presence through the written word and of infusing his poetry with the music of *jouissance* fails to circumvent deadlocks in *The Revolt of Islam*, despite the sexual union of its two main characters. The fusion of Laon with Cythna would seem on the surface to represent an ideal coupling of language and voice, as the gifts brought forth by each partner create a mutually supportive and inspirational arrangement.[6] Cythna could never have become Laone, a high priestess and spokeswoman for the revolution, without the mentorship of Laon, and Laon's hymns would never have fuelled social upheaval without Cythna's instrumental voice conferring upon them eloquent and widespread public expression. Fractures in the fantasy emerge primarily from the sexualized view of expression that schematizes the narrative structure. Cythna and the strand woman, who serves as her narrative precursor in the text, embody an almost infinite vocal range, and this characteristic becomes a likely sign of Shelley's desire.

In *The Revolt of Islam* Shelley flirts with the possibility that true expression is fundamentally feminine.[7] Laon, for example, acts "interpassively," that is, by

---

[6] See Richard Cronin's discussion of Shelley's recognition of the problematical nature of incestuous coupling, despite his fascination with that relationship in the context of art. According to Cronin, Shelley knew that exogamy was necessary for keeping desire alive, in art, in love and in life; see "Shelleyan Incest and the Romantic Legacy," *Keats-Shelley Journal* 45 (1996): 61–76.

[7] See Mladen Dolar's conclusion to his essay "The Object Voice," *Gaze and Voice as Love Objects*, ed. Renata Salecl and Slavoj Zizek (Durham and London: Duke UP, 1996): 7–31. Also see William Keach's discussion of *The Revolt of Islam* in *Arbitrary Power: Romanticism, Language, Politics* (Princeton: Princeton UP, 2004). Keach argues that Cythna represents Shelley's attempt to revise efforts by Mary Wollstonecraft and Robert Southey to envision an alternative to traditional figures of "discursive and political power" (96–7) and that she becomes the "core of Shelley's revolutionary revision." Keach responds to the argument made by Richardson, namely that male Romantic writers were out to "colonize" the feminine, and the argument made by Leask, that the marking off of Cythna's voice in quotation marks indicates Shelley's effort to speak for her, by saying: "in Shelley's revisionary revolutionary fiction Cythna claims her own mind as 'the *type* of all' by becoming self-consciously the producer of historically constrained yet liberating supplements. Shelley's representation of a woman's linguistic and political agency through the figure of Cythna is not just another instance of narcissistic Romantic ventriloquism. The

"proxy,"[8] through Cythna, a role traditionally appropriate to the heterosexual woman who lives through her man. She liberates herself from capture, sweeps him off his feet in the middle of a battle between revolutionary and counter-revolutionary armies and, metaphorically, transmits life by way of her magnificent voice back into his dead body from her seat in the temple. Despite Teddi Chichester Bonca's assertion that Shelley strove from a young age to eradicate from himself elements of masculinity in order to gain entrance into a sorority governed by a feminine ethos of passionate understanding and interdependence, the phantasmic features of *The Revolt* would seem indicative of Shelley's interest in protecting the male poet's most precious commodity, his voice.[9] Shelley guards himself and his male protagonists from threats to their vocality by making them custodians of narrative. A non-specific speaker tells the strand woman's story (and we should recall that, like Cythna, she received inspiration and direction from a now-dead male poet) and then Laon sets his involvement with Cythna within a narrative of his own framing. Despite the operation of fantasy features such as these designed to stave off what Lacan regards as the horror of the "real," the possibility that the male word is empty and that the "decentered" male poet trades his secret treasure for symbolic authority continues to surface through cracks in Shelley's phantasmic construct.

When he introduces himself to us, Laon initially seems to fit the conventional standard for the ideal poet. From the moment he pledges to "arise and waken" the benighted "multitude" (*SPW* 784–5). Laon commits himself to the hope that attends him everywhere he goes and to the job of broadcasting a language of change:

> These hopes found words through which my spirit sought
> To weave a bondage of such sympathy,
> As might create some response to the thought
> Which ruled me now—and as the vapours lie
> Bright in the outspread morning's radiancy,
> So were these thoughts invested with the light
> Of language: and all bosoms made reply
> On which its lustre streamed, whene'er it might
> Through darkness wide and deep those tranced spirits smite. (*SPW* 802–10)

---

ventriloquist does not quote the voice of another but produces an illusion that his voice is that other's voice. This is not the structure of Shelley's rhetorical fiction in *The Revolt of Islam*" (116). See Alan Richardson, "Romanticism and the Colonization of the Feminine," *Romanticism and Feminism*, ed. Anne K. Mellor (Bloomington: U of Indiana P, 1988) 13–25; Nigel Leask, *British Romantic Writers and the East: Anxieties of Empire* (Cambridge: Cambridge UP, 1992).

[8] Zizek 118.

[9] Teddi Chichester Bonca, *Shelley's Mirrors of Love: Narcissism, Sacrifice, and Sorority* (Albany: State U of New York P, 1999).

Laon's imagery identifies his mission with enlightenment and his poetry with a spell, or visual "trance." In addition, it reveals Shelley's familiarity with discourse informing the debate surrounding the merits of mesmerism. According to Tim Fulford, the British mind associated "magnetism" with France and its revolution, primarily because it represented a force that could promote political as well as personal upheaval. While reactionaries believed the events of the French Revolution contained the potential for mesmerizing the British population into training its sights on its own monarchy, liberals believed the British government itself had managed to mesmerize its citizenry to focus its attention on the "sensual gods of avarice, ambition and absolutism;" in this way it could be encouraged to participate in its own oppression.[10] Though Shelley's use of light imagery emerges from the stock-and-trade dark/evil, light/good dichotomy, it paradoxically indicates that the power of Laon's language transmits the light of reason into the "bosoms" of his auditors. Working in the way of the sun, implying, perhaps, that Laon employs a methodology used by the son of the Christian God, Laon is no selfish demagogue leading his followers toward some selfish end of his own.

Even though Laon speaks the language of thought, he manages to charge his words with emotion, which results in a commitment to social justice. The immediacy of the transaction—he says he can feel the "senses" of his "heart's brother ... swim" and "hear" the "swift gaspings of his breath" (*SPW* 814), for example—would seem to indicate that Laon works by way of the spoken as opposed to the written word, and the erotic nature of its results invests Laon with a vocality convention generally reserves for females. Other metaphors create a different impression, however; they associate him with the values of masculine contest and with tyranny. He recalls commanding a "magic store" from which "I drew / Words which are weapons," and he observes that "round my heart there grew / The adamantine armour of their power" (*SPW* 841–3). Perhaps unaware of the ramifications of the distinction he draws between the "hymns" (*SPW* 915) he composed and Cythna's performance of them, he reveals that "all things became / Slaves to my holy and heroic verse" (*SPW* 933–4). Laon's metaphors secure him to a masculine world of violence Bonca quite correctly argues Shelley aimed to vanquish. Laon's writing, in an irony of which Shelley was most likely aware, participates in the counterproductive cycle of revolution and counter-revolution. At this point in his career, Laon is unable to regard himself as a victim of a faulty, or failed, imagination.[11] He lacks the ability to free himself from history. Consequently, his songs ultimately support a masculine, symbolic order that breeds division and lacks the liberating capacity of *jouissance*, which Lacan perceives as non-historical and "'freefloating.'"[12]

---

[10] Tim Fulford, "Conducting the Vital Fluid," *Studies in Romanticism* 43 (2004): 73.

[11] See Cian Duffy's fine article on Shelley's evolving understanding of the "historical and political potency of the imagination" (401). "'The Child of a Fierce Hour': Shelley and Napoleon Bonarparte," *Studies in Romanticism* 43 (2004): 399–416.

[12] Zizek 50.

Narrative events indicate that Laon should have begun to recognize the faultiness of his language. Apparently, long before Cythna's voice transformed his "heroic verse" into a song of liberation, Laon experienced betrayal at the hands of a friend with whom he had kept "lofty converse" (*SPW* 825). Laon recalls "that this friend ... like other men could weep / Tears which are lies, and could betray and spread / Snares for that guileless heart which for his own had bled" (*SPW* 825–8). It is not so much that Laon, in the same fashion as the speaker of the essay "On Love," finds his "language misunderstood like one in a distant and savage land" (*SPP* 503); the problem lies more with the fact that the early returns Laon collects regarding the efficacy of his compositions are misrepresentative. Sincere expression and lofty goals prove in the end powerless to combat selfishness and subterfuge.

A model male poet emerges ostensibly in the form of the Hermit, who frees Laon from prison. A hybrid exhibiting masculine and feminine powers of expression, the Hermit speaks with uncommon eloquence and writes poetry capable of making parents "weep" as they read his "writings to their babes" (*SPW* 1522–3). Recalling his rescue from capture, Laon reports "that from stony gloom a voice arose, / Solemn and sweet as when low winds attune / the midnight pines" (*SPW* 1356–8). He says the Hermit came to the "lone column" to which Laon had been chained,

> And with his sweet and mighty eloquence
> The hearts of those who watched it did unlock,
> And made them melt in tears of penitence. (*SPW* 1505–7)

The old man strikes Laon's chains, cradles him in his arms and transports him by boat to a seaside chamber, pausing during the journey to refresh Laon with a "healing potion" and to speak to him in a "human tone" the "poor victim" joys to hear (*SPW* 1387–94). Though an intrepid father figure, the Hermit also possesses maternal qualities. Laon remembers that the "aged man, so grand and mild, / Tended me, even as some sick mother seems / To hang in hope over a dying child" (*SPW* 1401–3). The entire rescue scene, in fact, parallels Cythna's rescue of Laon from the battlefield in Canto VI, raising the possibility that both characters serve as phantasmic manifestations of the object voice that has been removed from Laon's secret treasury. Each constitutes Laon's image of himself as a poet-prophet, but at the same time both figures, Cythna more than the Hermit, represent a power of eloquence he has lost.

The Hermit drops below Cythna in stature, because he sequesters himself from the public, symbolic realm, even though he continues to write and inspire young "voices" in "the Golden City" to make "tyrants ... tremble" (*SPW* 1531–2). By his own admission, the Hermit is "both unknown and old" (*SPW* 1558) and relies on Laon's name and his "soul-subduing tongue" to serve as the collective "lance to quell the mailed crest of wrong" (*SPW* 1563–6). The Hermit's comparison of Laon's tongue to a piercing lance counters those attributes that situate him within a culture of feminine care and allies him with a masculine culture of violent change.

He discloses this orientation when he recounts that he has studied "the lore of bards and sages old" and that their influence has enabled him to "unfold / Truth to my countrymen" (*SPW* 1514, 1517–18). Given this lineage, furthermore, the lance metaphor only serves to amplify his earlier acknowledgement that "'I have been thy passive instrument'" (*SPW* 1549). It is to the Hermit's credit that he cannot generate the transformative but violent power of Laon's tongue; however, the Hermit's passivity, though he has been operating secretly in Laon's stead during the latter's imprisonment, mirrors Laon's own ineffectuality. Along with Laon's name and his tongue (an ironic metaphor given the fact that Laon's words lack the capacity to embody it), the Hermit has acted, paradoxically, as a passive agitator for change. He becomes the constitutive instrument, therefore, of Laon's inability to present himself and his ideas to an oppressed population.

Cythna serves as Laon's object of desire, because she embodies the presence and eloquence he lacks. An orphan taken in by Laon's parents, she begins her training as his protégée, but quickly becomes closer to him than his "own shadow ... A second self, far dearer and more fair" (*SPW* 874–5). Laon's characterization of Cythna's extraordinary capacity for expression indicates that she is a gifted, perhaps natural, poet:

> And, in the murmur of her dreams was heard
> Sometimes the name of Laon:—suddenly
> She would arise, and, like the secret bird
> Whom sunset wakens, fill the shore and sky
> With her sweet accents—a wild melody!
> Hymns which my soul had woven to Freedom, strong
> The source of passion, whence they rose, to be;
> Triumphant strains, which, like a spirit's tongue,
> To the enchanted waves that child of glory sung— (*SPW* 910–18)

Clearly, Laon has authored Cythna's "strains" and inspires her performance, suggesting that she has become both vessel and instrument for his words; however, even he recognizes that Cythna infuses those "hymns which my soul had woven" with a vitality they have lacked. Marveling that so much innocence and power can inhabit the same creature, he finds himself asking: "what genius wild / Yet mighty, was enclosed within one simple child" (*SPW* 953–4). Her ability to convert his "song" (*SPW* 928) into a "wild melody" suggests that out of the realm of dream and imagination she energizes Laon's compositions with *jouissance*. In fact, once he hears his own songs performed by her for him, he comes to a fresh understanding of their substance and "purpose, the vast theme / Of those impassioned songs" (*SPW* 921–2). The temporary fusion of her "impassioned" voice with his "conceptions" results in a superior form of communication within which the presence of both partners inheres: "Hers too were all my thoughts, ere yet, endowed / With music and with light, their fountains flowed / In poesy" (*SPW* 940–2).

The idea that Cythna remains "unconscious of the power through which she wrought / The woof of such intelligible thought," drawing fuel from "the visions of her eloquent sleep" (*SPW* 966–8), implies her passivity and, by extension, Laon's activity. He not only composed the songs she sings; he submits her performance to poetic narrative, providing a frame within which they become meaningful. Paradoxically, though, the maneuver raises the possibility that the activity is false and that Laon performs the role of passive auditor, allowing himself to become the object of perversion, his writings serving as Cythna's instrument, from which he receives erotic pleasure. In this case, fantasy allows Laon (and Shelley) to maintain control of an otherwise untenable situation.[13] If Cythna represents the living voice Laon lacks, he arranges by means of a phantasmic narrative construct to become himself the object of desire, turning the tables in his favor. His own imagery, however, fractures that construct. He describes the effect of his "conceptions" on Cythna as a wind-born cloud and his "thoughts" as a flow of poetic "fountains," illuminating the possibility that his song finds expression only through metonym, through stand-ins for the self-present voice he fails to command. He conceives of her as his mirror image, "in hers mine own mind seeing" (*SPW* 948), and observes that, once she concluded her song, she turned her dream-enchanted face on his "with speechless grace" (*SPW* 944). She reflects back to him the secret treasure he still believes he possesses, but the idea that her face is "speechless" implies that what he sees in this acoustic mirror is his own silent vacancy.

Cythna's violent capture by the Tyrant's forces and her subsequent rape reenacts Laon's castration, a repetition that inflames the original wound at the same time that it confirms subjectivity. Losing his "voice" in this way reminds Laon of his subjugation to what Lacan calls the "big Other," and his own subsequent capture and imprisonment reinforces his bondage within the symbolic world of words, signs and a spectral power that operates from some unidentifiable seat of origin. The idea that Cythna functions once again as the object voice Laon desires emerges with Laon's observation that the "great Altar of the Federation," at which Cythna, now Laone, serves as "Priestess of this holiest rite," remains covered by "morning mists" (*SPW* 2072, 2146, 2079). A "female Shape upon an ivory throne," she shields herself further from definition by means of a "veil" that "shrouded her countenance bright" (*SPW* 2106, 2115). Identifying herself by name with Laon suggests that she is both his offspring and his property. Her veiled appearance at this point in the narrative indicates, however, that she cannot be drawn back into the subject from which she originated.

Laon observes that Laone's voice continues to embody a quality of wildness, a *jouissance,* which invests her speech with uncommon passion and penetrative power. Her voice reaches and heals "restless multitudes" (*SPW* 2080). This is the power Laon and Shelley believe they once had, and it is the phantasmic goal of both poets to reclaim it through narrative. At this juncture of Laon's tale, his

---

[13] See Zizek's discussion of the phantasmic role played by perversion in *The Plague of Fantasies*.

characterization of Laone's voice reflects back to him his own diminished vocal stature, reduced as he is to the position of passive auditor; what he now perceives is a portrait of his own lacking. In the aftermath of Laone's address to the crowd surrounding her altar, Laone recollects

> She, like a spirit through the darkness shining,
> In tones whose sweetness silence did prolong,
> As if to lingering winds they did belong,
> Poured forth her inmost soul: a passionate speech
> With wild and thrilling pauses woven among,
> Which whoso heard, was mute, for it could teach
> To rapture like her own all listening hearts to reach. (*SPW* 2274–80)

Images of air and fluid convey the timeless and natural potency of Laone's voice. Her sweet "tones" seem born on "lingering winds," and she "pours" forth her "inmost soul" via "passionate speech." In the succeeding stanza, Laon notes that "her voice was as a mountain stream which sweeps / The withered leaves of Autumn to the lake" (*SPW* 2281–2). These tropes demonstrate, moreover, that she has mastered the art of unifying self with voice and with language. Paradoxically, because images identifying Laone with air and fluid consist of metonym, they reveal the horror fantasy aims to hide from Laon and from Shelley: self-presence, the "thing" both poets seek, is missing; as must be the case if subjectivity is to remain constituted, substitutes occupy its place.

Laon's first contact with Laone is aural, and he bears witness to the cleansing and revitalizing power of her eloquence.

> And, neither did I hear the acclamations,
> Which from brief silence bursting, filled the air
> … nor the vision fair
> Of that bright pageantry beheld,—but blind
> And silent, as a breathing corpse did fare,
> Leaning upon my friend, till like a wind
> To fevered cheeks, a voice flowed o'er my troubled mind.
>
> Like music of some minstrel heavenly-gifted,
> To one whom fiends enthral, this voice to me …. (*SPW* 2116–17, 2120–6)

Initially, it would seem that the encounter constitutes the fantasy reunion Laon had hoped for. As soon as he experiences the return of his lost object, he fills with renewed health and life. Laone's voice liberates him from the bondage that ensues from the moment one becomes a subject and is beset with desires, which cannot be satisfied. Laon's description of himself "as a breathing corpse" injects an element of instability into the arrangement, however, since the phrase generates the possibility that reunification with the vocal Laone compromises Laon's credibility as author of this narrative: corpses do not breathe. The error suggests that Laon has at least temporarily lost the ability to control his language. Contact with the self-presence and passion Laone represents threatens to dislodge Laon from his grounding in the symbolic.

Cythna rescues Laon from the battle that follows the Festival of Liberty and subsequently immerses him in a cloistered world of music. Their sexual union anticipates in every way the model Shelley lays out in the essay "On Love." Natural as well as psychosomatic harmonies inform their erotic correspondence. Their coupling, occurring as it does in the sixth canto of this 12-canto epic, appears to represent the apex of Shelley's fantasy, a bringing together of logos and *jouissance*, voice and word; however, one might argue that the true climax happens once Laon leaves Cythna behind in order to exercise successfully his revitalized power of public expression, something that remains trapped somewhere in Laon's past throughout most of the narrative.

Despite being surrounded by the clamor of battle and by "impotent ... tongues" of men as "they lolled into the air" (*SPW* 2478), Laon's attention locks onto to Cythna's approach on horseback, remarking that this bright "Phantom"

> ... relaxed its course
> As it approached me, and the wind that flows
> Through night, bore accents to mine ear whose force
> Might create smiles in death—the Tartar horse
> Paused, and I saw the shape its might which swayed,
> And heard her musical pants, like the sweet source
> Of waters in the desert , as she said,
> "Mount with me, Laon, now!"—I rapidly obeyed. (*SPW* 2507–14)

On the face of things it might seem that contact with the Tyrant has infected this sword-wielding Cythna with his ethos of violent contest, but the sexual pun in the last line of this passage as well as Laon's association of her with music and natural elements contradict that impression. Cythna has other things on her mind. She takes her partner to a "lone ruin" by the ocean, where Laon recalls hearing

> the murmur of the motion
> Of waters, as in spots for ever haunted
> By the choicest winds of Heaven, which are enchanted
> To music, by the wand of Solitude. (*SPW* 2535–8)

Though the presence of fantasy images involving air and fluid countervail the possibility that Cythna's bower will restore presence to Laon rather than constitutive absence, the predominance of "music wild and soft that filled the listening air" (*SPW* 2586) fuels the opposite possibility.

Laon and Cythna communicate primarily along somatic channels. Talk leads to silence, which in turn "causes / The baffled heart to speak with sighs and tears"

(*SPW* 2605–6). Laon reports that "wildering passion swalloweth up the pauses / Of inexpressive speech" (*SPW* 2607–8), thereby suggesting that their passion for one another eludes the grasp of words. In addition to shared upbringing and appearance, the sympathetic "blood itself which ran within our frames" (*SPW* 2608–10) culminates in the formation of a single "voice." That voice finds harmonic accompaniment in the form of a "wild Meteor by some wild wind sent" that orchestrates a symphony of light, sound and song: "A wondrous light, the sound as of a spirit's tongue" (*SPW* 2617–22). Laon characterizes the sexual union of their two "frames" as a rhythmic mingling, a "beating" (*SPW* 2633–5) of burning blood, anticipating the lyre metaphor Shelley uses to describe the merger of antitype and prototype, though Laon stops short of classifying the coupling as a string instrument performance. He avoids relegating it, therefore, to the realm of logos.

Even here, though, Laon's imagery betrays him. Like the meteor that marks its emergence, the conjoined voices of Laon and Cythna will inevitably crash to earth. Laon invests himself in the notion that he and Cythna have elevated their communication to the level of ideal expression, to make themselves, that is, present throughout the surrounding environment. He reports that

> The tones of Cythna's voice like echoes were
> Of these far murmuring streams; they rose and fell,
> Mixed with mine own in the tempestuous air,— (*SPW* 2704–6)

Laon's language indicates his belief that finding Cythna has restored him to his natural state, that she has realigned his ontological rhythms and introduced him to a superior plane of expression. More to the point, perhaps, is that Shelley, for whom Laon serves as interpassive object, demonstrates an inability to "traverse" the fantasy himself.

Laon's reunification with Cythna, his lost object voice, returns him to his social mission, except that now he possesses the capacity to reach directly hearts and minds with his eloquence, an ability he recounted earlier in the narrative but failed to demonstrate. He appears in disguise before the Tyrant and his senate in hopes of trading his life for Cythna's transportation to America. Recalling the episode in third person, Laon reports,

> Dark Priests and haughty Warriors gazed on him
> With baffled wonder, for a hermit's vest
> Concealed his face; but, when he spake, his tone,
> Ere yet the matter did their thoughts arrest,—
> Earnest, benignant, calm, as from a breast
> Void of all hate or terror—made them start;
> For as with gentle accents he addressed
> His speech to them, on each unwilling heart
> Unusual awe did fall—a spirit-quelling dart. (*SPW* 4342–50)

The scene is reminiscent of Laone's address to the multitudes from her altar seat, in that Laon in this instance manages to enchant the crowd not necessarily by way of words per se, but by means of intangible vocal qualities such as "tone" and "gentle accents." Despite evidence of these qualities in his "speech," qualities which convention associates both with music and feminine expression, Laon does not retrospectively invest his performance with qualities of air and fluid, as he does Cythna's.

The omission suggests that his eloquence embodies a symbolic pedigree, a possibility supported by his ability to sway enslavers who themselves have become slaves to such "symbols" as "purple, and gold, and steel" (*SPW* 4381–2). The omission further suggests that the voice Laon recalls hearing at this time was not a stand-in, an object he had lost, but the real, self-present article. Ostensibly, what influences those young warriors gathered around the Tyrant's throne is no wild magic or heavenly harmony, but the force of Laon's convictions and the tranquility of his spirit. According to Laon the young warriors "fed and hung" upon his "eloquent accents" as "bees ... mountain-flowers," and a slave who raised his sword to strike found that Laon's "voice unstrung his sinews, and he threw / His dagger on the ground, and pale with fear, / Sate Silently" (*SPW* 4391–2, 4402–4). Whereas Cythna characteristically appears as an angel or as a Shape speaking ethereally from behind a veil, Laon speaks from underneath a hermit's garb. Nevertheless, though Laon's voice apparently does not contain elements of air, fluid and wildness, it exhibits a similar ability to transform temporarily its auditor.

Earlier in the narrative, Laone recounted details from her captivity among the Tyrant's "thralls," remembering that one day

> The Tyrant heard her singing to her lute
> A wild, and sad, and spirit-thrilling lay,
> Like winds that die in wastes—one moment mute
> The evil thoughts it made, which did his breast pollute. (*SPW* 2862–5)

This passage suggests that music forms a rift Laon's imagination evidently cannot close, however. He continues to sexualize human expression. Laon claims that he has composed hymns, but the ability to perform them effectively in public—before his fellow citizens, before the Tyrant and senate, before the reader of this narrative—eludes him. Shelley fails to recognize and eliminate from his phantasmic narrative the conventional notion that music remains a woman's province and that a man lacks the ability to write his thoughts and feelings and then serve as his own instrument of expression in order to present himself to the world. Laon compounds the significance of this blindspot when he implies that his eloquence fails to sway the Tyrant's minions once he strips off the hermit's garb and reveals himself to them. Though the narrative indicates on its surface that the mob turns on the Stranger because it has agreed to take Laon's life in exchange for Cythna's, Laon's unmasking suggests the possibility that his rhetorical effectiveness surfaces only when he constitutes himself metaphorically through some object, in this case in character. Though the hermit and Laon are familiar, they are also estranged, in the same way each subject chooses to recognize itself in a voice to which he or she has become estranged. The episode indicates, therefore, that Laon wields the power to persuade only when he becomes a "decentered" subject.

Shelley compensates for Laon's failure to persuade the Tyrant to spare Cythna by removing his hero and heroine from the socio-symbolic world, projecting their relationship into an ethereal world of music:

> And is this death?—The pyre has disappeared,
> The Pestilence, the Tyrant, and the throng;
> The flames grow silent—slowly there is heard
> The music of a breath-suspending song,
> Which, like the kiss of love when life is young,
> Steeps the faint eyes in darkness sweet and deep:
> With ever-changing notes it floats along,
> Till on my passive soul there seemed to creep
> A melody, like waves on wrinkled sands that leap. (*SPW* 4594–602)

It would appear that Cythna and her daughter serve as stewards of this realm, since it is Cythna who wakes Laon from his death and introduces him to this musical paradise, and her daughter who captains the boat that will sail the trio off into eternity. Once again, however, it appears that Laon performs the truly active role, because he functions as narrator of these events, while the two females feed him their observations. Laon's acknowledgement, though, that "on my passive soul there seemed to creep / A melody like waves on wrinkled sands that leap" confirms the true operation of the dynamic in which he finds himself. He has become a passive conduit for impressions fed to him by mother and daughter. The final image from the passage quoted above captures this ambiguity. It is difficult to determine whether it is Laon's soul or the melody, "wrinkled sands" and "waves," respectively, that respond with a "leap." The word "creep" in this formation unsettles the image even further, because it suggests that melody jeopardizes Laon's male identity, washing away its distinctive "wrinkles."

The visionary narrator who opens *The Revolt of Islam* encounters a beautiful Woman "sitting beneath the rocks, upon the sand / Of the waste sea" (*SPW* 262–4). A musical creature, she commands extraordinary powers of expression. Characterizing her voice, he reports that it "was like the wildest, saddest tone, / Yet sweet, of some loved voice heard long ago" and her language he describes as a "strange melody" that "might not belong to earth. I heard, alone, / What made its music more melodious be, / The pity and the love of every tone" (*SPW* 316–7, 289–92). The "strain" she sings he labels as "unintelligible" (*SPW* 300) to anyone but the wounded Serpent, a Shelleyan symbol of social justice, to whom she ministers. He associates her expression with natural elements and marvels at its abundance and ubiquity:

> Loosening her star-bright robe and shadowy hair
> [She] poured forth her voice; the caverns of the vale
> That opened to the ocean, caught it there,
> And filled with silver sounds the overflowing air. (*SPW* 285–8)

As they always do in the phantasmic narrative Shelley's writing recycles, however, images of air and fluid mark the emptiness of the Woman's voice by suggesting that her "strange melody" lacks definition and therefore gestures toward something missing, something that cannot be captured by words. Though the trope specifies that her voice fills a vacancy, it implies that "the caverns of the vale" filled with absence, with the sound that constitutes her rather than the Woman herself.

The narrator's imagery, then, conveys both his lacking and the emptiness of his authority, especially if one considers that the bulk of the poem consists of revelation, the product of anxiety and dream. If the Woman on the strand figures forth the *jouissance* and potent vocality he has lost, her character also confirms that this collective "thing itself," the *objet petit a*, for which he searches cannot be captured. The Woman's story and the ensuing main narrative reflect the narrator and by virtue of that fact constitute him. His words fill out formerly blank pages in the same way the Woman's voice fills caverns, but ultimately both phenomena lack presence.

As a narrative construct, the confluence of the narrator's and Woman's resources seems to produce the results Shelley was looking for, since the Woman's musical enchantment of the narrator spawns 12 cantos in Spenserian stanza. At this early stage in the poem it would seem that the narrator serves as the Woman's instrument. However, it turns out that the Woman on the strand, who began life as an orphan living "far from men" (*SPW* 442), was influenced by

> A dying poet [who] gave me books, and blessed
> With wild but holy talk the sweet unrest
> In which I watched him as he died away—. (*SPW* 454–6)

The poet's mastery of books and his ability to balance the "holy" with the "wild" in his "talk" qualify him as the ideal mentor and speaker, though his death reveals that the ideal is flawed. Integrating speech with *jouissance* and writing cancels out subjectivity, because all three lose their object, and therefore constitutive, status.

Guardianship for the orphan apparently shifts gender after the poet's death, when Venus, "the Morning star" (*SPW* 485), begins visiting her "when [she] rose from sleep" (*SPW* 485). However, male authority reemerges in the form, apparently, of the dying poet's spirit, which bears the Morning star on his brow. Reminiscent of the veiled maid in *Alastor*, this "winged youth" (*SPW* 500) appears as a sexually potent shade surrounded by radiant light:

> ... a wild dissolving bliss
> Over my frame he breathed, approaching near,

> And bent his eyes of kindling tenderness
> Near mine, and on my lips impressed a lingering kiss,—. (*SPW* 501-4)

Youth and poet inspire the Woman in the same way Laon inspired Cythna when she was a child. Both women appear to become passive instruments of male inspiration and authority, though in that role they mirror clearly the genuine passivity of their male counterparts: the poet is dead; the "winged youth" paradoxically finds expression as "A Shape of speechless beauty" (*SPW* 497); Laon without Cythna remains an alienated auditor. Though Shelley's imagination tries to relegate woman to the realm of instrument, characterizing her as a resource that can be subjectivized and exploited, it cannot overcome the dynamics of subjectivity or eradicate the plagues of fantasy.

First impressions of *Rosalind and Helen* might suggest that Shelley's fantasy has short-circuited, because the heterosexual union of Lionel and Helen results in Lionel's death, an event he himself initiates. Helen's musical performance puts an end to his lingering poor health by killing him. The poem's imagery, delivered by Helen's narrative, suggests that the fault lies with the *excess* of her music (a "long quivering cry," "the awful sound of my own voice" and "sounds," produced by her harp "which my skill could ne'er awaken," *SPW* 1142, 1149, 1140), a supplementary circumstance brought on by Lionel. Evidently, he went too far. Lionel led Helen to his mother's favorite shrine, introduced her to his mother's harp and encouraged her to extend the performance begun by a nightingale, whose heavenly tune filled the twilight air with enchantment. In fact, the poem offers the possibility that Shelley has approached a point at which he might traverse his own fantasy, for it seems to caution its readers about the dangers involved when one indulges with abandon the desire for the lost object voice. Lionel succeeds at integrating himself within Helen's spirit and consciousness, representing a union of logos and *jouissance*, but he sacrifices both his authority and his subjectivity in the process. His undoing installs Helen in the role of narrator. Closer consideration of the episode reveals, however, that Lionel's orchestration of his life's final chapter qualifies as a masterstroke, establishing him as the ideal poet.

Lionel seems to have achieved that status long before his final moments. Helen observes that, from the time she met him, Lionel exercised uncommon powers of expression. Reminiscent of Laon standing before the Tyrant, Lionel "stood at the throne of armed power / Pleading for a world of woe;" his "words," she says, "could bind / Like music the lulled crowd, and stem / That torrent of unquiet dream, / Which mortals truth and reason deem" (*SPW* 630–1, 636–9). His voice rained "like dew from his sweet talk,"

> ... and through their ears,
> The subtle witchcraft of his tongue
> Unlocked the hearts of those who keep
> Gold, the world's bond of slavery. (*SPW* 643, 651–4)

Helen's testimony makes clear that Lionel's powers of persuasion were not limited to oratory. He also excelled as a writer:

> For he made verses wild and queer
> On the strange creeds priests hold so dear,
> Because they bring them land and gold.
> Of devils and saints and all such gear,
> He made tales which whoso heard or read
> Would laugh till he were almost dead. (*SPW* 680–5)

A master poet, Lionel channels the disruptive, "wild," energy of *jouissance* into satiric verses that bring readers pleasure by burlesquing clerical authority and by puncturing hypocrisy.

The extraordinary nature of Lionel's literary authority fails to spare him from the fate Shelley in *A Defence of Poetry* claims all poets suffer. Eventually, Lionel's words lost their saliency, as "public hope grew pale and dim / In an altered time and tide" (*SPW* 692–3). The blow to his authority drives Lionel away from his home, and it compromises his health. At this point he meets Helen and the narrative assumes a familiar pattern. Her love revitalizes him and soon the self-indulgent "mournful verses" (*SPW* 762) he composed evidently in the wake of a previous, failed union with a woman were replaced by "words" that "grew subtile fire, which made / The air his hearers breathed delight" (*SPW* 793–4). Putting his past behind him, "his talk, and looks, and mien ... did become infectious" (*SPW* 803, 808). Sexual union with Helen ("And so we loved, and did unite / All that in us was yet divided" *SPW* 844–5) restores him to his former prowess. Led off to prison as a subversive by "ministers of misrule" (*SPW* 857), Lionel forecasts the eventual fall of tyranny to a crowd of spectators,

> with voice that made them shiver
> And clung like music in my brain,
> And which the mute walls spoke again
> Prolonging it with deepened strain. (*SPW* 890–3)

Upon his release from prison, Lionel remains undaunted. His "words" bid his now-sympathetic jailers a "kind farewell" (*SPW* 913), and Helen's account reveals that the two lovers remain in tune with one another, body and soul. She testifies that the "blood in our fingers intertwined / Ran like the thoughts of a single mind" (*SPW* 940–1). When they retire at night, she says,

> ... new emotions came,
> Which seemed to make each mortal frame
> One soul of interwoven flame,
> A life in life, a second birth
> In worlds diviner far than earth,

> Which, like two strains of harmony
> That mingle in the silent sky
> Then slowly disunite, passed by
> And left the tenderness of tears,
> A soft oblivion of all fears,
> A sweet sleep. (*SPW* 977–87).

Recollections such as these make one wonder why Lionel embraces death rather than the possibility of a second restoration under Helen's care. Perhaps the answer rests with the fact that he has lost for a second time his stature as a poet capable of transforming the minds and hearts of his countrymen. His return home to his mother's estate, essentially removing himself from circulation and giving credibility to earlier criticism from his enemies that his denial of wealth, fame and power to which he might lay claim was unnatural, would seem to constitute a surrender to circumstances. Ultimately, his writing proved incapable of destroying for good entrenched oppression. It is possible, therefore, that Lionel's assisted suicide conveys through metaphor Shelley's recognition that voice and music will always exceed control by the word, and that any attempt to integrate the two by means of heterosexual coupling results in the destruction of male subjectivity. Helen's narrative extends the insight to the widest register when she implies that even before Lionel entered her sphere of influence, he inherited eloquence from a musical mother, whose magic he was able to unite to words. From within an "ivory dome" the sound of Lionel's mother's "harp would kindle there / The melody of an old air" (*SPW* 1097–9) capable of bringing the villagers listening below to tears. Though Lionel managed to conflate feminine music with masculine words, his verse failed to produce lasting results and to maintain Lionel as a threat to the "big Other," as his inexplicable release from prison suggests.

Helen's recollection of Lionel's final moments raises the possibility, however, that death consolidates Lionel's authority and ensures his survival through words. Helen says that in preparation for her musical performance, Lionel

> ... paused, and to my lips he bent
> His own: like spirit his words went
> Through all my limbs with the speed of fire ...
> Yes, 'twas his soul that did inspire
> Sounds, which my skill could ne'er awaken;
> And first, I felt my fingers sweep
> The harp, and a long quivering cry
> Burst from my lips in symphony:
> The dusk and solid air was shaken,
> As swift and swifter the notes came
> From my touch, that wandered like quick flame
> And from my bosom, labouring
> With some unutterable thing.

> The awful sound of my own voice made
> My faint lips tremble; in some mood
> Of wordless thought Lionel stood ....
> (*SPW* 1131–3, 1139–51)

Though Lionel's gesture is merely a kiss, the action of his lips becomes a metaphor of authorship. He pours his spirit into Helen and the initiative makes her capable of extraordinary expression, so much so that she becomes estranged from her own voice and her playing of the harp's strings. She recalls uttering "a long quivering cry" and remembers that her "bosom" labored to deliver "some unutterable thing." Helen's language suggests that her performance serves as a castration constituting her as a new subject, that is, as a hybrid subject that emerges as the vessel for Lionel's spirit. Helen becomes Lionel's composition, his masterwork, a living text capable of reproducing Lionel's life story for anyone willing to listen. Unlike his earlier writings, the textual Helen, even in exile, preserves his memory within her verse narrative.

Helen's activity remains under Lionel's control, making her his passive other, though her passivity, as it usually does in fantasy, mirrors (this time acoustically) Lionel's own. He stands in "wordless thought," despite performing "gestures" (*SPW* 1160) that amplify Helen's expressive power:

> And from the twinkling wires among,
> My languid fingers drew and flung
> Circles of life-dissolving sound.
> Yet faint; in aery rings they bound
> My Lionel, who, as every strain
> Grew fainter but more sweet, his mien
> Sunk with the sound relaxedly;
> And slowly now he turned to me,
> As slowly faded from his face
> That awful joy: with looks serene
> He was soon drawn to my embrace,
> And my wild song then died away
> In murmurs: words I dare not say
> We mixed, and on his lips mine fed
> Till they methought felt still and cold. (*SPW* 1164–78)

The possibility that Helen's abilities fall short of Lionel's designs arises with her confession that the lovers mixed intimate words in a private moment she now dares "not say." She withholds part of Lionel from public audition, suggesting, therefore, that the confluence of her "wild song" with his private words and gestures has given way to "unwritten rules" of which the symbolic world consists.[14] The

---

[14] Zizek 28.

temporary merger of *jouissance* and logos during Helen's performance, in other words, devolves to the status quo once that "wild song ... died away."

Despite the promise of the fantasy arrangement created by the binding of Lionel to the "aery rings" of sound produced by Helen, *Rosalind and Helen* hints at Shelley's reluctance to promote Helen's authority. Expressing a wish that she would rather die than live without Lionel, Helen remembers her responsibility to her child, Lionel's son, and declares "Alas, we know not what we do / When we speak words" (*SPW* 1193–4). This statement implies that Helen is a text prone to misrepresentation. Earlier in the narrative she reveals a penchant for instability when she loses her way to "Fenici's seat" (*SPW* 74). When Henry points out the error, Helen says "Yes: I know: I was bewildered" (*SPW* 77–8). Perhaps this is why Shelley employs an unobtrusive, third-person narrator (for example, "The boy / Lifted a sudden look upon his mother," 85–6). Helen's story, which is intertwined with Lionel's, requires male narrative support. Evidently, Shelley believes Helen is at her best when she serves as an instrument of male authority, although this reversion to convention in the end undermines what Lionel achieves in fantasy.

In *Prometheus Unbound*, Shelley presents a sexualized version of cosmic rejuvenation. If the first and second acts represent conditions governed primarily by logos and *jouissance*, respectively, the third and fourth acts represent phantasmic versions of what might happen if these two informing principles were to merge.[15] While it might be argued that the text's complex experimentation with form, style and phonics suggests that it achieves a fuller and more substantial version of Shelley's fantasy than *Alastor, The Revolt of Islam* or *Rosalind and Helen* manage to accomplish, the same types of fracture compromising the fantasies underwriting those poems surface in *Prometheus Unbound*.

With regard to the phantasmic narrative Shelley has scripted, three focal points emerge in the play's opening act: delivery of the curse to Prometheus by the Phantasm of Jupiter; the correspondence that unfolds between Prometheus and his mother, Earth, and the supplementary role of Asia's sisters, Ione and Panthea. The Phantasm of Jupiter serves as the acoustic mirror of Prometheus,

---

[15] Criticism devoted to *Prometheus Unbound* has long recognized Shelley's commitment to exploring the limitations of language and the possibility of carving out new possibilities for the future of human experience. Tetreault and Foss focus on Shelley's adoption of the lyrical drama model as the context for programming within the text a musical line of transmission; see Ronald Tetreault, "Shelley at the Opera," *ELH* 48 (1981): 144–71, and Chris Foss, "Shelley's Revolution in Poetic Language," *European Romantic Review* 9 (1998): 501–18. A number of other interpretations have concentrated on issues of utterance and authority, while feminist psychoanalytic readings of the play examine these and similar issues by applying models based on gender and family dynamics. See, for example, Susan Hawk Brisman, "'Unsaying His High Language': The Problem of Voice in *Prometheus Unbound, Studies in Romanticism* 16 (1977): 51–86; William Hildebrand, "Naming-Day in Asia's Vale," *Keats-Shelley Journal* 32 (1983): 190–203; Barbara Gelpi, *Shelley's Goddess* (Oxford: Oxford UP, 1992); Laura Claridge, *The Paradox of Desire* (Ithaca: Cornell UP, 1992).

reconstituting him as a vocal agent in the logocentric universe, and the curse it embodies, therefore, functions as the object voice, as the "thing," Prometheus has lost which remains his object of desire. If Prometheus were to reclaim and thereby reintegrate the curse, he would reestablish himself as co-sovereign of Jupiter's kingdom, but in the process he would sacrifice his subjectivity and become a non-entity, his Promethean stature subsumed by Jupiter. This is the threat raised by the Phantasm when it takes the form of Jupiter and not Prometheus. Were Prometheus to embrace the curse once again once the Phantasm recalls it, the two would merge, and the identity of Prometheus's identity defined by the traditional world of the symbolic would be lost. The idea that Prometheus fails to recognize and then reassume ownership over the curse establishes him in his own, separate, subjectivity. At the conclusion of the Phantasm's performance, Prometheus requests Earth's help. He asks, "Were these my words, O Parent?" and she replies "They were thine" (*SPP* 1. 302–3). The failure of Prometheus to recognize his voice or his words in the form of the Phantasm raises the possibility that this potential union represents the wrong fit, that the true acoustic mirror of Prometheus lies elsewhere, namely in Asia's vale.

At this point in the drama, Shelley's fantasy dictates that Prometheus must remain estranged from his voice in order to remain in a state of desire, which will lead to a merger with Asia and her music, the route to ideal authority and self-presence. Despite numerous indications in Act 1 that the desiring subject might readily achieve these goals, the dialogue ultimately suggests that ideal authority and self-presence occur in corrupted form only and, therefore, do not exist. For example, at the initial appearance of the Phantasm, Ione finds herself unable to distinguish between the "Shape" she notices and "a throng of sounds" (*SPP* 1. 226), implying that aural pronouncement conflates with visual inscription, and that some aspect of Jupiter retains, therefore, the potential to assume supreme authority. Panthea validates Ione's initial impression when she observes that the arriving "sound is of whirlwind underground," and that the Shape it accompanies "is awful like the sound" (*SPP* 1. 231, 233). This series of observations culminates when Prometheus addresses the Phantasm as "Tremendous Image!" and bids it to "Speak the words which I would hear" (*SPP* 1. 246, 248). The Phantasm itself counteracts the impression created, however, when it refers to itself as "a frail and empty phantom" that fails to recognize the "unaccustomed sounds" that "Are hovering on my lips" (*SPP* 1. 241–3). Prometheus punctures the Phantasm's illusion of authority once and for all when he determines that, even though the phantom serves as the conduit for words, "no thought inform[s] thine empty voice" (*SPP* 1. 249). Ultimately, Jupiter's Phantasm voids Jupiter's authority.

Shelley's characterization of Jupiter's Phantasm in many ways conforms to the rapacious and lecherous god of ancient mythology who assumes altered form in order to gain what he desires, using that form as the instrument of his will. The Phantasm demonstrates that capacity by means of reflexive inquiry when it inquires of itself, "Why have the secret powers of this strange world / Driven me, a frail and empty phantom, hither / On direst storms?" (*SPP* 1. 241–3), suggesting that, even though it merely shadows Jupiter's form, it commands self-presence. The phantom immediately undercuts that status, though, when it claims not to recognize the "unaccustomed sounds / ... hovering on my lips" (*SPP* 1. 242–3). The acknowledgement verifies the Phantasm's castration, and this formation, in turn, confirms Jupiter's lacking: the curse Prometheus spoke was neither Jupiter's nor Prometheus's; neither figure can "subjectivize" it. As a metaphor of the object voice, the curse escapes god and Titan, though it continues to define who they are.

In this respect, Phantasm and curse achieve the collective status of text. The curse in particular lacks its original vitality, and when it re-enters the world it is not the voice of Prometheus that speaks it. In this respect, it is no different than a poem. Despite its Promethean origin, the curse detaches itself from the Titan and when he utters it, and, once it enters the world, it becomes separate from him, though it figures forth the subject who finds his substance in that object reflection. In relation to Prometheus, the curse represents the secret treasure Earth and its elements revere. This collective other desires him on the grounds that he can be identified with the text he created. Prometheus acknowledges, however, that the words the Phantasm speaks carry no thought and that the voice that expresses them is empty. The situation reflects the status of authorship in the realm of the symbolic, where castration causes subjectivity and enables meaning but in the process alienates word from voice. Earth's injunction that "Grey mountains and old woods and haunted springs, / Prophetic caves and isle-surrounding streams" (*SPP* 1. 251–2) must mute their echoes once the Phantasm speaks creates a metaphor that marks the curse as void. Prometheus acknowledges its impotence when he remarks that the curse has perhaps devolved to a text that can be seen but not heard:

> I see the curse on gestures proud and cold,
> And looks of firm defiance, and calm hate,
> And such despair as mocks itself with smiles,
> Written as on a scroll ... yet speak—O speak! (*SPP* 1. 258–61)

As we know, once the Phantasm speaks, its words are empty and Prometheus fails to identify them as his own. If the curse represents the Promethean subject, the secret treasure that distinguishes him in this universe and induces Earth's desire, its value has been reduced to the level of silent gesture and inscription. Prometheus retains his subjectivity and isolates himself from Jupiter by disowning his former words, but in the process confirms, nevertheless, his immersion in the symbolic. Making matters worse is the fact that Prometheus's condition requires him to enlist the aid of an instrument to reenact the curse. The Phantasm, therefore, serves as proxy and acts the part of passive figure repeating an empty curse that has lost its bite and no longer embodies an intention that lies beyond its own author's recognition.

The relationship between Prometheus and the Phantasm of Jupiter twists the "interpassive" dynamic in several ways. First, Prometheus's refusal to capitulate to Jupiter's desire (that the Titan reveal the secret of the tyrant's downfall) resonates with a strategy used by the neurotic-hysteric who "wants to be the object of the Other's *desire*, not the object of his *enjoyment*."[16] Such behaviors surface because of pressure imposed on the subject, as he or she negotiates with symbolic codifications. As Zizek explains, the subject in this case knows that "the only way to remain desired is to *postpone* satisfaction;"[17] the subject resists becoming the instrument of the Other, manipulated by him or her, a feat Prometheus has achieved successfully for millennia. Second, a feminine disposition informs Prometheus's activity, in the sense that, throughout the first act, he lives through his others: Earth, the Phantasm of Jupiter, the Oceanides and even the Furies. His activity points subversively, therefore, to the possibility that the subject's true status is feminine. Zizek asks,

> What if the "original" subjective gesture, the gesture constitutive of subjectivity, is not that of autonomously "doing something" but, rather, that of the primordial substitution, of withdrawing and letting another do it for me, in my place? Women, much more than men, are able to enjoy by proxy, to find deep satisfaction in the awareness that their beloved partner enjoys (or succeeds, or has attained his or her goal in any other way).[18]

Living by proxy, Prometheus's existence mirrors that of the female agents—Earth and the Oceanides, including Asia—and counters the ethos that informs the actions of Jupiter and the masculine order, manifest for example in the Furies, which engage in "compulsive rituals" aimed at keeping "the other mortified, that is," preventing "him from enjoying."[19] Though still bound and subject to Jupiter's torture at this point in the drama, Prometheus moves in the direction of Asia. He underscores his changed outlook when he remarks that "words," which represent the footings of all symbolic structures, are, by themselves, "quick and vain" (*SPP* 1. 303).

Earth represents an alternative form of expression, corresponding with Prometheus not by way of words but directly to his brain and body by means of "awful thoughts, rapid and thick" (*SPP* 1. 147). Her son can no more integrate these transmissions than he can his own voice. Employing metonym, Earth asserts that her "tongue is known / Only to those who die" (*SPP* 1. 150–1). Her use of the metaphor "tongue" suggests that Prometheus currently lacks something his mortal children apparently have: the power to transact will through language. He is the lacking father, who is much less dangerous now that he has spoken his curse than

---

[16] Zizek 33.
[17] Zizek 33.
[18] Zizek 118–19.
[19] Zizek 126.

he would be had he never spoken at all.[20] Because he lacks a mortal's "tongue," moreover, Prometheus figuratively lacks the ability to incarnate himself into the text of the material world. Gelpi contends that this wordless exchange qualifies as an example of "affect attunement," indicating that Earth "casts Prometheus into that stage of an infant's life before words became arbitrary 'signs' of presence and are introjected as such."[21] In alliance with Prometheus, Earth, in other words, loosens memories within her son's mind of pre-subjective correspondence with her—exchanges characterized by nonsensical transmissions that, from a certain perspective, threaten patriarchal prerogative and order. She does so in order to free him from the systemic cycle in which a castrated son eventually replaces his castrated father at the top of the symbolic order. From Gelpi's perspective, then, *Prometheus Unbound* consists of "a series of mirrorings, initiated and then overseen by mother Earth, that guide the protagonist into ever-deeper levels of self-knowledge."[22]

While it appears obvious that Earth plays the role of medium orchestrating the titan's experience by carefully indulging his wishes and needs, it becomes equally apparent that she mirrors her son's failings, and thereby performs a constitutive function. Prometheus initially identifies her as a "melancholy Voice" (*SPP* 1. 153), confirming her figurative status as his lost object. The idea that she appears to him as a "Voice" who cannot communicate with him through words verifies his *and* her castration. She is voice without word; he is word without voice. Even if one were to accept the text's suggestion that the dialogue appearing on the page merely "suggests," or dramatizes, their correspondence, Prometheus's prior communication with Earth's elements is dialogic. When he queries "What was that curse? for ye all heard me speak" (*SPP* 1. 73), voices from Mountains, Springs, Air and Whirlwinds respond. Earth acknowledges that her constituents "preserve" the curse Prometheus spoke, and she refers to it as a "treasured spell" (*SPP* 1. 184). Her perspective verifies her position as Prometheus's other—she who recognizes a secret "treasure" within him, which he, correlatively, regards as the measure of his present value. Prometheus desires the desire of another world that perceives him as spokesman for rebellion and justice.

Ione and Panthea provide the reader with exposition throughout the opening act, and in this regard they serve as faculties of Prometheus, filling in the narrative gaps Prometheus creates as he interacts with a host of entities, particularly when those interactions overwhelm him. For example, Earth's confirmation that the Phantasm reiterated the very curse Prometheus had spoken fills the Titan with remorse, causing him to concede, "I wish no living thing to suffer pain" (*SPP* 1. 305). Prometheus also fails to mark the coming of Mercury and the Furies. However, Ione observes the "golden-sandalled feet" of "A Shape ... / Stretching

---

[20] See Zizek's discussion of Lacan's concept of power exercised, in *The Plague of Fantasies* 63.

[21] Gelpi 148–9.

[22] Gelpi 167.

on high from his right hand / A serpent-cinctured wand," and Panthea supplements the characterization by confirming that "'Tis Jove's world-wandering Herald, Mercury" (*SPP* 1. 319–25). Later, after Mercury fails to persuade Prometheus to reveal his secret and Prometheus says "How vain is talk! / Call up the fiends" (*SPP* 1. 431–2), Ione calls out

> O sister, look! White fire
> Has cloven to the roots yon huge snow-loaded Cedar;
> How fearfully God's thunder howls behind! (*SPP* 1. 432–4)

Mercury departs at this sign from Jupiter and Panthea remarks: "See where the child of Heaven with winged feet / Runs down the slanted sunlight of the dawn" (*SPP* 1. 437–8). At this moment, the Furies, according to Ione "come, they come, / Blackening the birth of day with countless wings, / And hollow underneath, like death" (*SPP* 1. 440–2).

Because the Oceanides supplement the Promethean narrative, acting as additional sets of eyes and ears supplying detailed images that invest Prometheus's story with richer texture, they represent, in terms of Prometheus's subjectivity at this point in the drama, lost objects. Simply put, they speak for him when he is unable or unwilling to speak for himself. Once Prometheus reunites with Asia in Act 3, he demonstrates narrative mastery, describing their future, commanding the Spirit of the Hour and bestowing upon her the "that curved shell, which Proteus old / Made Asia's nuptial boon" (*SPP* 3. 3. 65–6), the sound of which broadcasts the emergence of a new cosmic order. Until that point, the Oceanides supply the voice Prometheus lacks. In fact, the idea that they speak and see in lieu of him implies his separation from both voice and gaze.

With respect to gaze, Prometheus has difficulty identifying the Phantasm of Jupiter, whom he speculates must be Jupiter's shadow, and his response to the Third Fury points to the same disability, as he addressed the tormenter indefinitely as "some dreadful voice" (*SPP* 1. 444). Prometheus's impaired eyesight combines with his awareness that chained to the crag he has become the object of cosmic gaze, the focal point of the universe. Though Prometheus turns this disadvantage into his advantage by denying Jupiter the information he desires, therefore short-circuiting the tyrant's pleasure, Prometheus's position also locates him firmly within Jupiter's domain of perversion. He becomes the "interpassive" instrument of Jupiter's satisfaction, the enduring text that inscribes publicly Jupiter's authority.

The substance of the remarks made by Ione and Panthea not only consists of visual and aural detail, but produces additionally an undercurrent of phonic harmony that countervails Prometheus's suffering.[23] The way in which Ione's and Panthea's comments resonate with one another serves as a model register in

---

[23] See Chris Foss's insightful Kristevan analysis of Shelley's employment of phonics in *Prometheus Unbound*. Foss demonstrates that subtle sound patterns in the drama disrupt narrative authority and symbolic constructs.

which words and sounds work together. For example, when Ione describes the rising Phatasm of Jupiter as "A Shape, a throng of *sounds*," Panthea amplifies the remark by noting that "The *sound* is of a whirlwind under*ground*, / ... The Shape is awful like the *sound*, / Clothed in dark purple" (my italics; *SPP* 1. 226, 231, 233–4). Other observations occurring throughout the act chime together with these. Panthea describes the Furies as "Jove's tempest-walking *hounds*" and Jove as one who "bursts Heaven's *bounds*," and Ione, later on marking the arrival of the Chorus of Spirits, says, "More yet come, one by one: the air *around* them / Looks radiant as the air *around* a star" (my italics; *SPP* 1. 331, 334, 692–3).

Phonic familiarity such as this is not limited to the Oceanides's observations, of course, but their role in the drama as substitutes for Asia serves as a phonic marker of something else Prometheus has lost: his Asia and her music. However, Ione and Panthea, functioning as Asia's "interpassive" objects and constituting her, therefore, in the first act, ultimately confirm Asia's inertia, as she waits in her vale for liberation. Metaphorically, music without word suffers it own bondage. This might explain why Ione and Panthea so often cover their eyes and ears in the first act and why they evidently lack the power to intercede on Prometheus's behalf. Music on its own cannot effect liberation. Panthea's visual portrait of the departed Chorus of Spirits perhaps unwittingly underscores this limited efficacy of music. When Ione asks, "Where are the Spirits fled?" Panthea replies,

> Only a sense
> Remains of them, like the Omnipotence
> Of music when the inspired voice and lute
> Languish, ere yet the responses are mute
> Which through the deep and labyrinthine soul,
> Like echoes through long caverns, wind and roll. (*SPP* 1. 801–6)

What remains is not the presence of music so much as its absence. Even the traditionally perfect expressive economy composed of "voice and lute" exhibits its temporal mortality, as the music the arrangement produces quickly transforms into cavernous "echoes." The trope exposes a break in Shelley's fantasy by suggesting that not even the combination of voice and word ensures eternal presence. If confluence of the two results in "Omnipotence," that power remains bound within time, eventually rolling away with the wind in the same fashion that words, even curse words, roll away with their speaker's breath.

Prometheus never sets foot in Asia's vale during Act 2; however, he makes himself present nonetheless and orchestrates by proxy the actions of Asia and Panthea. The arrangement raises a familiar paradox in the sense that Prometheus constitutes himself by means of objects operating "interpassively" in his stead, while those same objects, performing their passive, instrumental role, imply both his absence and his inertia. It is this contradiction that Shelley's fantasy fails time and again to resolve. By way of Panthea's agency, Prometheus introduces himself into Asia's vale first through inscription and then through voice. By these means he manages to conduct Asia toward a meeting with Demogorgon and to catalyze her transformation from dormant to active expression.

Panthea has apparently served as a medium for the two lovers, feeling the burden of their separation as she carries "the music ... / Of thy most wordless converse" (*SPP* 2. 1. 51–2) between the two realms. Her conversation with Asia indicates that she bears the "shadow" (*SPP* 2. 1. 31) of Prometheus to Asia and represents Asia to her beloved by wearing her sister's image. She becomes, therefore, a text in which each lover recognizes a semblance, rather than a direct presence, of the beloved. As long as the two remain separate, something will be lacking. The first indication that this situation is about to change occurs when Asia greets Panthea and comments that "my heart was sick with hope, before / The printless air felt thy belated plumes" (*SPP* 2. 1. 33–4). Asia's use of the word "printless" suggests a significant ontological enhancement of Panthea's role. She continues to be a Promethean text Asia can read, but at this moment she enables the titan by proxy to "imprint" himself into Asia's surroundings.

Asia verifies her sister's continued status as textual carrier of Prometheus when she bids Panthea to "Lift up thine eyes / And let me read thy dream" (*SPP* 2. 1. 55–6). Panthea continues to speak, describing the dream in which she became dissolved and "absorbed" within the being of Prometheus and then eventually "condensed" (*SPP* 2. 1. 76, 82, 86). Asia complains,

> Thou speakest, but thy words
> Are as the air. I feel them not .... oh, lift
> Thine eyes that I may read his written soul! (*SPP* 2. 1. 108–10)

Panthea's characterization of herself under Prometheus's influence by means of liquid-metaphors combines with Asia's pronouncement that her sister's "words / Are as the air" to suggest paradoxically Prometheus's lack of presence. His influence on both sisters reduces to metonym, that is, it remains in things associated with voice: the "wandering dew" (*SPP* 2. 1. 78) and "air" produced by speech, the "written soul" produced through inscription. At this point, at least, Asia's vale remains a realm of "shadow," as all three characters mirror one another, thereby constituting each subject only through their own object status. Panthea concedes this point when she asks as Asia reads her eyes, "what canst thou see / But thine own fairest shadow imaged there?" (*SPP* 2. 1. 112–13).

Shelley's phantasmic agenda maintains the primacy of male authority by associating Prometheus and not Asia with *jouissance*, but not without calling into question the constitutive power of voice and music. Panthea's verbal account of her dream recalls that

> ... the azure night
> Grew radiant with the glory of that form
> Which lives unchanged within, and his voice fell

>   Like music which makes giddy the dim brain
>   Faint with intoxication of keen joy .... (*SPP* 2. 1. 63–7)

Prometheus speaks, and his erotic form, amplified by the power of his voice, draws Panthea into a state of perfect correspondence, of which she remembers that she "saw not—heard not—moved not—only felt / His presence flow and mingle through my blood" (*SPP* 2. 1. 79–81). However, the blood communion he initiates is evidently fleeting, devolving to spoken "accents" that "lingered ere they died / Like footsteps of far melody" (*SPP* 2. 1. 88–9). Prometheus presents himself erotically and directly to a sleeping Panthea, inscribing himself into her consciousness, but Panthea's observation that "His voice" and the "accents" in which he finds expression "die," despite lingering momentarily. Though one might observe that Panthea carries the substance of her dream, and therefore the spirit of Prometheus in her memory, preserving it and him for future iteration, both manifestations survive as constitutive objects only, each a "shadow" as opposed to the thing itself.

In addition to *jouissance*, Prometheus introduces desire into Asia's vale. At the opening of Act 2, Asia welcomes the return of spring, but expresses impatience over Panthea's delayed arrival: "At sunrise thou shouldst come, sweet sister mine ... / Too long desired, too long delaying, come!" (*SPP* 2. 1. 14–15). Asia, as she has evidently done for millennia, desires news about Prometheus, though the implication emerges that no news other than her beloved's liberation would satisfy her. Panthea, moreover, implies that Prometheus's appearance to her in dream elicited a sympathetic reaction from Ione, who apparently woke suddenly and asked:

>   'Canst thou divine what troubles me tonight?
>   I always knew what I desired before
>   Nor ever found delight to wish in vain.
>   But now I cannot tell thee what I seek;
>   I know not—something sweet since it is sweet
>   Even to desire—it is thy sport, false sister! (*SPP* 2. 1. 94–9)

It would appear that Prometheus's influence jolts the Oceanides out of lethargy, but herein lies another faultline in Shelley's fantasy. Asia prepares herself to reunite with Prometheus; however, if desire exists beyond all possibility of specification and satisfaction, as it must in the symbolic realm, it is desire that will maintain subjectivity as a matter of constitution through one's lost objects and one's others.

Asia's metamorphosis at the conclusion of Act 2 obviously aims at eliminating such foreclosure. She transforms into the embodiment of pure spirituality and pure music, modes of being theoretically without boundaries and without the need for supplementation. Her transformation sets the stage for her reunion with the liberated Prometheus in Act 3, a marriage that represents the unification of word with music and marks, as it should given the arrangement, the end of all desire. Absence of desire, however, produces stasis and eliminates subjectivity, thus putting an end to sexualized expression, upon which the desire for immortal self-presence through the living word relies. The existence Prometheus forecasts for himself and his family consists precisely of these conditions, and this situation likely provides an additional explanation regarding why Shelley saw the need to recast the conclusion of his lyrical drama.[24]

Though still bound to the precipice, Prometheus conducts Asia and Panthea to Demogorgon's cave. With the emergence of Panthea's second dream, implicitly initialized by Prometheus, who also authored her first dream, the sisters notice that the phrases "*O follow, follow,*" "*Follow, O follow*" (*SPP* 2. 1. 141, 153) and similar variants have become "stamped" (*SPP* 2. 1. 139, 155) on their surroundings. The verb "stamped" connotes official in addition to legal approval, and the noun "stamp" creates the suggestion of an image permanently affixed to something. Combined, these implications indicate that even in his absence Prometheus compels the Oceanides to follow orders. Panthea's initial recollection of the appearance of the suggestion to "follow" in her dream dislodges within Asia's mind the memory of a dream in which the same phrase "Athwart the purple mountain slope was written" (*SPP* 2. 1. 152). Perhaps Prometheus's coalescence with Panthea via dream enhances his authorial capacity, since the stamped and written word "follow" quickly finds aural transmission by way of Echoes, which at first Panthea observes mocking their own voices. Asia attributes the sound to spirits uttering "The liquid responses of their aerial tongues," and Panthea notices that "the strain floats nearer now" (*SPP* 2. 1. 171–2, 189). Asia makes the decision to pursue the strain after a group of Echoes bids her to return to the place where she and Prometheus parted long ago in order to "commingle now" (*SPP* 2. 1. 205).

On the surface, at least, it would seem that, even in his absence, Prometheus undergoes a transformation of sorts, as his influential presence moves along the spectrum of expression, from word (in the command to "follow"), to disembodied sound, and finally to "notes [that] sink upon the ebbing wind!" (*SPP* 2. 1. 195). Given the features of Shelley's fantasy, it would appear that over the course of Act 2 Prometheus graduates in expressive stature. Asia's imagery and the continuation of mirroring foreclose on that progress, however. Panthea's proclamation that "The crags, this clear spring morning, mock our voices, / As they were spirit-tongued" (*SPP* 2. 1. 163–4) renders authorship ambiguous. While it is true that, as each sister shares the contents of her dream within which the word "follow" plays a pivotal role, the vale acoustically echoes what each sister says, it is also true that the dream originates from Prometheus's influence on a sleeping

---

[24] Gelpi and Claridge both point out the double-bind Shelley creates in his effort to escape the bondage of language and the Law of the Father that underwrites it. The subject's desire to reach that moment prior to his or her entry, via the threat of castration, into the symbolic world is essentially a desire for self-annihilation, since the price of success in this endeavor would be the sacrifice of one's subjectivity. The desire for the feminine as alternative to the masculine, then, very much amounts to a death wish.

Panthea. In this respect, though the vale echoes the voices of Asia and Panthea, it also functions, in fashion similar to the instrumental Oceanides, as the acoustic mirror of the Promethean word. Separate from Asia, Prometheus fails to present himself directly, paradoxically losing and constituting himself by means of echo. Though this condition might qualify as a failure in terms of Shelley's phantasmic metaphysics, it offers the male writer consolation by assigning traditional authority to Prometheus.

The conclusion of Act 2 unites Asia with a singing Voice, troped as a continuum of "silver waves" on which the "enchanted Boat" of her soul now rides (*SPP* 2. 5. 73–6). The Voice sits at the helm of her soul, and Asia observes that, in the hands of this pilot, "The boat of my desire is guided" (*SPP* 2. 5. 94). The merger parallels the reunion in Act 1 between Prometheus and the curse, except that here unification breeds healing and marks the end of loss as the means to subjectivity. Furthermore, the Voice now conducting Asia's soul serves as an extension of the voice that guided her with the words "*O follow, follow*" throughout the act. Evidently, the voice belongs to Prometheus and its integration with Asia's soul figures forth the coupling Shelley's fantasy is designed to construct. Whereas Ione complained of experiencing desire lacking a specified target, it appears Asia's pilot will guide her desire toward some satisfying end. The perfection of this fantasy construct notwithstanding, the idea that the boat of Asia's soul "floats" on waves (a reference to water) supplied by the Voice, "Whilst all the winds with melody are ringing" (a reference to air; *SPP* 2. 5. 77), implies that this Voice is a stand-in for the real thing.

In Act 3, a liberated Prometheus foretells that he and Asia will exist, essentially, in cold storage. From the "curved roof" of the cave they will occupy eternally with Panthea and Ione, "the mountain's frozen tears / Like snow or silver or long diamond spires / Hang downward, raining forth a doubtful light" (*SPP* 3. 3. 15–17). In this sheltered environment, he foresees, they "will sit and talk of time and change / As the world ebbs and flows, ourselves unchanged" (*SPP* 3. 3. 23–4). Ione "shall chant fragments of sea-music" to buoy their spirits and they will, together, "weave harmonies divine, yet ever new," and they will listen to "echoes" of life in "the human world" (*SPP* 3. 3. 27, 38, 44). The Promethean narrative portrays an ideal existence in which language and music have conjoined, but the problem with his vision in terms of Shelley's phantasmic mission is that he and Asia will cease to play a vital role in the new order they have established. Man, the main character in the text they have composed, will continue to grow "wise and kind / And veil by veil evil and error fall" (*SPP* 3. 3. 61–2), but Prometheus and Asia remain separate from that process, existing in a state of inertia. Though humanity becomes the beneficiary, the passive recipient and instrument, of the freedom Prometheus and Asia bestowed upon it, humanity also constitutes its benefactors in the world outside their cave. The arrangement figures forth the situation in which even the most accomplished author finds himself or herself.

Prometheus enlists the aid of a "curved shell" (*SPP* 3. 3. 65), given to Asia by Proteus as a wedding gift, as the means of proclamation. He instructs Ione to present the shell, which produces a "sound ... at once both sweet and strange" (*SPP* 3. 3. 75), to the Spirit of the Hour, and he commands the Spirit to

> Go, borne over the cities of mankind
> On whirlwind-footed coursers! once again
> Outspeed the sun around the orbed world
> And as thy chariot cleaves the kindling air,
> Thou breathe into the many-folded Shell,
> Loosening its mighty music;—it shall be
> As thunder mingled with clear echoes.—Then
> Return and thou shalt dwell beside our cave. (*SPP* 3. 3. 76–83)

The Shell's dual lineage, once owned by Proteus and now by Asia, implies that the emerging law and order bears masculine and feminine signatures equally; however, it is obvious that Prometheus has assumed ownership of the device, bidding Ione to secure it from its hiding place "in grass under the hollow rock" (*SPP* 3. 3. 68), and that the breath, therefore, that produces the Shell's "mighty music" extends, though indirectly, from Prometheus.

The conch shell upon which Prometheus relies for broadcasting his law based on mutual love, interdependence and harmony performs the same equivocal function as the bull's horn, or shofar, in Hebraic tradition. The shell presents Promethean law throughout the world, confirming its ubiquity, and it implies, therefore, the embodiment of Prometheus within that law. At the same time, however, the "mighty music" the shell has converted from divine breath represents the object voice and, as such, pronounces the separation of Prometheus both from his law and from his "own" voice. By employing the conch shell, in other words, he constitutes himself by means of an object, implying his absence from the law and announcing the vacancy that lies at the core of his subjectivity. Prometheus himself is no more than a shell. His imagery communicates this possibility. Signaling the clash of atmospheric pressures, "thunder" represents the result of that clash and is not the thing itself. Furthermore, the image of "thunder mingled with clear echoes" only amplifies the idea that the Promethean voice is a remainder, in the sense that thunder, once removed from the conditions that caused it, becomes twice removed when it transforms into echo.

An additional sign that Prometheus has failed to achieve eternal presence in his words occurs when he kisses the Earth, engaging, perhaps, in a more intimate form of communication with her. She responds to the gesture in a speech laden with erotic imagery:

> I hear—I feel—
> Thy lips are on me, and their touch runs down
> Even to the adamantine central gloom
> Along these marble nerves—'tis life, 'tis joy,
> And through my withered, old and icy frame

The warmth of an immortal youth shoots down
Circling.— (*SPP* 3. 3. 84–90)

The exchange recalls Lionel's initiation of Helen's singing performance when he places his lips on hers. In this case, Prometheus returns Earth to its former state of *jouissance*, but, again, the gesture suggests what Prometheus lacks rather than what he is. Lips transmit his influence in a pulse that "shoots" deep into Earth's frame, but, no less than words, the orifice functions constitutionally. Earth, in fact, now becomes an extension of Prometheus's orality, and the transformation she undergoes italicizes her stature as his revision. As textual object, Earth's reaction to her son's kiss indicates that his secret treasure finds expression not within himself, but within her. The erotic transaction sets in motion the celestial ballet that takes place in Act 4, and this shift in Prometheus's attention from Asia to "Mother Earth" (*SPP* 3. 3. 84) suggests, perhaps, a change in strategy. By redirecting his desire toward another object, Prometheus renews the possibility of entering and then remaining an expressive force in the world.

Ione's description of the Spirit of the Earth replicates the strand Woman's portrait in *The Revolt of Islam* of the dying poet, who served as her mentor. Ione points out to Panthea that "on its head there burns / A light like a green star, whose emerald beams / Are twined with its fair hair!" (*SPP* 3. 4. 2–4). Panthea extends the characterization in Act 4, referring to the Spirit of Earth asleep in its "chrystal" sphere as a "child" whose "forehead" bears a "star," from which "shoot, ... / Vast beams like spokes of some invisible wheel" (*SPP* 4. 239, 263, 270, 274). If the Spirit of the Earth arrives as a result of the kiss Prometheus gives his mother, the Spirit then would be Prometheus's son. In Act 4, Earth and the rejuvenated spirit of the moon engage in correspondence redolent with erotic energy and imagery. The Moon refers to Earth as "Brother mine" and characterizes herself as his lover:

> I, thy chrystal paramour
> Borne beside thee by a power
> Like the polar Paradise,
> Magnet-like, of lovers' eyes;
> I, a most enamoured maiden
> Whose weak brain is overladen
> With the pleasure of her love—
> Maniac-like around thee move,
> Gazing, an insatiate bride,
> On thy form from every side …. (*SPP* 4. 325, 463–72)

By reproducing himself in the form of the eternally youthful male spirit of Earth, Prometheus, in effect, creates a living replica of himself, a text that will remain vital and dynamic rather than lifeless and still. Furthermore, the marriage of masculine Earth and feminine Moon, abundant with images of healing interpenetration (Earth, for example, tells the "gentle Moon" that its "chrystal accents pierce / The caverns of my Pride's deep Universe," providing "balm" for its "wounds," *SPP* 4. 499–502), projects the mortal heterosexual coupling upon which Shelley's fantasy depends into celestial terms. Moon and Earth mirror one another mutually in visual and acoustic registers, though the complex interplay of sound characterizing their dialogue suggests that Earth and Moon perform an improvisational duet meant to represent the dynamic music of the spheres. Consider, for example, Moon's figurative depiction of its devotion to Earth and Earth's reply:

> THE MOON
> As a grey and watery mist
> Glows like solid amethyst
> Athwart the western mountain it enfolds,
> When the sunset sleeps
> Upon its snow—
> THE EARTH
> And the weak day weeps
> That it should be so. (*SPP* 4. 487–94)

Earth completes its partner's metaphor, reproduces long *e* and long *o* sounds, and matches phonically Moon's final couplet, "sleeps / snow," "weeps / so." Meter, rhyme and line sets, however, vary consistently in character, type and length. If such prosodic elements remained regular throughout the dialogue between Earth and Moon, each would serve as its other's perfect mirror image, creating an arrangement in which each sphere would constitute its partner, granting it subjectivity, but in the process rendering it vacant, or void. Shelley's irregular patterning creates a union based on harmonic correspondence that resists codification and "decentered" existence in the symbolic.

Lunar and terrestrial cycles deliver opportunities for eternal iteration and potentially fresh reiteration. However, the idea that both spheres consist of "chrystal" implies that they are ontologically fragile, that the renovated state in which they find themselves now could shatter, something Demogorgon's warning, which concludes the drama, would seem to verify. In addition, Moon's figurative depiction of herself as a "Maenad" introduces a menacing note into her relationship with Earth that threatens the entire phantasmic construct:

> Gazing, an insatiate bride,
> On thy form from every side
> Like a Maenad round the cup
> Which Agave lifted up
> In the weird Cadmaean forest.— (*SPP* 4. 471–5)

The Moon's reference to herself as "Insatiate" implies that desire motivates her, and it suggests that her mate, Earth, will never satisfy her. The term also suggests that Moon has become who she is because she has lost something, ostensibly

Earth, but that the wound of castration cannot be undone. This status fuels her desire for Earth, but it also constitutes her as separate from him. Her status as Maenad indicates, moreover, that, as was "Agave," she is capable of killing her own blood, Earth, essentially annihilating herself in the process, since Earth represents a part of herself she has lost. Without him, she cannot be.

This deadlock draws attention to the incestuous nature of Prometheus's coupling with Mother Earth, which produces the star-crowned male poet heir, and Earth's orgiastic interaction with Moon. Familial reproduction promises to overturn the process of subject formation in the sense that the other with which one mates technically fails to qualify as other, since both partners share the same genes. In this respect Prometheus and the Spirit of Earth find expression reflexively through themselves, thus eliminating the gap required for subject formation, and, with regard to writing, the gap required for traditional authority. Author and text become one and the same. The prospect that nothing is produced offsets this dynamic, though. Conceivably, without a legitimate other, subjectivity becomes impossible, and this includes the production of text, which constitutes its author in the world of signs, but in that process establishes his absence. Incest ultimately fails to reproduce sound and resilient offspring, and the line it aims to prolong eventually disappears.

Demogorgon's appearance at the play's conclusion complicates the model of expression formed by Earth and Moon. Panthea's description of the entity in Act 2 renders it sexless:

> I see a mighty Darkness
> Filling the seat of power; and rays of gloom
> Dart round, as light from the meridian Sun,
> Ungazed upon and shapeless:—neither limb
> Nor form nor outline, yet we feel it is
> A living Spirit. (*SPP* 2. 4. 2–6)

The observations she and Ione deliver when Demogorgon resurfaces in the final act reveal its mastery of voice and word, implying that the entity's expressive force combines what our culture has traditionally considered to be masculine with feminine strengths. As the "stream of sound" generated by the correspondence of Earth and Moon ebbs "away," Ione reports that "there is a sense of words upon mine ear," to which Panthea adds that it is "A universal sound like words" (*SPP* 4. 506, 517–18). The idea that one sister hears something resembling a "sense of words" and the other a "sound like words" connotes equivocally that Demogorgon conveys wisdom via some supercharged linguistic medium, or that its expression fails to solidify in language. The former connotation would establish this "Spirit" as the ideal poet Shelley has in mind—a combination of Lionel and his harp-playing mother—while the latter connotation locates it in the realm of *jouissance*, qualifying Demogorgon as a revolutionary force inimical to the existing symbolic order. It has already taken down Jupiter. Ominously, it might someday threaten the harmonies initiated by Prometheus and Asia and then (if one reads Act 4 as the narrative conclusion to Acts 1 through 3) carried out by Earth and Moon.

The combined voices of all mortal spirits would seem to reinforce the possibility that Demogorgon commands comprehensive expression when they respond to his summons by asserting, "Speak—thy strong words may never pass away" (*SPP* 4. 553). Metaphors employed by Earth, Moon and voices representing all corners of creation amplify the observation. Responding to the summons of Demogorgon, Earth proclaims, "I am as a drop of dew that dies!" and Moon says, "I am a leaf shaken by thee!" while a Voice ostensibly representing the dead states, "we change and pass away" (*SPP* 4. 523, 528, 538). Demogorgon's voice and its words promise to outlast them all. The problem, of course, is that all of these entities apparently identify Demogorgon with the voice that speaks for him, in place of him. Prior to his articulation onto the cosmic stage, Demogorgon finds expression, according to Panthea, as

> ... —a mighty Power, which is as Darkness,
> ... rising out of Earth, and from the sky
> Is showered like Night, and from within the air
> Bursts, like eclipse which had been gathered up
> Into the pores of sunlight—the bright Visions
> Wherein the singing spirits rode and shone
> Gleam like pale meteors through a watery night. (*SPP* 4. 510–16)

Panthea's impression that Demogorgon resembles "Darkness," "Night," and an "eclipse" suggests that nothing, that no being, can be seen. Ironically, in the same way that the "singing spirits" have constituted themselves by means of luminous marks, which, "like meteors," are sure to burn out, Demogorgon registers its presence by means of a voice that emerges from the voids of darkness and space. The Voice representing the lesser creatures of nature and its elements introduces the possibility of finitude when it compares Demogorgon's voice to "wind among still woods" (*SPP* 4. 548). Wind eventually dies down. If for Shelley Power represents divine expression originating from an unknowable source, and if Demogorgon serves as the nebulous incarnation of that Power, the conclusion to *Prometheus Unbound* conveys the idea that even Power fails to present itself consistently as a fundamental poetic force in the world humans perceive.

On the surface it would appear that *Epipsychidion* represents a different category of expression than *Prometheus Unbound*, *Rosalind and Helen*, *The Revolt of Islam* and *Alastor*, because it involves actual rather than fictional characters in its vision of the ideal heterosexual union. In this poem, Shelley envisions running off with Teresa Viviani, the soulmate he calls Emily, to an island paradise filled with exotic fragrances and soothing harmonies. Teresa's father, the governor of Pisa, had confined his 19-year-old daughter to the Convent of Santa Anna, a conservatory school with ties to the Tuscan state, while she awaited marriage.[25] She received visits from Percy, Mary and Claire and it would seem that the combination of her captivity, her attractive appearance and her stimulating conversation must have struck Shelley hard. Though unlike Jane Williams, Sophia Stacey and Claire Clairmont, Teresa failed to exhibit a talent for musical performance, Ann Wroe observes that Teresa evidently "sadly spoke and sang" to a caged lark that hung in the parlor of the two-room apartment she occupied.[26] Wroe writes that Shelley told Claire

> What he felt for Emilia contained no mixture 'of that which you call *love*' ... He had hinted rather boastfully to Byron, however, that something more had gone on in Emilia's case, and that 'Mary might be very much annoyed by it': a sign that his sexual virtue was sometimes no more than a pose.[27]

Bieri evidently believes the two might have known one another sexually. "Shelley's letters and poetry to Emilia suggest they shared physical intimacies," he says, adding, "his description of sexual intercourse with her in *Epipsychidion* is the most vivid erotic encounter in his poetry."[28]

Despite its autobiographical underpinnings, though, *Epipsychidion* belongs in the same discussion as the narrative and dramatic poems portraying heterosexual unions, because it tells the story of twin beings separated by worldly circumstance that, under ideal conditions, should be together. The poem's opening lines refer to Emily as "Sweet Spirit! Sister of that orphan one, / Whose empire is the name thou weepest on" (*SPP* 1–2), and the image suggests that Shelley, whose soul would be that empire, has managed to capture Emily's emotional interest. Later in the poem he defines their relationship as a musical performance, querying,

> We—are we not formed, as notes of music are,
> For one another, though dissimilar;
> Such difference without discord, as can make
> Those sweetest sounds, in which all spirits shake
> As trembling leaves in a continuous air? (*SPP* 142–6)

The construct reproduces the trope he uses to describe the coupling of prototype and antitype in the essay "On Love," and it underscores the idea that when the right heterosexual partners discover one another, their union consists of harmony, a blend of different notes that becomes sweeter than either partner would be

---

[25] James Bieri, *Percy Bysshe Shelley: A Biography*, 2 vols. (Newark: U of Delaware P, 2004) 2: 214.
[26] Ann Wroe, *Being Shelley: The Poet's Search for Himself* (New York: Pantheon Books, 2007) 45.
[27] Wroe 79–80.
[28] Bieri 2: 221.

capable of generating on his or her own. His use of the trope "trembling leaves in continuous air" to describe the sounds issuing from this ideal arrangement suggests that the music he and Emily will make will be spiritual and natural, ostensibly existing outside the bounds of convention. The metaphor folds back in on itself, however, because the word "leaves" connotes leaves of text and projects their relationship back into the realm of language and art, identifying it as a literary artifact that will eventually wither and fall. This connotation supplies an unsettling reason for why the leaves tremble. Shelley echoes the metaphor at the poem's conclusion, again proposing,

> We shall become the same, we shall be one
> Spirit within two frames, oh! wherefore two?
> One passion in twin-hearts, which grows and grew. (*SPP* 573–5)

Because Shelley casts his relationship with Emily within a narrative construct, however, the arrangement becomes vulnerable to the same paradoxes and instabilities that inevitably plague all narratives. Most prominent among them is the element of "interpassivity," the most basic condition of subjectivity. Though Emily apparently lacks the ability to sing or play music, she functions as the instrument of Shelley's expression, enabling him to compose *Epipsychidion*, which he calls "My Song" (*SPP* "Advertisement"). Initially, it appears that she serves as the passive other to the active author who conceives of her and of their relationship within the scope of this poem. However, by displacing his inertia onto Emily, who consequently emerges, then, as the inert object of the poem, Shelley ends up confirming his own; Emily mirrors back to him the vacancy that lies at the heart of all his "interpassive" gestures. In this regard, she doubles as the mirror image of *Epipsychidion*. Because they serve in the capacity of others, Emily and the poem create the appearance of vivacity and fullness, but ultimately remain silent iterations on a blank page—withered and fallen leaves.

Shelley might have regarded Emily as the perfect vehicle for initiating the process of retrieving what he had lost, since she no doubt appeared to be a fixed target. He addresses her by way of metaphors that emphasize her captivity and, therefore, her passivity. The opening of the poem suggests that, from Shelley's perspective, Emily needs someone to act for her, on her behalf, since she has no choice otherwise. First, she is a

> Poor captive bird! who, from thy narrow cage,
> Pourest such music, that it might assuage
> The rugged hearts of those who prisoned thee,
> Were thy not deaf to all sweet melody. (*SPP* 5–8)

Next, she becomes a "High, spirit-winged Heart! who dost for ever / Beat thine unfeeling bars with vain endeavor" (*SPP* 13–14), and she then metamorphoses into myriad celestial phenomena, that nevertheless remain even if only in part hidden, obscured or shrouded by other forces: a "Seraph of Heaven" inhabiting "that radiant form of Woman;" "Thou Moon beyond the clouds! Thou living Form / Among the Dead! Thou Star above the Storm!" (*SPP* 21–8). Embracing the opportunity to sing of what Emily is, Shelley creates the impression that he acts in Emily's stead, that he and his vivacious metaphors articulate her substance and her value to the world.

The activity exemplifies the conventional arrangement in which a woman lives through her man and a man desires only what is desired by another as the means to eliminating it. In this case, Shelley, perhaps, takes pleasure in writing this poem to Emily primarily because it enables him to deprive other men of the pleasures she offers. The other men in this case would be Emily's father, who takes pleasure in possessing her through confinement, and Emily's future husband who will inevitably claim Emily as his own and deprive Shelley of pleasure. As Zizek points out, however, the dynamics of this arrangement only complicate our conventional perception of it as a construct expressive of innate sexual difference, in the sense that it might ultimately point "towards the feminine status of the subject," because to be a subject means to have someone else do it "for me, in my place." This possibility exposes a fracture in Shelley's fantasy, because it undermines the central principle on which it is based, that is, the idea that one might achieve ontological healing by uniting logos and *jouissance*, word with voice and music. As Zizek indicates, such a union might produce a most unexpected and most unwelcome result: feminine as opposed to masculine authority. Shelley's own language betrays this possibility.

Prior to the close of *Epipsychidion* he confesses,

> The winged words on which my soul would pierce
> Into the height of love's rare Universe,
> Are chains of lead around its flight of fire.—
> I pant, I sink, I tremble, I expire! (*SPP* 588–91)

Because the passage indicates that Shelley shares Emily's captive status, it closes the gap convention would impose between them, and in the process Shelley assumes Emily's passive stature. Though his "winged words" evidently fail his soul, they nevertheless constitute him in his subjectivity. In the process of identifying Emily, therefore, he constitutes himself through this poem. The signs and metaphors that form the basis of his effort to constitute Emily illuminate the substance of his subjectivity. The poem hints at this specular passivity in the opening four lines, where Shelley tells Emily that "In my heart's temple I suspend to thee / These votive wreaths of withered memory" (*SPP* 3–4). The verb "suspend" generates the paradox that Shelley is actively passive and passively active. The image of "votive wreaths," moreover, amplifies the paradox in the sense that it marks the futile cyclicity not only of memory, but of all narrative, as well. To write over and over about searching for and eventually finding a soulmate amounts to making no progress at all.

Nonetheless, Shelley chooses to write about Emily, whom he refers to as

> Thou mirror
> In whom, as in the splendour of the Sun,
> All shapes look glorious which thou gazest on!
> Aye, even the dim words which obscure thee now
> Flash, lightning-like, with unaccustomed glow;
> I pray thee that thou blot from this sad song
> All of its much mortality and wrong .... (*SPP* 30–6)

If Emily serves as Shelley's mirror, she serves as his constitutive other, reflecting back to her "decentered" subject his secret treasure, the "splendour" of what he is when the two come in contact. His belief that her gaze brings out the best in him rings true in the terms of "intersubjectivity," because she conveys to him that he is desired. At the same time, however, the arrangement they share constitutes her. The equivalent of her gaze would be his words, which recognize her, though the phrase "which obscure thee now" chafes against that prospect, implying that there is something about Emily, her bright Spirit, perhaps her presence, that words fail to constitute. The trope assigns passivity and activity to both sides of the formation. Her influence inspires the words rendering her in the form of sign and metaphor; his words actively obscure her presence in the process of passively receiving the "flash" of her divine "splendour."

Critics of *Epipsychidion* have commented extensively on Shelley's self-conscious use of metaphor, though none has viewed the phenomenon as the product of fantasy.[29] While the more obvious purpose behind Shelley's prolific

---

[29] D. J. Hughes, for example, claims that *Epipsychidion* has no definitive theme, because "it is more self-reflexive than referential; it is about itself, its attempt to become and its attempt to be, and, being about itself, it is, inevitably in Shelley, about the processes of mind and the limits of poetry and the limits of thought" (279). See "Coherence and Collapse in Shelley, with Particular Reference to *Epipsychidion*," *ELH* 28 (1961): 260–83. Frank McConnell contends that Shelley's self-critical use of metaphor enunciates the incompatibility of phenomenon and figure, while Angela Leighton sees the poem as a complex of "peculiar tension" (224) generated by Shelley's refusal to separate figures caught in the nexus linking the rhetorical to the historical, the autobiographical to the literary. "Shelley's high-flown figures," she says, "whether impelled by self-pity, sexual hypocrisy or literary imitation, are nonetheless loaded with tell-tale frictions and salutary skepticisms" (231). See Frank McConnell, "Shelleyan 'Allegory': *Epipsychidion*," *Keats-Shelley Journal* 20 (1971): 100–12; Angela Leighton, "Love, Writing and Scepticism in *Epipsychidion*," *The New Shelley: Later Twentieth-Century Views*, ed. G. Kim Blank (New York: St. Martin's, 1991) 220–41. Earl Schulze says he fails to see how Shelley's skepticism leads to self-defeat. In his view, Shelley uses Dantean allegory to affirm the limitations of metaphor but also to explore and celebrate imaginative creativity. See "The Dantean Quest of *Epipsychidion*," *Studies in Romanticism* 21 (1982): 191–216. Barbara Gelpi argues, "the hold which Teresa Viviani took on Shelley's imagination had its roots in

use of metaphor might be to represent as well as enact his perception that Emily's nature exceeds language, and, as such, serves as a metaphor of the creative process, which resists settling on any given image, his use of metaphor might also indicate that objects of desire resist capture, because desire always exceeds the object. If Emily gives positive shape to what Shelley believes he has lost, the loss that formed him as a desiring subject in the first place, she must remain elusive. Elusiveness of this kind breeds frustration, but in the process sustains desire, which, in turn, brings about pleasure. If Shelley managed to arrest and then assimilate Emily, he would cease to be a subject poet, and Emily would cease to be the subject his desire constitutes.

It might appear that Shelley approaches recognition of this possibility when he refers to *Epipsychidion* as a "rose," whose "petals pale / Are dead," assuring Emily that it will not harm her: "But soft and fragrant is the faded blossom, / And it has no thorn left to wound thy bosom" (*SPP* 9–12). As a representation of Emily, this song in words constitutes her to a degree, but it also lacks something. It plays the role of other which gives substance to vacancy. Standing in for, or rather *as*, its author, furthermore, the poem lacks his presence and, therefore, lacks ideal authority. That which marks each counterpart in this "intersubjective" arrangement is what conventional thinking would regard as the effect of some cause, specifically a set of faded petals that recall the rose's former color and a fragrance, perhaps now more intense, reminiscent of the flower's living perfume. Interpreted from this perspective, the "rose" Shelley conceives is no longer a rose, but a remnant. However, these signs embody what a rose is in the same way that Shelley's song constitutes Emily. Emily, the real article standing before him, would be no less a sign than the rose growing in the soil of someone's garden.

The possibility that Shelley recognized the ramifications of seeking a union with Emily diminishes because a version of the dead flower image appears in at least two other lyrics Shelley wrote for women he associated with music: in a poem he composed for Sophia Stacey called either "On a dead Violet" or "On a Faded Violet" and in a poem he composed for Jane Williams called "Remembrance." In addition to serving as a stock image of mortality, Shelley's flowers in these poems stand multi-valently for loss, lacking and absence, and they represent variously Shelley, the poem he has written, or the woman for whom he writes.

---

part in aspects of his personal psychological history" (185). She adds, "the language both of her letters to him and of *Epipsychidion*" confirms that "the relationship between Shelley and Viviani is constructed by and through the discourse of sentimentalism" and "participates in an exploratory psychic narrative" (185) that is universal and theoretical more than it is cultural. See "Keeping Faith with Desire: A Reading of *Epipsychidion*," *Evaluating Shelley*, ed. Timothy Clark and Jerrold E. Hogle (Edinburgh: Edinburgh UP, 1996) 180–96. Finally, Nancy Moore Goslee concentrates on Shelley's drafts and his revisions to consider the possibility of including them as a part of the poem, a poem that intends to represent a figuration of collapse through inclining and declining imagery. See "Depersoning Emily: Drafting as Plot in *Epipsychidion*," *Keats-Shelley Journal* 42 (1993): 104–19.

Shelley's recycling of the trope for phantasmic purposes illustrates one of the problems with narrative. In autobiographical narrative, the author visualizes life before the point of loss, an impossibility given what must happen in order for subjectivity to emerge in the first place. This faded rose of a poem he creates for Emily conveys the idea that he, it and she were once whole—perhaps that each or all were at one time active and alive. *Epipsychidion* is "dead," however, in the sense that Shelley has transferred to it all of his own inertia, thereby establishing himself by way of the transaction, but that subject becomes one whose emptiness is mirrored by his creation. Shelley's fantasy designates music as the corrective to this unfortunate formation, but forecloses on its own success by finding expression in the form of verse narrative, a form that attempts to bring together word and music, but one that nonetheless inherently lacks the certainty, continuity and spontaneity of performance.

Shelley portrays Emily as an image of ideal illumination, primarily following models supplied by the conventions of courtly love poetry and by Dante, whose Beatrice exudes "an inner light that shines forth especially from her smile and eyes (those parts in medieval tradition, which most closely communicate her soul)."[30] As much an abstract embodiment of ideal love and beauty as a genuine figure in Shelley's life, Emily lights Shelley's way through the poem as she guides him on his life path. In his mind's eye she takes the form of "Sweet lamp!," "star," "beloved light" and "Seraph of Heaven" who veils "beneath that radiant form of Woman / All that is insupportable in thee / Of light, and love, and immortality!" (*SPP* 53, 60, 63, 21–4). The "wells" of her eyes capture "sun-beams ... which ever leap / Under the lightings of the soul" (*SPP* 88–9). As much as Emily represents light, however, she also represents music. Shelley calls her, for example, a "gentle tone / Amid rude voices" (*SPP* 62–3) and "A lute, which those whom love has taught to play / Make music on, to soothe the roughest day" (*SPP* 65–6). The latter image resonates sharply with Shelley's depiction of Jane Williams in the lyric "With a Guitar. To Jane," where he attributes to Jane and the guitar he has given her the capacity to alter for the better the consciousness of any listener her song reaches.

Shelley's association of Emily with music bears the familiar trademark of fantasy, however. Certainly, he locks in on Emily's eyes and on her smile as Brown observes, anatomizing her in the way Petrarch's imagination breaks down Laura, for example, but throughout the poem Shelley associates Emily's expression with fluid and air, and he repeatedly identifies her lips as the focal point of desire as well as the transmitter of *jouissance*. Signature metonyms such as these in Shelley's writing paradoxically signal both a woman's presence, specifically in the form of her voice, and a woman's absence, that is, the vacancy, or void, to which those signs refer. They suggest, furthermore, that Shelley remains twice removed from the object that has temporarily caught his desire. If fluid, air and lips stand in

---

[30] Richard E. Brown, "The Role of Dante in *Epipsychidion*," *Comparative Literature* 30 (1978): 232. See also Earl Wasserman's discussion of the biblical underpinnings of Emily's character.

for voice, voice stands in for nothing. Shelley fails to consider this deadlock and instead indulges the prospect that he and Emily will share one another's presence unadulterated by words or signs:

> And we will talk, until thought's melody
> Become too sweet for utterance, and it die
> In words, to live again in looks, which dart
> With thrilling tone into the voiceless heart,
> Harmonizing silence without a sound.
> Our breath shall intermix, our bosoms bound,
> And our veins beat together; and our lips
> With other eloquence than words, eclipse
> The soul that burns between them .... (*SPP* 560–8)

The synesthesia occurring in the phrase "looks, which dart / With thrilling tone into the voiceless heart" conveys the extraordinary nature of the lovers' communion as much as it demonstrates Shelley's point, that language lacks the capacity to capture what lies beyond it. What Shelley apparently does not realize, however, is that the objects that constitute him and Emily—"breath," "bosoms," beating "veins" and "lips"—also constitute their coupling.

By Shelley's own account, sharing Emily's presence differs little from suffering her absence. He recalls a point earlier in his journey when

> In solitudes
> Her voice came to me through the whispering woods,
> And from the fountains, and the odours deep
> Of flowers, which, like lips murmuring in their sleep
> Of the sweet kisses which had lulled them there,
> Breathed but of *her* to the enamoured air;
> And from the breezes whether low or loud,
> And from the rain of every passing cloud,
> And from the singing of the summer-birds,
> And from all sounds, all silence. (*SPP* 200–9)

On its surface, this passage testifies to Emily's constancy, her ubiquity, her elemental purity. By equating her voice with "flowers" and "breezes" and "rain," Shelley suggests that, even when she is not near him, he can hear and feel her substance. The imagery conveying this belief, however, "desublimates" Emily. Rather than an omnipresent whole finding expression through a variety of media, Emily becomes a "hole" that exists everywhere and nowhere. This fact about her might be the "tiny detail," the zero point of her being, which represents the "Other in her moment of *jouissance*,"[31] Shelley cannot tolerate, and it might explain why

---

[31] Zizek 49.

he ultimately renounces her from his reality. When her "voice" comes to him, it does so by means of media resembling, that is, standing in for, "sweet kisses," "lips" and "breathing" he can never transcend.

Ironically intolerable, expressions of Emily's *jouissance* occur in the form of "thought's melody," "veins" beating "together," "whispering woods" and "the singing of summer birds." In a direct address to the reader as "Stranger" (*SPP* 72), an effort to make himself palpably present, Shelley observes of Emily,

> ... from her lips, as from a hyacinth full
> Of honey-dew, a liquid murmur drops,
> Killing the sense with passion; sweet as stops
> Of planetary music heard in trance. (*SPP* 83–6)

The "liquid murmur" uttered by her "lips" is "sweet" and nourishing, but the empty calories it provides "kill" the "sense with passion." The trope implies on the one hand that Emily's expression traverses the bounds of mortality, but on the other hand that the secret treasure it represents, both what Shelley perceives as Emily's ideal self and that perfection in himself she mirrors back, becomes lethal to the subjectivity that feeds off of it.

As a narrative, *Epipsychidion* focuses on the condition of lacking produced by castration, specifically the loss of Emily, who represents music and voice, and envisions a fantasy state of restoration. The entire construct exhibits the typical contradiction compromising all narrative, that is, the subject's presupposition of his own existence prior to the event that established his subjectivity.[32] In some ways, such a deadlock serves Shelley's purpose in the poem, since he wants to suggest that before Emily his life was empty. However, if she represents what he lost and has always sought, *he* could not have experienced her as a pre-subjective vision. In language echoing *Alastor*, he describes life without Emily's influence as a frustrating emptiness and himself as "a man with mighty loss dismayed" (*SPP* 229). He recalls a conversation with a disembodied "voice" that asked

> ... "O Thou of hearts the weakest,
> The Phantom is beside thee whom thou seekest."
> Then I—"where?"—the world's echo answered "where!"
> And in that silence, and in my despair,
> I questioned every tongueless wind that flew
> Over my tower of mourning .... (*SPP* 232–7)

The recollection confirms that a wounding loss results in Shelley's sense of himself, his subjectivity. The "world's echo" of his query indicates that the object voice constitutes him and that he shares the emptiness that lies at the heart of the echo. The world acoustically mirrors his question "where?" imperfectly in the form of

---

[32] Zizek.

the exclamation "where!," emphasizing that he and his voice have paradoxically become alienated at the same time that they have become mutually dependent on one another.

Shelley's corrective for this condition involves running off with Emily as part of a pre-castration fantasy, but liability inheres to the conventional romance environment he chooses:

> The blue Aegean girds this chosen home,
> With ever-changing sound and light and foam,
> Kissing the sifted sands, and caverns hoar;
> And all the winds wandering along the shore
> Undulate with the undulating tide. (*SPP* 430–4)

The island becomes an extension of Emily's being, and as an emanation of fluid and air, water and wind, it functions as sign rather than as transcendental signifier. However, the island also becomes a place of balance and harmony, where the sea meets the land. It provides "clear exhalations" (*SPP* 471) that immerse its inhabitants in a fantastic atmosphere of healing fulfillment, bathing them in music:

> And every motion, odour, beam, and tone,
> With that deep music is in union:
> Which is a soul within the soul—they seem
> Like echoes in an antenatal dream.— (*SPP* 453–6)

On the one hand, the subject finds himself echoed everywhere. In this regard, the island delivers to the subject constant confirmation of its value in "every motion, odour, beam, and tone." In addition, the "deep music" played back for the subject indicates the depth of the subject's, or, from Shelley's perspective the individual's, core being—the substance of his or her presence. That the island expresses itself in "echoes of an antenatal dream," however, suggests the true nature of what one hears: the replay of the pre-castration fantasy. Ironically, Shelley's decision to escape the world of loss and responsibility and retreat to the island only repeats the necessary moment of mutilation. When he cuts himself and Emily off from the world, he severs himself from words and by extension from poetry. Fantasy escape would restore voice and music to his language, but at the same time it would paradoxically excise him from language, erasing all trace of him and Emily from the world of reality.[33]

When Shelley posits that his new home will provide the right conditions for his relationship with Emily to graduate to its proper, more natural form, he uses a familiar metaphor to define its transformation, predicting that they "shall

---

[33] See Ghislaine McDayter's illuminating discussion of this dimension of *Epipsychidion*. "'O'er Leaping the Bounds': The Sexing of the Creative Soul in Shelley's *Epipsychidion*," *Keats-Shelley Journal* 52 (2003): 21–49.

become the same, we shall be one / Spirit within two frames" (*SPP* 573–4). The term "frames" obviously refers to their bodies, but it also denotes, as it does in the essay "On Love," that each partner will function as a musical instrument playing the same song. Two instruments united by one spirit contribute to the same erotic composition. The connotation of harmony, of differences blended into a singular expression, created by this metaphor falters, because it comprises one feature of a larger relational profile.

Throughout *Epipsychidion*, Shelley insists that, because he and Emily are twin spirits, they are related in the same way as sister and brother. He calls her "my heart's sister" (*SPP* 415), asks her to become a "vestal sister" to whatever remains of his "dull mortality," serving as "bride" to that "imperishable" part of his being (*SPP* 389–93). After confessing his love for her, he expresses the wish,

> Would we two had been twins of the same mother!
> Or, that the name my heart lent to another
> Could be a sister's bond for her and thee,
> Blending two beams of one eternity! (*SPP* 45–8)

Projecting their relationship outside the bounds of the law of the "big Other," Shelley defines his bond with Emily as incestuous. Sharing his bloodline, she becomes his walking reflection, insurance for his subjectivity; however, this specular relationship forecloses on any additional gains, because within the arrangement each partner simply confirms his or her counterpart's vacancy, not his or her core substance. What emerges is an economy that insures value as far as subject formation is concerned, but this result runs counter to what Shelley's fantasy means to achieve. Ultimately, though, that fantasy provides compensation, perhaps what it is designed to do in all the narrative and dramatic poems, because it bestows upon Shelley the resources necessary—desire and its product, language— to sustain him as a writer.

The faultlines characterizing Shelley's fantasy as it cycled its way through successive narrative and dramatic iterations reminds us of at least two things: first, while fantasy conceals the horror of the "Real," it paradoxically "creates its 'repressed' point of reference."[34] Second, the controlled order and sequence of narrative cannot eliminate the "repressed antagonism" it means to resolve.[35] Outside the fictional environment of the narrative and dramatic poems dedicated to the reconciliation of sexualized expression, Shelley found himself contending with additional sources and types of instability. The personal poems he wrote for Jane Williams, Claire Clairmont and Sophia Stacey exhibit even greater signs of stress, as Shelley struggled to resolve tensions inherent to the more immediate symbolic structures from which he could not and would not extricate himself. In those poems he is unable to avail himself of "interpassive" protagonists as the

---

[34] Zizek 7.
[35] Zizek 10–11.

means to creating the illusion of authorial mastery, and he finds himself similarly hard-pressed to relegate female musical performers to instrumental stature. His strategy for approaching in the hope of integrating their expressive capacities involves corresponding with them by means of somatic signals tuning both partners into the "real."

Chapter 3
Sounding the "Real"

Musical women framed Shelley's desire. Claire Clairmont, Sophia Stacey and Jane Williams possessed beautiful singing voices, which separated them from other women in Shelley's experience. Shelley's fantasy of integrating voice and word in order to achieve self-presence informs the poems he wrote for these women as pervasively as it does the narrative and dramatic poems, which feature fictional characters and scenarios. In these personal poems, however, the relationships and situations involve Shelley and the women whose voices fuelled his desire as positive objects directly. The poems achieve levels of tension, intensity and richness perhaps unparalleled anywhere else in Shelley's writing, because they bear the marks of Shelley's struggle to prosecute a phantasmic narrative within the confines of the symbolic system, permeated by the laws, protocols and strictures of a spectral "big Other." The clash produces not pathological expression, but, rather, modes of correspondence revelatory of a "normal" individual forced to cope with the deadlocks and paradoxes that characterize human experience.

Critics have long recognized the volatile and unstable character of the poems Shelley wrote for Claire, Sophia and Jane. For example, Michael O'Neill contends that in them Shelley barely managed to keep the raw feeling of his "deepest obsessions" under artistic control,[1] and William Keach believes the lyrics to Jane Williams represent sites where life and poetry exert mutually shaping force on one another. "Shelley's stylistic choices and performances," he says, "are inextricably enmeshed in the choices and performances of living."[2] Susan Wolfson takes a similar approach, concentrating on Shelley's sensitivity toward the unknowable factors that shape a poem's reception. She focuses on Shelley's efforts to conduct

---

[1] O'Neill and Donald Reiman write that Shelley's "reputation as a poet of amorous longing rests on the poems he wrote for—or at least gave to—three women with whom he is not known to have been sexually intimate—Sophia Stacey, Emilia Viviani, and Jane Williams. According to the common wisdom, he wrote no such poems to his wives, except a few posthumously published lyrics that reflect his later estrangement form Harriet Shelley shortly before his elopement with Mary Godwin and from Mary during the last year of his life. Though PBS is likely to have been sexually intimate with Claire Clairmont early in 1815," only one completed poem addressed to her "bears any mark of emotional involvement." See "Poems Given to Sophia Stacey: Headnote," in Donald H. Reiman and Michael O'Neill, eds, *The Manuscripts of the Younger Romantics. Fair Copy Manuscripts of Shelley's Poems in European and American Libraries. Percy Bysshe Shelley*, vol. 8 (New York and London: Garland Publishing, 1997) 277–9.

[2] William Keach, *Shelley's Style* (New York and London: Methuen, 1984) 202.

Jane's reaction by manipulating the "phonic field" of each poem he wrote for her. As an example, she cites his use of rhyming words compatible with Jane's name in order to invoke her presence and vent the pain she caused him without having to mention either explicitly. Wolfson points out that Shelley's recognition of the problematical nature of lyric expression, inner-directed and private, but at the same time outer-directed and public, inflects the composition of each poem. This "doubleness" pervades the lyrics to Jane, "eroding their self-authorized aesthetics with urgencies of correspondence and response that take shape as a series of calculated performances" that find expression in the "phonic field" of each poem.[3]

A common thread in these readings is that writing for Shelley forms a symbolic arena in which desire, expectation and intention contend with convention. While the struggle results in poetry of great richness, it also forces compromise. As much as Shelley masters diction and adjusts meter to conform to his wishes, the world of sign and structure—the law of the "big Other"—asserts its own authority. Though it is likely that Shelley counted on the instability of language to secure him an advantage in the personal lyrics as O'Neill, Keach and Wolfson demonstrate, it is also true that he sought to stretch his expression beyond the perimeter of the symbolic system that in part determined him. At least a portion of his motivation derived from the effect Jane's, Claire's and Sophia's voices must have had on him. Perhaps in a fashion similar to the prima donnas whose performances he witnessed at the London opera houses, the combination of voice and somatic movement produced by these three intimate acquaintances touched him in visceral and emotional ways to which no combination of words could do justice. Ann Wroe suspects that "the impact of song on him was often unbearable in its physical intensity. When women played, they played him; when they sang, they stole his breath from him. He was in love with them, ached with wanting them, whatever his reasonings otherwise."[4] By focusing intently on diction, form, rhyme and meter, Shelley might succeed at delivering the same kind of experience to his chosen female auditor.

In this respect, the personal lyrics Shelley wrote for Claire, Sophia and Jane end up serving as acoustic mirrors of what he found most essential and, therefore, most desirable about each of them. The poems attempt to retrieve the thing, the "*agalma*"—the object voice and the vocal indelibility it promises, perhaps—Shelley the poet could never quite capture.[5] These poems also satisfy the requirements of

---

[3] Wolfson, *Formal Charges* (Stanford: Stanford UP, 1997) 208–9. Wolfson's overall argument with respect to Shelley argues that, whether he was writing for a public or a private audience, he understood that poetic forms "cannot ultimately legislate reading by their marks, and that other self-devitalizing relations, unapprehended in the poet's conception, may evolve in the convergence of text and reader that brings a poet's work into existence," 195.

[4] Ann Wroe, *Being Shelley: The Poet's Search for Himself* (New York: Pantheon Books, 2007) 243.

[5] Slavoj Zizek, *The Plague of Fantasies* (London and New York: Verso 1997) 8–10.

Shelley's fantasy in a slightly different way, in the sense that they give expression to what he imagined to be the thing that made him desirable to his others, his secret treasure. In this case, that secret treasure would be his ability to shape his experience with each woman in poetry. Ostensibly, none of the three women in question possessed the talent for such expression, despite exhibiting vocal, musical or emotional fluency. Deadlock of course, cripples such an agenda, because even though written language becomes the instrument of audition, it also harnesses and structures the sound it issues. Ultimately, written language evacuates sound, in the same way it evacuates presence. If Shelley viewed the poems for Jane and the others as instruments of transmission, effectively, that is, as acoustic reflections of his own voice and, therefore, his presence, in the end he would find each lyric effort self-defeating. Writing would remind him that he and the voice ostensibly inhabiting the poems he composed could never be anything but estranged from one another. In this regard, none of these personal poems—written performances in their own right—reproduces the experience of listening while a woman sings.

A psychoanalytic approach to the rhetorical and social ambiguities that typify the poems Shelley devoted to musical women creates the possibility that, within the scope of fantasy, Shelley sought to communicate with Sophia, Claire and Jane on a level approaching the Lacanian "real." Lacan defines the "real" as an unknown value that exists outside the symbolic and resists construction. It consists not of the symbolic matrix which covers and supports the subject—this, in fact, is what we regard as "reality"—but remains a third term, separate from the imaginary and the symbolic, which forecloses on analysis. Alan Sheridan, translator for the Norton edition of *The Four Fundamental Concepts of Psychoanalysis*, explains that, in the case of the subject, the "Real" involves "the organism and its biological needs," remaining something that at best might only be supposed.[6] At one point during a discussion of the concept of "repetition," Lacan posits that, "the subject in himself, the recalling of his biography, all this goes only to a certain limit, which is known as the real."[7] In a subsequent discussion of the relationship between the "real" and phantasy, he asserts that "the place of the real ... stretches from the trauma to the phantasy—in so far as the phantasy is never anything more than the screen that conceals something quite primary, something determinant in the function of repetition."[8]

Each of the poems in question demonstrates that Shelley's fantasy of becoming intimate with a musically fluent woman, as the means to capturing and then reintegrating something he lost, necessitated evading the biographical facts—the frustrating social deadlocks to which Keach refers—of his own life. Doing so would entail pushing poetry, a manifestation of the symbolic, until it gives. The

---

[6] Jacques Lacan, *The Four Fundamental Concepts of Psychoanalysis*, ed. Jacques-Alain Miller, trans. Alan Sheridan (New York and London: W. W. Norton & Company, 1981) Translator's Notes 280.

[7] Lacan 49.

[8] Lacan 60.

lyrics to Sophia, Claire and Jane suggest that Shelley's strategy involves reaching what he targets as a positive object of his desire by means of a fundamental music, that is, by means of the psychosomatic sounds of his own being. Clever deployment of resonant and rhyming syllables—the hard *a*, *ane* and *ain* sounds Wolfson discusses from the Jane Williams lyrics—deliver something essential about Shelley's experience not just to Jane's consciousness, for example, but to Jane's vocal chords, to her throat and sinus cavity. By uttering Shelley's words, Jane, Sophia and Claire speak Shelley; he becomes poignantly though deceptively present during each recitation or performance.

At times in the poems, deliberate adjustments in meter, furthermore, become Shelley's means for conveying the psychosomatic pulses of his being, theoretically in its raw, biological and emotional states, unadulterated by law, custom or sign. The speaker guided by Shelley's lines and measures finds her body—her respiration, heart rate and somatic articulations—and her mood tuning into Shelley's body and mood. But this is not all. The poems also serve as recordings of actual or imagined encounters with these women, and, as such, they articulate Shelley's perception of correspondent expressions of psychosomatic states experienced by them. In this way, the poems represent efforts to capture and render aspects of erotic connection that travel outside the symbolic field. Listening to Sophia, Jane and Claire sing to instrumental accompaniment weakens or strengthens his heart as much as it quickens or slows his pulse rate. These effects, the poems seem to say, occur prior to linguistic processing, though the fact that he chooses to express them in poetic language suggests that fundamental physical expression does not do them justice. Correspondence in the "real," Shelley must have found, amounts to correspondence without meaning.

The poems Shelley devoted to Claire, Sophia and Jane prosecute his phantasmic agenda by manifesting this sexualized economy of communication in which the masculine word, embodying the masculine spirit and consciousness, mixes with the feminine voice, embodying the feminine spirit and consciousness. He supplies the score the female singer lacks, and the female singer supplies the voice and *jouissance* lost to the male subject. At such moments, the two would become fully integrated, sharing one being and performing together, voice and word, *jouissance* and logos, in perfect partnership. Repetition, which underlies the fantasy narrative inherent to each poem, offsets the accomplishment, though. As is often the case when someone reprises the same musical number or role, Shelley's pursuit of ideal correspondence in each of the poems gains nothing new, addressing over and over again the same trauma of loss.

In his essay on Schumann, Zizek writes,

> What is music at its most elementary? An act of *supplication*: a call to the figure of the big Other (beloved Lady, King, God …) to *respond*, not as the symbolic big Other, but in the real of his or her being (breaking his own rules by showing mercy; conferring her contingent love on us …). Music is thus an attempt to provoke the "answer of the Real"; to give rise in the Other to the "miracle" of

what Lacan speaks apropos of love, the miracle of the Other stretching his or her hand out to me.[9]

Shelley's "attempt to provoke the 'answer of the Real'" forecloses on itself at every turn. The personal lyrics differ little from their narrative and dramatic counterparts in this regard. Both modes expose the horror of the "real" Shelley's fantasy means to conceal. Specifically, communion with a woman's vocality and the *jouissance* underwriting it amounts to meaningless communion; it is a communion that cannot be represented and leads to a dead end. Ultimately, the outstretched hand of the "Other" Zizek mentions threatens subjectivity and the complete authority about which Shelley fantasized. Cardio-respiratory rhythms and emotionally charged syllables possess dubious communicative value outside the realm of the words and measures that codify them. And, though they might command a value beyond the linguistic, that value according to Lacan remains an x-factor, an unapproachable commodity that lies outside of speech. Perhaps all too often Shelley's fantasy construction of "real" communication clashes with one of the most basic functions of fantasy, which is to shield the subject from the "horror of the real." Contacting the kernel of a woman's being threatens to short-circuit the very fantasy that initiates that objective.

As is the case with all fantasies, Shelley's fantasy contains the means of its own undoing, because it seeks to conceal a desire incompatible with its mission of achieving a confluence of voice and word, paradoxically in the process catering to an opposite desire to possess the singular authority of a poet. As much as he sought the object voice, the thing he lacked and the thing that made him the poet he was, Shelley could not embrace an economy of expression that entailed surrendering his birthright. Nor would he surrender himself to the promising ministry of the female voice, though the poems supply ample evidence that he envisioned it to be a cure for the wound of castration. It might be true that at least a portion of each woman's charm consisted of her inaccessibility; however, it is also true that Shelley's phantasmic aspirations required him to keep his distance from those charms. If, despite their phonic complexities, the personal poems function primarily as recordings of Shelley's psychosomatic states, therefore serving as objects that reaffirm their subject poet's vacancy, they also serve as monologues that mark absence or distance from the object voice Shelley desired. His words evoke the presence of Sophia, Claire and Jane, but in all cases conveniently fail to make them present, underscoring the possibility that, when it comes to expression, the written word remains the final and only achievable kind of authority. Paradoxically, then, by projecting the female voice out of reach, Shelley gets what he really wants, or at least what he fears losing. As much as any other factor, this dynamic becomes a powerful source of instability and tension in the personal poems.

Sophia Stacey was the ward of Shelley's uncle, Robert Parker, and was indirectly tied, therefore, to Shelley's family at Field Place. Touring the continent

---

[9] Zizek 192.

in 1819 with her chaperone, Miss Corbet Parry-Jones, Sophia, intrigued by stories she had heard about the family's "disreputable black sheep,"[10] met and then spent time with the Shelleys in Florence. James Bieri writes,

> She was a talented harpist with an attractive singing voice, qualities—along with her orphan status—that soon established her as Shelley's new *inamorata*. The five or more lyrics and fragments Shelley wrote for the well-named Sophia are among his most erotic. He kept them from Mary, who gave them misleading dates when she published some after his death.[11]

Mary's journal makes scant mention of Stacey, though in a letter to Mrs Gisborne she comments explicitly on Sophia's musical talent, observing that "the younger lady ... sings well for an English dilettanti & if she would learn the scales would sing exceedingly well for she has a sweet voice" (*MWSL* 302).

Scholars have disagreed about the nature and extent of Shelley's relationship with Sophia Stacey. O'Neill and Reiman, for example, assert, "there is no hint that MWS was jealous of Stacey. Nor is there evidence that PBS found Stacey attractive in any other way then her singing voice, and only the texts of the lyric poems he gave her hint that he might have considered her more than a social acquaintance through family ties."[12] The editors of Mary Shelley's journals, Feldman and Scott-Kilvert, would seem to agree, suggesting that Shelley was primarily "impressed with her singing and playing on the harp" and Richard Holmes reports that Shelley "made a point of helping her with her Italian, and taught her the words of a Carbonari ballad and a local love-song. They seem to have gone visiting galleries together, probably with Claire and Miss Jones as well, making a voluble and attractive female party, and perfectly adapted to Shelley's social tastes."[13] On one particular occasion, writes Holmes, Shelley nursed Sophia through a toothache by applying "a cotton lint to the offending molar at the back of her mouth."[14]

Newman Ivey White insists on the innocuous nature of Shelley's relationship with Sophia and on the generic character of the poems he wrote for her, some of which, Bieri contends, were "probably composed to be sung."[15] According to White, "Shelley was charmed with the company of Sophia Stacey, but the beautiful lyrics that she inspired, and even, for the most part, the poem directly addressed to her, were not personal tributes, but tributes to the power of music. Some other lovely

---

[10] Richard Holmes, *Shelley: The Pursuit* (New York: Elisabeth Sifton Books, 1975) 564.

[11] James Bieri, *Percy Bysshe Shelley: A Biography*, 2 vols. (Newark: U of Delaware P, 2004) 2: 170.

[12] Reiman and O'Neill 278.

[13] Paula Feldman and Diana Scott-Kilvert, eds, *The Journals of Mary Shelley: 1814–1844* (Baltimore and London: The Johns Hopkins UP, 1987) 302; Holmes 565.

[14] Holmes 565.

[15] Bieri 2: 171.

voice singing impassioned or sentimental lyrics would have done as well."[16] White refers to those critics who might be tempted to cite the poems Shelley wrote for Sophia as evidence that the two were intimate as "suspicious," claiming that they display the same innocent devotion he directed toward Elizabeth Hitchener, Teresa Viviani and Jane Williams.[17] Nathaniel Brown disagrees with Holmes' assessment. "The true nature of Shelley's impulses" regarding Sophia Stacey, he says, "emerges plainly from the record of his poetry, however strenuously disguised, suppressed, or sublimated."[18] Responding to Mary's comment that "'you never see anyone except those whom you shut out when you can,'" Bieri points out that Shelley "did not shut out Sophia; his love lyrics to her imply some physical intimacy."[19]

Regardless of the extent to which Shelley pursued a physical connection with Sophia, the poems he composed for his uncle's ward establish her as one more positive object of desire, and they identify her as medium capable of providing phantasmic fulfillment.[20] Approaching the lyrics from this angle bolsters White's insistence that they primarily represent "tributes to the power of music" and reinforces his assertion that "some other lovely voice singing impassioned or sentimental lyrics would have done as well;" it also validates Bieri's assumption that Shelley's erotically laden responses to Sophia's music reveal extraordinary personal involvement. Collectively, the lyrics for Sophia focus on the effects that linger after a physical encounter in which Shelley found himself captivated by her voice and by her body's movements. Her influence also registers with him in the form of an infectious psychosomatic rhythm—the beats of her being to which his becomes attuned—apparently only he can hear and feel. The Sophia Stacey poems also feature a preoccupation with oral gratification, specifically in the form of kisses feared, desired or recalled. Sophia's mouth generates her music and promises the physical contact for which Shelley longs; however it also becomes a representation of the thing Shelley has lost and consequently desires even more than sexual intercourse. Oral coupling figuratively represents for Shelley the confluence of separate forms of expression, his capacity for uttering the poetic word and her capacity for song. In the same way that the transmission of her voice by way of controlled, moist exhalation functions as a metonym for the thing he

---

[16] Newman I. White, *Shelley*, 2 vols. (New York: Alfred A. Knopf, 1940) 2: 175.

[17] White 2: 174.

[18] Nathaniel Brown, *Sexuality and Feminism in Shelley* (Cambridge: Harvard UP, 1979) 65.

[19] Bieri 2: 171.

[20] The poems written for Sophia include "To Sophia," "On a Faded Violet," "Time Long Past," "To—('I fear thy kisses gentle maiden')," "Goodnight" and "Love's Philosophy." Bieri includes the poem eventually titled "Indian Serenade" and "The Indian Girl's Song" in the Sophia Stacey set. Given that the poem was apparently recycled for Jane Williams, and given that all of the personal poems written for musical women contain the same phantasmic signature, I will discuss "The Indian Girl's Song" with the poems written for Jane.

desires, however, kisses serve as stand-ins offering temporary gratification, but ultimately no satisfaction.

The opening stanza of "To Sophia" portrays her as music in motion:

> Those soft limbs of thine, whose motion
> Ever falls and shifts and glances
> As the life within them dances. (*SPW* 4–6)

Shelley's language suggests that Sophia's body becomes the direct and outward expression of a being whose natural state qualifies as a form of musical performance. If her body serves as the sign of that state, it becomes a sign in flux, one that refuses to settle into a predictable or codifiable pattern and, by implication therefore, evades representation or reproduction. The second stanza concentrates on the spellbinding power of her eyes, which he calls "a double Planet" (*SPW* 7), identifying them with the planet Venus, which serves both as morning and evening star. The figure conveys the power of her gaze, which remains as singular as the appearance of Venus, often the only star that can be seen in twilight, and thus the disorientation he experiences when she looks at him: one planet appears to be two. Though both stanzas attempt to render Sophia's substance and influence by way of literary figure, the note of ephemerality inherent to Shelley's images—that is, comparing her to "Nymphs of earth or ocean" and linking the fire in her eyes to "thoughts of tender gladness / Which, like zephyrs on the billow, / Make thy gentle soul their pillow" (*SPW* 2, 10–12)—indicate that Sophia's presence never fully concretizes. At the same time, however, the association of her with air and water suggests that Shelley bears witness to a substitute for self-present expression, a series of amorphous fill-ins that gesture toward but fail to manifest the thing itself. The performance of Sophia's being remains ontologically equivalent to Shelley's characterization of it.

Apparently, Sophia's eyes dominated her appearance. In this poem, they dominate Shelley. In the poem's second stanza he observes that her Maenadic "Gaze" has the ability to drive "the wisest into madness" (*SPW* 8), associating it with *jouissance*, and the poem's third stanza advises,

> If, whatever face thou paintest
> In those eyes, grows pale with pleasure,
> If the fainting soul is faintest
> When it hears thy harp's wild measure,
> Wonder not that when thou speakest
> Of the weak my heart is weakest. (*SPW* 18)

The word "gaze" introduces the first note of loss into the poem. The "pale" image Shelley recognizes in the portrait supplied by Sophia's eyes constitutes him at the same time that, in the return gaze of the image, he remains an irrevocably lost object. Her ability to render him "faint" and ostensibly "mute" (*SPW* 22) whenever she plays the harp compounds the image of loss, because it reminds him of his own lost voice, his diminishing presence, growing ever more "faint," and his waning authority. Sophia is the one who commands narrative power according to Shelley, for she is the one who will "speakest / Of the weak."

The "wild measure" of Sophia's harp playing makes Shelley paradoxically "pale with pleasure," indicating that the "*jouissance*" she generates musically acts upon him as a kind of poison. When she plays, the balance between "*jouissance*" and logos and between music and word tilts dramatically in her favor. Shelley redresses the imbalance by encapsulating what he has witnessed in the form of a tribute poem, consisting of 24 lines, predominantly in trochaic meter, effectively confining Sophia and her music within a symbolic construct. The poem's final line closes a series of similes conveying the idea that Sophia's influence agitates him into a state of speechlessness:

> As dew beneath the wind of morning,
> As the sea which whirlwinds waken,
> As the birds at thunder's warning,
> As aught mute yet deeply shaken,
> As one who feels an unseen spirit
> Is my heart when thine is near it. (*SPW* 19–24)

In the same way that a thunder clap abruptly quiets chirping and singing birds, the proximity of Sophia's heart, ostensibly manifest in rhythms swept out by her "limbs" on the harp, momentarily stops Shelley's heart when he listens to her play. Shelley communicates his condition, a pleasant, but potentially threatening arrhythmia, to Sophia by shifting from trochaic to iambic meter in lines nine, 19 and 23 of the poem. To illustrate, the stressed syllables in lines 22 and 24 would be: "*As* aught *mute* yet *deep*ly *shak*en;" "*Is* my *heart* when *thine* is *near* it." In line 23, however, the meter moves from trochaic to iambic, placing stress this way: "As *one* who *feels* an *un*seen *spir*it." If by chance she were to recite "To Sophia" aloud, moreover, her voice might stumble, or become temporarily "faint," when it navigated each of these lines; she would feel, in other words, the same loss of self-mastery as Shelley. His words and measures in the end would take charge of Sophia's voice.

Two months after Sophia's departure from Florence, Shelley appended, without Mary's knowledge, the poem called "On a dead Violet" (later titled "On a Faded Violet") and an accompanying note to a letter Mary was about to send to Sophia. The note reads as follows:

> I promised you what I cannot perform; a song on singing:—there are only two subjects remaining. I have a few old stanzas on one which though simple & rude, look as if they were dictated by the heart.—And so—if you tell no one whose they are you are welcome to them. (*MYR* 301)

Because of its ambiguity, the note resembles those Shelley attached to poems he gave to Jane Williams. Apparently unable to compose a "song on singing," Shelley has chosen to send along stanzas on the theme of lost love and, while he attests to their sincerity ("they were dictated by the heart"), he hides behind the equivocal qualifier "look as if." Shelley never clarifies what the other "remaining" subject, fit for Sophia to sing, might be. Though the song is not about singing, the note highlights its nature and its purpose. Shelley outfits his heartfelt stanzas for Sophia's voice.

A multi-valent figure, the "flower" of the poem "On a Faded Violet" stands for the departed Sophia, the loss of her music and, more generally, the object voice Shelley desires. The first stanza reads,

> The odour from the flower is gone
> Which like thy kisses breathed on me;
> The colour from the flower is flown
> Which glowed of thee and only thee. (*SPW* 1–4)

The "kisses" Sophia "breathed" on Shelley share a flower's evanescence and fragility. Though it laments the loss of physical contact with Sophia's mouth, the touch of her lips and moist breath, the metaphor registers the absence of Sophia's voice. The image injects an element of instability into the fantasy narrative of this poem by acknowledging the possibility that, even though Sophia is now physically removed from Shelley, her kisses and breath lingering in his memory, her former mode of expression never enabled him to close in on her core substance. Ostensibly empty of sound, kisses and breath mark metonymically not just the absence of voice, but mark the absence of presence. In fact, the conspicuous absence of Sophia's voice from the poem enunciates its otherwise vacant status, despite an implication generated by the reference to Sophia's breath that some essential, some "real," part of her entered Shelley's nostrils and mouth. The state of absence and abandonment Shelley articulates in the poem will characterize that poem once it reaches Sophia. Though constituting him, the words she reads will reflect a familiar lack of voice and presence.

Stanza two intensifies the motif of lacking by summoning through metaphor an image of castration:

> A shrivelled, lifeless, vacant form,
> It lies on my abandoned breast,
> And mocks the heart which yet is warm,
> With cold and silent rest. (*SPW* 5–8)

If the clipped flower represents Sophia, her departure has cut away from Shelley something vital and beautiful. By losing her and the music she performed for him, that is, he has lost a part of himself. Phallically and ontologically, he is now the "shrivelled, lifeless, vacant form." The flower shrivels, because it lacks water, and

Shelley's comment in stanza three that his "tears revive it not!" (*SPW* 9) confirms that the loss he suffers is irreversible. Shelley shrivels because he no longer has access to Sophia's breath. The arrangement implies that a return of Sophia's breath would revive him; however, her breath could never become more than a substitute for the thing he has lost: her/his voice.

The hard "k" sound in the verb "mocks" resonates phonically with the same sound contained in the words "va*c*ant" and "*c*old," creating an effect that something has been cut. It also generates telling ambiguity. As an emblem of the heart beating inside Shelley's "abandoned breast," the flower "mocks," or copies, the emotional lifelessness belied by the heart's "warmth." As a more accurate sign of Shelley's feelings, the flower "mocks," or derides, the heart for creating an impression of continued life and health in Sophia's absence. The figure seems to confess, then, that, even though Shelley continues to be physically sound, his heart suffers a "silent rest," no longer beating in response to Sophia's influence. To the extent that the "shrivelled" violet becomes an emblem of Shelley's castration, the fact that it now lies "mute" (*SPW* 11) figuratively ties the loss to Sophia's voice, an embodiment of the object voice, which has "flown." Despite his generous offer to transfer ownership of his stanzas to Sophia ("you are welcome to them"), Shelley's action represents an effort to recover her voice by containing it within his words.

Anxiety forms the signature note of the poem "To—('I fear thy kisses, gentle maiden'):"

> I fear thy kisses, gentle maiden,
> Thou needest not fear mine;
> My spirit is too deeply laden
> Ever to burthen thine.
>
> I fear thy mien, thy tones, thy motion,
> Thou needest not fear mine;
> Innocent is the heart's devotion
> With which I worship thine. (*SPW* 1–8)

Ostensibly, Shelley fears letting himself fall victim to Sophia's charms, which would draw him into an illicit relationship. At the same time, however, he fears burdening innocent Sophia with all the baggage that would come with having an affair with a married man. It is possible, however, that a more compelling motive fuels Shelley's confession: perhaps he fears what Zizek refers to as the loss of loss. A situation in which love is not returned or not consummated delivers the lover, in this case Shelley, to a state of *jouissance*.[21] If Shelley were to receive Sophia's "kisses," hear her "tones" and witness her "motion," he would enter into a condition of psychosomatic intimacy with her.

---

[21] Zizek 46–8.

However, experiencing these erotic expressions of Sophia's being would ironically remove him from *jouissance* in the end, because it would inevitably result in Sophia's "desublimation." It would be better for him to live, therefore, in a state of suspension, a state of loss in which desire remains unfulfilled. Fear, in this regard, qualifies as an advantage, for it provides the surplus pleasure necessary to inspire Shelley to write, insuring his authority. Without fear of her gifts, there would be no need for poetry. Receiving her music, in other words, would foreclose on his poem, effectively silencing him. This interpretation accounts for Shelley's acknowledgement that his heart will continue to "worship" Sophia's. Acceptance of an arrangement such as the one Shelley portrays in the poem aligns him with the castrato, who sings sublimely to heaven as a result of his mutilation rather than avenge himself on those who have made him what he is.[22] According to Zizek, "this is (the singing) *voice* at its most elementary: the embodiment of 'surplus enjoyment' in the precise sense of the paradoxical 'pleasure in pain.'"[23] It is important that Shelley, at least within the scope of this poem, allows fear to support his renunciation of Sophia, since giving in to temptation might give unbearable definition to the "mien," "tones" and "motion" he cherishes, persuading him not to subject them to utterance.[24]

Shelley also strives after renunciation in the poem "Good-Night," despite apparently expending all rhetorical effort at forestalling the termination of a social outing with Sophia. Shelley reasons that the night is not over until someone, ostensibly Sophia, utters the phrase "*good* night," and he insists that the night qualifies as "*good*" only so long as the couple remains together. Her closing wish prompts him to consider,

> Good-night? ah! no; the hour is ill
> Which severs those it should unite;
> Let us remain together still,
> Then it will be *good* night.
>
> How can I call the lone night good,
> Though thy sweet wishes wing its flight?
> Be it not said, thought, understood—
> Then it will be—*good* night.
>
> To hearts which near each other move
> From evening close to morning light,
> The night is good; because, my love,
> They never *say* good-night. (*SPW* 1–12)

---

[22] Zizek 47.

[23] Zizek, 47.

[24] See Zizek's application of the "Kierkegaardian triad" to Wagner in Slavoj Zizek, "There Is No Sexual Relationship," *Gaze and Voice as Love Objects*, ed. Renata Salecl and Slovoj Zizek (Durham and London: Duke UP, 1996) 208–49.

Prolonging the evening indefinitely preserves its ideal character. Terminating it returns the evening to the temporal and, by extension, reaffirms the mortality of Shelley and Sophia. Beyond this agenda, it also appears that Shelley wishes to prevent Sophia not only from uttering the phrase "*good* night" once again, but wants to prevent her from speaking at all. He seems to have in mind that postponing departure and refusing to allow "good night" to be "said, thought, understood" will clear the way for an alternative form of communication, in which two hearts "move" together apparently in harmony.

Suspending time and remaining with Sophia paradoxically bestows upon him the excessive pleasure of subjecting to inquiry the wish for a "*good* night." When he asks "How can I call the lone night good…?" he implies that his superior judgment should give him the final say. Consider, however, that Shelley employs the words "good" and "night" 12 times over the course of the poem. The repetition, an oral and written pulsation of desire, discloses Shelley's contradictory wish that Sophia would leave but also stay, and it also creates an acoustic mirroring effect that results in the mutual constitution, the confluence, of both partners. Her words constitute her but verify at the same time "her" inaccessibility. Transported into Shelley's poem, furthermore, her words now become his and constitute his subjectivity in the process. All considered, the rhetorical arrangement of the poem creates a deadlock that makes it impossible to distinguish authority and, perhaps, this is the situation Shelley desires most of all. Sophia's words are also his words; Sophia's voice becomes in the poem his voice. "Good-Night" asks its auditor to accept the following phantasmic proposal, which, given the requirements for subject formation, is an impossibility: lovers who never "*say*" the phrase "good night" mutually forestall the loss of one another "to morning light" and, theoretically, heal the wound of castration by circumventing the loss of the object voice.

Sophia's mouth serves as Shelley's object of desire in the poem "Love's Philosophy." Kissing it, the poem's conventional logic suggests, promises an intimacy consistent with "a law divine" (*SPW* 6) that apparently finds expression throughout the natural world. Shelley implies that love motivates all elements of creation to unite and concludes that humans should be responsive to the same motivation:

> The fountains mingle with the river
> And the rivers with the Ocean,
> The winds of Heaven mix for ever
> With a sweet emotion;
> Nothing in the world is single;
> All things by a law divine
> In one spirit meet and mingle.
> Why not I with thine?—
>
> See the mountains kiss high Heaven
> And the waves clasp one another;

> No sister –flower would be forgiven
> If it disdained its brother;
> And the sunlight clasps the earth
> And the moonbeams kiss the sea;
> What is all this sweet work worth
> If thou kiss not me? (*SPW* 1–16)

Shelley's illustrations form two categories, consisting of attraction among elements that share the same substance or properties, and elements that are fundamentally distinct. Water "mingles" in the form of "fountains," "rivers" and "Ocean;" "waves clasp one another" and "winds of Heaven mix," apparently in a spirit of "sweet emotion," though the locution also seems to say that winds blend themselves with "sweet emotion." A supplement to this "law divine" in which "all things ... / In one spirit meet and mingle" is the conjoining of elements different from one another. "Mountains kiss high Heaven," as "the sunlight clasps the earth," "as the moonbeams kiss the sea," and each flower devotes itself to a sibling.

Intended for Sophia, the poem raises several questions: to which category do she and Shelley belong? What is the nature of their relationship? Are they so alike in spiritual substance that they will "mingle" like water, or are they so different in social status, perhaps (Shelley a married man and Sophia an unmarried woman), that they can embrace only to the extent that "sunlight clasps the earth," but not as "waves clasp one another"? Shelley's proposal that "No sister-flower would be forgiven / If it disdained its brother" clouds further the arrangement he has in mind, because its reference to sibling affection conjures an image of innocence, while also striking a note of incestuous coupling. The "natural attractions" Shelley has in mind theoretically qualify as erotic behaviors that stand outside the realm of symbolic construction and gesture, therefore, in the direction of the "real." Social stature within this construct becomes under these terms an artificial encumbrance, an intrusion on his and Sophia's natural feelings for one another. The sibling-flower metaphor implicitly sexualizes their attraction, however, and commits them to the kinds of separation upon which the symbolic order relies, foreclosing on the possibility that they might ever "clasp" one another in the more "real" fashion of the evidently sexless "waves."

Serving as a metaphor in which Shelley's fantasy of integrating masculine word with feminine voice in the seamless way in which "all things ... / meet and mingle in one spirit," the poem counteracts that possibility, because Shelley expresses his desire in silent, figurative form. The failure of Shelley's phantasmic agenda surfaces in his desire to be kissed by Sophia. Her action would bring him into contact with the instrument of her voice, rather than the thing itself, though the request maintains marginal integrity in the sense that this expression of her affection for him would qualify as wordless and, consequently, "real." Shelley might have been trying to compensate phonologically for this deadlock. "Love's Philosophy" is rich in nasal syllables, but especially in nasal endings. Rhyme endings "Ocean / emotion," "divine / thine" and "Heaven / forgiven" combine with interior resonances present in words such as "fountains," "mountains," "winds" and "disdained," for example. When recited, nasal consonants fill the performer's nasal passages with sound and promote vibration. If Sophia were to read "Love's Philosophy" aloud, she might experience this effect; it would amount to a mingling of Shelley's words with her voice and her body, a situation which might be best captured by the metaphor "The winds of Heaven mix for ever / With a sweet emotion."

Except for the simile "A tone which is now forever fled," which Shelley cites in order to get a fix on "Time long past" (*SPW* 2–3), the poem "Time Long Past" explicitly involves neither music and voice, nor the desire for Sophia. In fact, its most jarring image, a comparison of the "regret, almost remorse" felt over lost time to "a child's beloved corse / A father watches" (*SPW* 13, 15–16) probably has more to do with the death of William Shelley than it does the imminent departure of Sophia.[25] With that said, the poem appears to devote itself to the more general phenomenon of temporal loss, a condition that marks Shelley's irreversible separation from a former state in which "There were sweet dreams in the night" (*SPW* 7). Within the schema of Shelley's phantasmic narrative, the poem describes the wound of castration by means of the compensations that issue from it, that is, by means of the subjectivity that results from the sense of irrecoverable loss and by means of figurative language, where similes stand in for a concept, the past, which resists recovery through definition.

Because Shelley apparently wrote the poem into a copy of Hunt's *Literary Pocket-Book* of 1819 and then gave it to Sophia, it would appear that she, at least at that moment, more than William represents the poem's focal point. No doubt it was with her that he experienced "A love so sweet it could not last" (*SPW* 5) and the now absent "tone" which brought him pleasure and "Beauty" (*SPW* 17). Clipped rhyme endings, formed by the letter *t*, dominate the poem, finishing 14 of its 18 lines, and underscore the theme of castration, that is, of something vital being removed over the course of time. Though Sophia's recitation of the poem would give voice to this unpleasant reality, repetition over time would, in terms of fantasy, overcome the loss by filling otherwise silent voids with sound. Sophia verifies and amplifies the absence Shelley experiences whenever she recites in succession "last," "past," "night," "past," "delight," "cast" (*SPW* 5–10) and so on. Paradoxically, however, the prospect that her voice will articulate that loss overturns the condition. Because they promise to activate Sophia's voice in the future, Shelley's words retain the potential to make him present, recovering the past in the process.

Shelley's desire for what musical women represented finds its most intense expression in the poems he wrote for Jane Williams.[26] As could Sophia, Jane could

---

[25] Reiman and O'Neill 279.

[26] Jerome McGann argues that the poems Shelley wrote in 1822 display a movement away from his early pursuit of the "Promethean norm of perfection" and toward "a more anthropocentric attitude toward life, love, and reality" (34). Shelley, McGann, contends,

sing and play a musical instrument, in her case a guitar, and the bond between her and Shelley might have intensified as a result of her ability to calm his nervous tremors by performing on him the art of mesmerism. Though Jane was an amateur at this ministry, it added another component of verbal and physical intimacy to her repertoire. Bieri estimates that "Jane's solace through hypnosis veiled [Shelley's] erotic enticement and her seductiveness. Perhaps the trance-inducing warmth of Jane's hand on his brow was the extent of their physical contact."[27] Bieri revises the assessment later in his discussion of Shelley's relationship with Jane when he observes that even though "it is uncertain what closeness Shelley and Jane had shared by the time he left Villa Magni, some physical intimacy possibly passed between them."[28] According to Susan Wolfson, by June of 1822 Shelley was in love with her.[29] The comforts Jane supplied were evidently timely, as a recent miscarriage that almost killed Mary put further strain on Shelley's marriage. Her presence in the cramped and damp beach house near San Terenzo increased that strain, however.

At first, Shelley judged Jane to be pretty but intellectually limited. That impression quickly changed, however, once he heard her sing and play guitar. In a letter to John Gisborne, Shelley confesses that witnessing Jane sing and play guitar had become a sublime pleasure. He could listen, he reports,

> The whole evening on our terrace to [Jane's] simple melodies with excessive delight. I have a boat here ... Williams is captain, and we drive along this delightful bay in the evening wind, under the summer moon, until earth appears another world. Jane brings her guitar, and if the past and the future could be obliterated, the present would content me so well that I could say with Faust to the passing moment "Remain, thou, thou are so beautiful." (*PBSL* 2, 434)

Experiences such as these inspired Shelley to respond to Jane by way of lyric missives, many of which he dispatched to her without Mary's knowledge, though he employed Edward, difficult as it is to believe, as courier. Reiman and O'Neill note that these poems "make their way" along "an emotional cliff-edge,"[30] and Keach reminds us that "they were not only written for Jane but were shown or

---

"had learned to accept and even enjoy the conditions of human existence," in which "the perception and the loss of beauty must live in hostile coexistence" (33–4). Though this reading might apply to Shelley's philosophical outlook, and though it is possible to argue that Shelley the love poet found joy in renunciation, the lyrics to Jane seem to lack the detachment McGann's perspective would assign them. See "The Secrets of an Elder Day: Shelley after *Hellas*," *Keats–Shelley Journal* 15 (1966): 25–41.

[27] Bieri 2: 311–12.
[28] Bieri 2: 319–20.
[29] Wolfson 207.
[30] Reiman and O'Neill xv.

given to her as half-furtive, half-open acts of personal communication."[31] Wolfson believes Shelley wrote the poems not only anticipating that Jane would recite them but that Edward might read them aloud, as well.[32] He might have reasoned that both occurrences would bring him closer to Jane, maybe even closer than Edward, his instrument, since the sounds of his words would enter Jane.

Including "Remembrance" and "The Indian Girl's Song," it appears Shelley wrote at least 11 poems for Jane Williams.[33] Most of them seem designed to cue a range of favorable responses from Jane, as Wolfson argues, but much about the poems seems intended either to replicate the aural moment of Shelley's enchantment (lyric features intoning the expressions of a hypnotic performer), or pay tribute (through a specular, and perhaps spectral, process of oral testimony) to the sonic aura of Jane's voice; in many cases the poems aim at both. These aspects of the poems Shelley wrote for Jane place Shelley in the equivocal position as composer (auditioning his lyric talents and his voice for Jane's reception) and as desirous and dependent listener (hoping to draw Jane's voice and consciousness inside a textual world he has constructed). In one way or another, almost all of the poems pay homage to Jane's capacity through musical and physical magnetism for shifting and orchestrating the ontological rhythms of Shelley's experience. Adopting the perspective that the poems serve as responses in kind raises the possibility that Shelley hopes to correspond with Jane on wavelengths that invoke or approach the "real."

The poems to Jane involve transmitting or calling forth somatic rhythm in the form of heart rate and respiration, and if each poem in the group qualifies as a performance in its own right, that performance, in the scope of Shelley's fantasy, is meant to be private. From this perspective, it would seem that Edward as carrier and co-performer facilitates the intimacy Shelley seeks, to the extent that he and the poem he brings collectively become Shelley's constitutive object. At least one portion of the "cliff-edge" Shelley walks involves his struggle, paradoxically, to indulge the desire to become one with Jane's voice, while at the same time preserving his authority. Escaping the pressures of the socio-symbolic structure by reaching after the "real" means losing one's power to make things meaningful. As is the case with all the personal lyrics Shelley wrote for musical women, the hypothetical prospect of linking word with voice and music here undergoes

---

[31] Keach 216.

[32] Wolfson 207.

[33] O'Neill believes "Remembrance" might have been written before Shelley met Jane and then reproduced for her. See "Poems Given to Jane Williams: Headnote," *The Manuscripts of Younger Romantics* 351–3. As for "The Indian Girl's Song," Chernaik, and Reiman and O'Neill posit that the poem was written for Jane to be sung to an Indian air; however, Bieri maintains that an early version of the poem might have been written with Sophia Stacey in mind. See Judith Chernaik, *The Lyrics of Shelley* (Cleveland and London: Case Western Reserve UP, 1972); "Poems Given to Sophia Stacey: Headnote," *The Manuscripts of the Younger Romantics* 277–9.

considerable strain in the face of actual circumstances and the conventional ways in which we negotiate with them.

The poem titled "The Magnetic Lady to Her Patient" recounts a hypnosis session during which the calming influences of Jane's attractive voice and touch temporarily relieve Shelley's suffering. The form of the poem, a transcript of what Jane said and of how Shelley responded, gives it a look of authenticity; however, the poem's status as a retrospective raises the possibility that imagination as much as reality have shaped it. Tim Fulford points out that even after Mesmer's practices had been rejected by the Academy of Sciences, mesmerism retained its allure as a psychosomatic treatment. Though many became increasingly convinced that no one could take electromagnetic control over someone else, people continued to believe that mesmerism could work by means of imagination, every individual's own healing agent, freeing that person from the limitations of status quo medical science.[34] This poem articulates Shelley's belief/desire that Jane does transfer the most essential parts of her being through her fingers and her voice, but it is also clear that, in liberating Shelley from his "'hour of woe'" (*SPW* 7), Jane also reanimates his imagination, giving him a reason to write. Jane restores her patient's poetic voice.

Jane's voice initiates and then sustains the hypnotic spell under which Shelley falls, but her influence also channels itself to Shelley by means of her enchanting touch:

> "Sleep, sleep on! forget thy pain;
> My hand is on thy brow,
> My spirit on they brain;
> My pity on thy heart poor friend;
> And from my fingers flow
> The powers of life, and like a sign,
> Seal thee from thine hour of woe ...." (*SPW* 1–7)

"Jane's" assertion that her own "powers of life" will "seal thee from thine hour of woe" enunciates her capacity to protect him from the pains of mortality, but "her" use of the verb "seal" in this statement of assurance connotes that her influence closes up a hole or a wound. Within the scope of Shelley's fantasy, the psychosomatic effect of her spell heals the wound of castration. Intimate contact with Jane restores him to the object voice, despite her (and his) conscious

---

[34] Tim Fulford, "Conducting the Vital Fluid," *Studies in Romanticism* 43 (2004): 57–78. Also see Nigel Leask, "Shelley's Magnetic Ladies," *Beyond Romanticism*, ed. Stephen Copley and John Whale (London and New York: Routledge 1992) 52–78. Leask observes that Shelley linked the healing powers of mesmerism to poetry, but remained mistrustful of the power exercised by the mesmerist over the subject, particularly when the subject was a female. In "The Magnetic Lady" Shelley inverts the dynamic, making himself the subject of Jane's power; the poem he writes, however, makes Jane his subject.

recognition that the most essential parts of her being "'may not blend / with thine'" (*SPW* 8–9) and her acknowledgement that "'I love thee not,'" and that "'I can never / Be thine'"(*SPW* 10, 26–7).

Stanza four of "The Magnetic Lady to Her Patient" recycles the image of a dying flower Shelley employs in the poem "On a Faded Violet" he wrote for Sophia Stacey. In this case, Shelley imagines himself as a "'withered flower'" rescued by Jane's moisture:

> "Like a cloud big with a May shower,
> My soul weeps healing rain
> On thee, thou withered flower!
> It breathes mute music on thy sleep;
> Its odour calms thy brain!
> Its light within thy gloomy breast
> Spreads like a second youth again.
> By mine thy being is to its deep
> Possessed." (*SPW* 28–36)

The passage reveals that Jane revives Shelley by reaching out with her soul. The tropes in her description of the soul's avenues of expression (its tears of "'healing rain,'" its breath carrying "'mute music'" and its "'odour'"), however, also identify through metonym Jane's soul with Jane's vocal expression. Both bathe Shelley in vital moisture. In the same way that a flower assimilates the water provided by a "'May shower,'" Shelley, the poem's phantasmic figures propose, assimilates the expressiveness of Jane's soul. It would appear that mesmerism permits communication not with a stand-in, paradoxically, but with the thing itself. That the soul identified with Jane's core being presents itself through instrumental means, however, compromises this prospect.

Shelley's troping of Jane's soul in action with "'a cloud big with a May shower'" characterizes their intimacy as incestuous. The simile suggests that when the water of Jane's soul breaks, Shelley experiences a rebirth, "'a second youth again.'" Figuratively, the arrangement indicates that Shelley and Jane are related biologically, that they are connected by blood, despite the separation represented by birth. Though now two separate parts, the other continues to constitute its biological partner, promising to make it whole, despite the frustrating reality that the two can never again be reintegrated. Support for the positive aspects of this fantasy occurs elsewhere in the text. When Jane assures Shelley that she places her "'pity'" on his "'heart'" and when she admits that "'my heart bleeds / For thine'" (*SPW* 17–18), she implies that she contacts Shelley on a level untouched by social and legal regulation, a level that approaches the "real." Even though she "can never / Be thine," because both are married and she apparently does not love him, her being "possesses" his nonetheless during those moments when he submits himself to her hypnotic spell.

Once Jane releases a now revived Shelley from her power, she asks him what would animate his spirits when he is "'suffering and awake'" (*SPW* 40), perhaps when she is unavailable. He replies,

> "What would cure, that would kill me,
> Jane:
> And as I must on earth abide
> Awhile, yet tempt me not to break
> My chain." (*SPW* 42–6)

The "chain" Shelley resists breaking refers primarily to his marriage, but the phonic compatibility of "chain" with "Jane" creates the possibility of another kind of coupling and asserts his desire for an alternative union, one that transcends conventional expression. To be chained to Jane's voice and body means never losing a vital part of himself. The economics of hypnotic enchantment complicate Shelley's fantasy aspirations, however, because within that economy he assumes the role of Jane's instrument responding to her touch, especially when he commemorates the event in lyric poetry, as though he were no different than her guitar. If the process goes no further than this point, Shelley succumbs to perversion, finding joy in his manipulation by the other. The situation is counterbalanced, however, by the consideration that, in recording the event in writing, Shelley composes and conducts Jane's performance perhaps as much as he composes his own spirits—practicing a form of self-hypnosis by creating poetry. Deadlock emerges either way, though, because in one case Shelley remains "'possessed'" by Jane's voice, and therefore sleepily silent; in the other case, he remains locked and mute within his own fantasy world of words.

Bieri comments that the poem "When the Lamp is Shattered" "is Shelley's most personal lament of emotional bereavement among his last lyrics, expressing an inability to respond or seek restored love."[35] Shelley originally composed the poem to be part of a drama he never finished,[36] but he eventually presented it to Jane.[37] If the poem qualifies as a stock lament over love's inconstancy, its images narrow Shelley's concern to the sort of loss that fuels desire, earmarking the poem as a phantasmic construct. Perhaps Shelley gave the poem to Jane because he identified her as the type of positive object who promised to fulfill his desire. The two stanzas that conclude this four-stanza lyric consist of a conceit figuring two hearts in love as birds sharing a nest, which one bird abandons, leaving behind its frailer mate. The abandoning heart belongs to Jane and the jilted heart belongs to Shelley, forced to suffer its fate alone. The conceit generates a complex tenor indicative of emptiness and vacancy. The loss of Jane's heart, an organ fundamentally tied not just to love and fidelity but to rhythm, constitutes a reopening of the wound caused

---

[35] Bieri 2: 291.
[36] Bieri 2: 291.
[37] Keach 209; Reiman and O'Neill 352.

by castration. The loss of Jane amounts to the loss of vital music and suffering amounts to existing in a state of arrhythmia, a condition identified metaphorically when Shelley says Love's "passions will rock thee / As the storms rock the ravens on high" (*SPW* 25–6).

The nature of the heart's expression serves as the axis metaphor of stanza two:

> As music and splendour
> Survive not the lamp and the lute;
> The heart's echoes render
> No song when the spirit is mute:—
> No song but sad dirges,
> Like the wind through a ruined cell,
> Or the mournful surges
> That ring the dead seaman's knell. (*SPW* 9–16)

Imagery in this passage seems to suggest that the heart functions as the spirit's agent, but because the heart transmits the spirit by means of "echoes," its relationship with spirit would have to be indirect. As acoustic mirror, in other words, the heart constitutes the lover's spirit, the core of his or her being, but in the process establishes the spirit's emptiness. The heart is once removed from the spirit's original expression, which apparently cannot be heard, and removed once again from the spirit itself. The relationship created by nesting hearts Shelley describes in stanzas three and four, therefore, falls far short of the "real" correspondence—a bare biological exchange—he idealizes. Supplementary images of air and fluid ("wind through a ruined cell, / Or the mournful surges") amplify this note of absence to the extent that, as utterances, they serve as carriers of expression and fail to manifest the substance of expression. The heart, it would seem, speaks absence, not presence.

Perhaps from Shelley's perspective this is why mortal love can never extricate itself from loss. The tropes Shelley has chosen to communicate the inevitable impact of loss and abandonment in this poem compromise the heterosexual model of integration that forms the mainstay of Shelley's fantasy. This might explain why, in the first stanza of the poem, Shelley states that nothing survives the instrument or the agent. So often in his poetry Shelley espouses the value of what remains after an event or an action, indicating that this condition represents the essence of human experience, that is, to be always lacking and regretting. He writes,

> When the lute is broken,
> Sweet tones are remembered not;
> When the lips have spoken,
> Loved accents are soon forgot. (*SPW* 5–8)

Though he might have presented Jane with this poem because the sentiment recorded here captures how empty he feels whenever she leaves, the passage also articulates a prospect he sought consistently to overcome: the idea that presence evades all expression, even when it is vocal or musical. The elegiac tone informing this and the other poems Shelley wrote for Jane emerges, perhaps, from this perception most of all.

Renunciation and loss characterize what might be the most evasive and challenging poem Shelley wrote for Jane. In their note to "The Serpent is Shut Out from Paradise," Reiman and Fraistat point out that Shelley enclosed its stanzas in a note he gave to Edward Williams, with the instruction that he "show them to no one else except Jane Williams, and preferably not even to her" (*SPP* 475, note 1). A note in Edward's journal suggests that he did allow Jane to read the poem, and Reiman and Fraistat remark that, despite appearances, Shelley composed "The Serpent is Shut Out from Paradise" "primarily with Jane in mind" (*SPW* 475, note 1). Keach explains that "the poem dramatizes its own uncertainty in ways that complicate rather than clarify what it asks of readers—of Jane and Edward Williams, but also of us," and adds that "the poem's words leave the reader with ... a sense of unrelieved, even unrelievable, frustration."[38] O'Neill says the poem "both withholds and discloses a mesh of difficult emotions [that have] to do with PBS's feelings about his wife and about Jane (and Edward) Williams. In the act of communicating this self-division, however, PBS displays control and perceptiveness."[39] Wolfson concludes that Shelley counted on Edward reading the poem to his wife, in which case Shelley would be able to use "Edward's voice as his own (hardly idle) mask for communicating to Jane, making Edward accommodate him and making both aware, in amusement or unease, of his superimposition."[40]

Rhetorically, Shelley struggles to communicate what he dares not say openly to his friend's wife. Innuendo and ambiguous pronoun references surface throughout the text. Viewed through the lens of psychoanalysis, the frustration Shelley felt and the restraint he found himself forced to exercise, paradoxically, power his expression. As in the case of the castrato, wound and loss enable him to sing, and song becomes the avenue to *jouissance*. Shelley alludes to this paradox in the poem's final stanza:

> I asked her yesterday if she believed
> That I had resolution. One who *had*
> Would ne'er have thus relieved
> His heart with words, but what his judgment bade
> Would do, and leave the scorner unrelieved.—
> These verses were too sad
> To send to you, but that I know,
> Happy yourself, you feel another's woe. (*SPP* 49–56)

---

[38] Keach, *Shelley's Style* 218–19.
[39] Reiman and O'Neill 352.
[40] Wolfson 209.

Ambiguity complicates the first line of the passage. "Her" most likely refers to Mary Shelley, but the fact that the poem was given to Edward adds the possibility that "her" might also be Jane. Shelley asserts that the resolute individual, in his case the resolute author, to which he makes earlier reference in stanza four, would remain silent, showing no sign of weakness. The author who has lost something he desires, however, endeavors to fill the void, to relieve his wounded heart, "with words." The poet evidently uses words to compensate himself for loss. In this case, the loss of Jane represents the loss of something essential, something life-threatening. It is precisely this loss of Jane's loving touch and her music—this loss of a loss—that makes him the poet he is.

Loss also becomes a strength in the sense that, by renouncing Jane, Shelley forecloses, at least within the space of this poem, on the risk of uncovering the horror of the "real" Jane—perhaps the Jane who shares Edward's bed—beneath the surface ideal about which he fantasizes. Sounding very much like Petrarch in the sonnets to Laura, Shelley confesses that he is unable to relinquish the comfort that accompanies the pain of seeing Jane (and Edward):

> Therefore, if now I see you seldomer,
> Dear friends, dear *friend*, know that I only fly
> Your looks, because they stir
> Griefs that should sleep, and hopes that cannot die.
> The very comfort which they minister
> I scarce can bear; yet I,
> (So deeply is the arrow gone)
> Should quickly perish if it were withdrawn. (*SPP* 17–24)

Ambiguity characterizes the pronoun "they" appearing in line 21. It most obviously refers back to the comforting "looks" his "dear *friend*" Jane directs toward him; however, reference for the pronoun "they" might also include the "Griefs that should sleep, and hopes that cannot die," which fuel his writing and bring him, therefore, the comfort of words. Renouncing Jane by flying from her "looks" intensifies the "griefs" and "hopes" that beset him, and these, in turn, become the inspiration for writing. Ironically, if any of Jane's gifts were to be withdrawn—"looks," "griefs" or "hopes"—Shelley the poet would perish, because being with Jane forecloses on the need for poetry.

As it does in "When the Lamp is Shattered," Shelley's use of metaphors involving nesting birds reveals the key component of his fantasy agenda, that is, overcoming the condition of lacking. Stanza one reads,

> The widowed dove must cease to haunt a bower
> Like that from which its mate with feigned sighs
> Fled in the April hour.— (*SPP* 4–6)

Stanza six amplifies this image:

> The crane o'er the seas and forests seeks her home.
> No bird so wild, but has its quiet nest
> When it no more would roam. (*SPP* 41–3)

An abandoned or empty nest becomes an image of both loss and absence. However, whereas all birds find nests waiting to fulfill their needs when they are done roaming (done, that is, desiring), the nest to which Shelley returns is a "cold," as in emotionally empty and unsupportive, "home" (*SPP* 25), no doubt a reference to his and Mary's mutual estrangement. Shelley apparently sees himself as the "widowed dove" jilted by a disingenuous lover. Whether Jane or Mary perform the role of the dove's mate, the tenor of the metaphor is that something vital has been stripped from Shelley, rendering him incomplete.

The doubleness and doublespeak Keach, O'Neill and Wolfson see in this poem stem from the fact that Shelley is not at liberty to express himself as candidly as he would like. Nonetheless, though a prisoner of sign and symbol, Shelley capitalizes on the capacity of language to create latitude and slippage when it comes to meaning. When, in stanza two, he says "But not to speak of love, Pity alone / Can break a spirit already more than bent" (*SPP* 12–13), it is difficult to determine whether he means that pity ranks second to love in its capacity to break the lover's spirit, or if he means, in code, that he cannot or will not speak his love for Jane, restricting his observations to the effects of Pity. In stanza five he confesses a reluctance to render the meaning of the "'she loves me, loves me, not'" game he played with flowers, writing parenthetically "(but I dread / To speak what you may know too well)," and then adding, "Still there was truth in the sad oracle" (*SPP* 35, 38–40). The word "still" remains charged, since whatever Jane knows "too well," the "oracle" delivered an equivocal message. Perhaps Jane is ambivalent, treating Shelley's nervousness with mesmerism, singing to him when they are sailing alone, pitying him and even loving him in a way, while still remaining faithful to Edward. She loves him and loves him not.

Shelley alludes to Jane's destabilizing influence on not just his emotions and spirit but on his stature as a poet, and on his writing, therefore. In stanza four he proclaims,

> When I return to my cold home, you ask
> Why I am not as I have lately been?
> *You* spoil me for the task
> Of acting a forced part in life's dull scene,
> Of wearing on my brow the idle mask
> Of author, great or mean,
> In the world's carnival. I sought
> Peace thus, and but in you I found it not. (*SPP* 25–32)

Shelley seems to be saying that his love for Jane has cursed him with seriousness and sincerity, rendering him unable to masquerade in that play in which authors adopt a narrative "mask" and write about fictional characters and events. If we can trust Shelley's assessment, however, it would mean that under Jane's influence he speaks nothing but the truth. The character of the very poem in which he makes this confession indicates the faultiness of Shelley's assessment, though. "The Serpent is Shut Out from Paradise" constitutes a mask behind which Shelley hides.

According to Reiman and Fraistat, the poem's title puns on Shelley's name in Italian, "bischelli" (which means "a small snake") for Bysshe Shelley. Shelley is the "serpent" shut out from experiencing paradise with Jane, and the poem means to convey Shelley's frustration without coming right out and saying it. In fact, in serving as Shelley's mask, this poem acts as a "medicine" (*SPP* 16) easing the pain Shelley feels from the injury Jane has caused him. In the opening stanza he represents himself as a "wounded deer" suffering from a sick heart, an animal which "must seldom seek again / Near happy friends a mitigated pain" (*SPP* 2, 7–8). Again, Shelley heals his wound with words, though doing so means, perhaps, never corresponding with Jane by means of pure expression outside the encumbrances laid on him by etiquette, law and, ironically, by poetry. Communicating with her by way of the poetic word only confirms their separation; each poem he writes for her renews the wound of castration, and it cuts him a little deeper.

This consideration adds significance to Shelley's claim that his heart has been compromised, the "arrow" (*SPP* 23) of comfort shot by Jane's "looks" penetrating too deep to be extracted. In stanza six he observes,

> The sleepless billows on the Ocean's breast
> Break like a bursting heart, and die in foam
> And thus, at length, find rest.
> Doubtless there is a place of peace
> Where *my* weak heart and all its throbs will cease. (*SPP* 44–8)

The passage seems to say that Shelley's heart will eventually find "peace" in death; however, combined with the reference in the preceding lines to the roaming bird that eventually finds its "quiet nest," the entire stanza might also suggest that Shelley's nest is Jane. He "hopes," perhaps, that his "bursting heart" will release itself on Jane's breast in the fashion of "sleepless billows" breaking on the "Ocean's breast." There he might find the "peace," but also the "piece" of himself, he has lost. If he were to merge his heart with Jane's breast, the poet he is would "cease" to exist, since there would no longer be a need to compose lyrics for Jane.

Reiman and Fraistat comment that Shelley probably composed "Lines written in the Bay of Lerici" "within three weeks of his death" (*SPP* 480, note 1). The poem records the toll Jane's absence takes on Shelley's "faint heart" (*SPP* 35). It opens by first associating Jane with the moon, which he calls "Bright wanderer, fair coquette of Heaven" (*SPP* 1), perhaps because Jane delivers light without physical warmth and because she seems so close but cannot be touched. Shelley counters this implication later in the text, however, when he speaks of being haunted by the memory of her magnetic touch. This heavenly body, apparently, entered Shelley's emotional orbit and, no doubt disruptively, pulled him toward itself. As is the case so often in poems Shelley wrote for or about Jane, "Lines written in the Bay of Lerici" generates at least one evasive note. Shelley advises the moon not to

> Envy ... this dim world, for never
> But once, within its shadow grew
> One fair as [thou], but far more true. (*SPP* 4–6)

The poem's reader is left to resolve a contradiction: how could Jane be "far more true" than the phase prone moon, when the moon appears every evening, while Jane, within the context of the poem, abandons Shelley to a state dominated by silence and memory.

Shelley utters twice the phrase "She left me" (*SPP* 7, 15), emphasizing his perception that Jane is gone for good, and that he has no choice but to deal with the impact. Perhaps she "left," because she sought to stay true to Edward. Figuratively, perhaps once her influence achieved its zenith, it never waxed and waned, but in the fashion of moonlight, nonetheless, illuminated for Shelley alternative life possibilities, what, in other words, are commonly called fantasies. In this regard, maybe Shelley judged his fantasy life with Jane to be "far more true" than his actual life with Mary. The images he uses to describe the aftermath of Jane's departure are redolent with the idea of figurative castration. Consequently, they reveal seams, or splicings, in the fabric of his fantasy, so that the "horror of the real" emerges amidst a construct designed to pay tribute to a recent past in which he and Jane exchanged "real" transmissions to escape the framework of the "big Other." Shelley recalls,

> She left me and I staid alone
> Thinking over every tone
> Which though now silent to the ear
> The enchanted heart could hear
> Like notes which die when born, but still
> Haunt the echoes of the hill:
> And feeling ever—O too much—
> The soft vibrations of her touch
> As if her gentle hand even now
> Lightly trembled on my brow;
> And thus although she absent were
> Memory gave me all of her
> That even fancy dares to claim.— (*SPP* 15–27)

The absence of Jane's healing "tone" condemns Shelley to a visual atmosphere of silence, an emotional space in which he confesses, "I dare not speak / My thoughts" but instead quietly watches "vessels glide / Along the ocean bright and wide" (*SPP* 35–8). As a representation of the object voice, Jane becomes the reason for his speechlessness, and her leaving delivers him to the silent, visual world of written poetry. His heart, he claims, stores the memory of that "tone." The implication that it serves him better than his "ear" suggests that his method of communication with Jane transpired over unconventional channels. However, the trope he chooses to define the heart's capacity for receiving and then recording Jane's expression conveys the possibility that he currently is not once but twice removed from Jane's presence.

As "notes which die when born, but still / Haunt the echoes of the hill," Jane's "tone" has become an empty echo, a vacancy that creates the illusion of presence. Even when Shelley stood in close proximity to that "tone," however, perhaps when Jane practiced mesmerism to calm his nerves, that utterance was theoretically never anything more than the object voice, an acoustic formation of Jane, as opposed to Jane "herself." Shelley's fantasy offsets this unsettling possibility by shifting the point of contact from Jane's voice to "the soft vibrations of her touch." His impression that Jane's "gentle hand even now / Lightly trembled on my brow" casts him in the role of Jane's instrument, implying that the two performed in perfect harmony and that her efforts composed him. The arrangement, in turn, would constitute a perfect constellation of music and language, with Jane and Shelley sharing authorship.

The final 23 lines of "Lines written in the Bay of Lerici" puncture the vision of collaboration Shelley's memory creates, though. The reality of Jane's departure has left him able to write but not speak, and his now "faint heart" appears to be functioning on life support. Perhaps it has become as empty as the echoed "notes" of Jane's influence it preserves. Notwithstanding, fantasy maintains its hold on Shelley's consciousness by transforming his surroundings into a realm of enchantment permeated by Jane's presence and her influence. He imagines that the ships he sees in the bay

> ... sailed for drink to medicine
> Such sweet and bitter pain as mine.
> And the wind that winged their flight
> From the land came fresh and light,
> And the scent of sleeping flowers
> And the coolness of the hours
> Of dew and the sweet warmth of day
> Was scattered o'er the twinkling bay. (*SPP* 43–50)

Air and fluid, in the form of "wind," "dew" and "twinkling bay," stand in for Jane's voice. These elements minister to Shelley's failing spirits, yet at the same time they poignantly remind him of what he has lost. "Wind," "dew" and "the scent of sleeping flowers" enter his nostrils, but leave behind only vestiges of themselves, particles reminiscent of the original. This sentiment finds amplified expression in the poem's final image, a fish lured to a fisherman's lamp and then speared, which loops back to the poem's opening comparison of Jane with the moon. Shelley and the fish have found themselves lured toward emptiness, toward a substitute for the thing itself.

Shelley alters the terms of his relationship with Jane in the poem "One Word Is Too Often Profaned" by implying that Jane has renounced or continues to renounce him, a turn of events that would suit his phantasmic agenda by minimizing the likelihood that some "real" aspect of his constitution would be exposed and then rejected by Jane. Such exposure would vanquish his hope of becoming the object of Jane's desire, supplanting Edward in the process, and it would force him to acknowledge that no secret treasure lies within him. The poem's second stanza exposes the economy of their relationship by means of metaphors that portray Jane as an unattainable commodity that elicits desire and Shelley as the desiring subject that futilely pursues an unreachable goal. On the surface, the arrangement appears to idealize Jane, suggesting that Shelley has chosen the tack of renouncing her to avoid the horror of the "real:"

> The desire of the moth for the star,
> Of the night for the morrow,
> The devotion to something afar
> From the sphere of our sorrow. (*SPP* 13–16)

By identifying Jane as a "star," as "the morrow" (which always remains locked away in the future) and "something afar" occupying a "sphere" separate from ours, Shelley insures that Jane maintains her status as object that focuses the aim of desire, but offers no capacity to satisfy it.

The second stanza opens, however, by suggesting that Jane refuses, or is perhaps at least reluctant, to let Shelley get too close to her. He asks,

> But wilt thou accept not
> The worship the heart lifts above
> And the Heavens reject not? (*SPP* 10–12)

Heaven might not reject the earnest prayers of the faithful, but the fact that Jane's receptiveness to Shelley's desire remains in question preserves the possibility that she might reject him, renouncing the message he sends from his heart. Within the lexicon of Shelley's fantasy agenda, an offering from the heart qualifies as an essential, secret transmission out of order with the symbolic. Shelley's tropes suggest that Jane might "reject" just such a transmission, putting her in a category of one, separate from all those things and places that seem to welcome the desire they set in motion.

Nasal syllables, which dominate the poem's title and arise prominently throughout the poem's opening stanza, seem designated to prevent the rejection of Shelley's advances. Consider the first four lines of the text:

> One word is too often profaned
> For me to profane it.
> One feeling too falsely disdained
> For thee to disdain it. (*SPP* 1–4)

If the poem were to be read aloud by Jane, the nasal sounds of Shelley's words—"profane" (repeated in the first two lines), "often," "me," "one" and "disdain"—might fill Jane's head, evoking far more than what they denote as words: his desire to fuse with Jane; his feeling of lacking something essential. At the same time, though, Jane would be filled by nothing more than the sound of her own voice, an echo of Shelley's, an emptiness confirming his "decenteredness." In this regard, she might recognize what Shelley does not want her to perceive: the emptiness within himself he wishes, paradoxically, to deny—that kernel of the "real" of his being, that "tic,"[41] which would "desublimate" him.

The arrangement Shelley conceives in this poem, then, ends up being a trap. If Jane renounces him, there is a good chance he might remain a distant ideal in her imagination, representing a fantasy partner who worships her from afar. Correspondence with her would go the way of prayers sent to "the Heavens:" sometimes they are heard and granted; sometimes they are not. The alternative, though, might be even worse. If Jane were to reconsider Shelley's erotic overtures, something the poem seems designed to promote, she would likely find herself face to face with a negative value, "the intensity of the real of *jouissance*," that lurks "'beyond the wall of language.'"[42] One aspect of the image with which Shelley concludes "One Word Is Too Often Profaned" (that is, "The devotion to something afar / From the sphere of our sorrow") might serve to defuse this outcome. Earlier in the lyric, Shelley refers directly to himself as "me" and "I" and apparently to Jane as "thee" and "thou." The pronouns confirm that a gap separates them, a gap which the image cluster involving the moth and star from stanza two figures as unbridgeable. When, however, Shelley refers to the "sphere of our sorrow," he relocates Jane from her sublime perch to the mundane turf he currently occupies. The linguistic gap between them closes, but one unfortunate consequence is that Jane in the process suffers "desublimation." The poem ends in deadlock.

Early in 1822 Shelley walked with Mary and Jane in the Cascine Forest near Pisa. He commemorates the occasion in two poems titled "To Jane. The Invitation" and "To Jane. The Recollection." As the titles suggest, Jane, not Mary, occupied the center of Shelley's attention, and the awkward composition of the walking party might explain why allusions to silence and images of visual beauty rather than aural harmony dominate both lyrics. However, the fact that he wrote and then gave the poems to Jane without Mary's knowledge should have mitigated self-restraint, providing the opportunity for him to express himself freely. Evidently this was not the case. In both poems he employs stock conventions—referring to Jane

---

[41] Zizek, *Plague* 49, 67–9.
[42] Zizek, *Plague* 49.

as "prophetess of May" (*SPP* "The Invitation" 17)—and resorts to ambiguity—referring vaguely to "*one* fair form that filled with love / The lifeless atmosphere" (*SPP* "The Recollection" 51)—most likely in order to channel away spousal suspicion. An additional consideration is that Shelley might have been unsure of Jane's feelings, as many other poems he wrote for her indicate, and might have found it necessary to guard against making himself vulnerable to rejection.

It would seem that another kind of pressure compounds the social pressure evident everywhere in these lyrics, though. Shelley's trope selection suggests that issues involving subject formation and vocal presence inflect all aspects of the correspondence he fabricates—anticipated, recalled or inscribed. These issues spawn, moreover, correlative signs of instability that elucidate the contradictory nature of all fantasy, that which qualifies it as a necessary plague.

The opening of "To Jane. The Invitation" pays tribute to Jane's capacity for enchantment, equating her influence to a visitation from "the brightest hour of unborn spring" (*SPP* 7) that temporarily reanimates all that winter has frozen. Shelley figures himself in the poem as "the rough year just awake," as "the forehead of the earth," as the "silent sea," as "the frozen streams" and "mountains," and as "the barren way" (*SPP* 5–18). Jane's spirit of warmth touches these elements primarily by means of oral contact and oral expression:

> It kissed the forehead of the earth
> And smiled upon the silent sea,
> And bade the frozen streams be free
> And waked to music all their fountains,
> And breathed upon the frozen mountains .... (*SPP* 12–16)

Jane makes Shelley's "wintry world appear / Like one on whom thou smilest dear" (*SPP* 19–20). The spirit of Shelley's testimony is that Jane's presence delivers the world and those sensitive enough to appreciate her to life and expression. The problem is that Shelley relegates Jane's vocality, the music she initiates, to the level of metonym.

Kisses and smiles stand in for orality, which in turn gestures toward vocal expression turned toward the outside world. Jane's breath evidently thaws "frozen mountains" and turns "frozen streams" into musical "fountains," but each of these figures isolates Jane's effect in an action or an object, something separate from "her" and something suggestive of her voice. Jane becomes present to Shelley through oral expression, but that oral expression, while constituting Jane, fails to become manifest as the thing itself, the *agalma* at the center of it all. Shelley's lyric portrait of Jane's influence mirrors this condition, because beneath the acoustic surface of bouncing couplets lies the silent word, that which constitutes Shelley the poet by standing in as his substitute. If Shelley is a "frozen stream" Jane has set free, the metaphor conveys absence: fluid expression represents a part of the object voice. Fountains and streams babble while words lie silent on the page. What should qualify as the confluence of two formerly separate elements, two separate beings, Shelley and Jane, emerges as a mutual confluence of object-others which makes the two partners what they are, but fails to integrate voice and word.

Shelley fantasizes that he and Jane will reject the world of "men and towns" and escape to

> To the wild wood and the downs,
> To the silent wilderness
> Where the soul need not repress
> Its music lest it should not find
> An echo in another's mind
> While the touch of Nature's art
> Harmonizes heart to heart. (*SPP* 21–8)

The "wild woods" represents a realm of *jouissance* that stands opposed to the world of "men and towns," to the written note Shelley leaves on his door to announce, ironically, his absence, and to the "unpaid bill" (*SPP* 35) that never goes away. This is the symbolic realm where subjectivity is established and where desire, insatiable as Shelley's creditors, dominates. "Nature's art" provides an alternative—a poetry of presence and direct contact in which souls are at liberty to express their music to one another without restraint. The construct slips when it asserts in the negative that the soul can be assured of finding "an echo in another's mind," though. Shelley and Jane will function as mutually acoustic mirrors to one another, but that which registers in each soul will be an "echo" of presence, not the core, the secret treasure, itself. Echo confirms for each partner that the other is "there," but that the "substance" of that other remains absent.

The final passage of "The Invitation," beginning with Shelley's address to Jane as "Radiant Sister of the day" (*SPP* 47), implicitly equates Jane with the sun, connoting that she is the source of life and warmth, a presence that can be found everywhere on this special day. Jane's influence contributes to the appearance of "pools" created by "winter-rains" that lie beneath the "wild woods and the plains" and "Image all their roof of leaves" (*SPP* 49–51). The conceit within which the pool-metaphor occurs challenges the possibility of presence. Within each pool,

> ... the pine its garland weaves
> Of sapless green and ivy dun
> Round stems that never kiss the Sun—. (*SPP* 52–4)

The surface of each pool bears the sunlit image of the world around it and in this sense becomes a specular iteration of sunny Jane. If one were to conflate Shelley with the pool figure, basking as he is in Jane's influence, the result would be that he becomes the bearer of Jane's image but not her presence. At the same time, however, Jane's influence establishes each "pool" in its subjectivity, though that subjectivity remains confined to the surface, covering the emptiness beneath it. The reference to "stems ... never" kissing "the Sun" suggests that the image in each pool is neither "the thing itself" (Shelley), nor the celestial other that defines it (Jane as the "Sun"), yet without the "Sun" each pool loses its image and becomes what it is, a dark vacancy. Shelley implies that without Jane he is nothing. What occurs by way of this phenomenon serves as the visual correlative of the soul's "echo" Shelley mentions earlier in the poem. The conceit counterpoints the passage involving the prospect of a direct correspondence of souls by defining the relationship between Shelley and Jane as silent and as empty as an image appearing in a pool.

Images of infancy and rebirth occur throughout "The Invitation." For example, Shelley writes that Jane's influence comes to "the rough year just awake / In its cradle on the brake" (*SPP* 5–6), and Jane, the "brightest hour of unborn spring," is to "hoar February born" (*SPP* 10). As the radiant sun, she shines on young flowers that "yet join not scent to hue," but nevertheless "Crown the pale year weak and new" (*SPP* 60–1). The world Shelley imagines entering with Jane is a world of immanent fullness without the threat of loss. It is a world in which "all things seem only one / In the universal Sun" (*SPP* 68–9). The poem's final image, ocean's "multitudinous / Billows murmur at our feet" (*SPP* 65–6), substantiates Shelley's pronouncement, because it raises the possibility that his natural union with Jane exists outside the matrix of the symbolic and will consist of a glossolalic "murmur," an alternative to language that nevertheless signals their intimacy. The assertion prompts its reader to wonder why Shelley found it necessary to validate the experience in poetry. One answer might be that poetry preserves his authority while it reduces Jane to the level of instrument. Another might involve the possibility that without poetry no desire remains and without desire there is no subject Shelley and, therefore, no need for Jane.

"To Jane. The Recollection" records what happens when anticipation meets reality. The poem insists that Shelley's excursion to the Cascine Forest with Jane fulfilled his fantasy agenda. Shelley's record of the encounter, however, bears the marks of compromise. To begin with, "The Invitation" foresees a situation in which "the soul need not repress / Its music lest it should not find / An echo in another's mind," but "The Recollection" reveals that reality (in the form of Mary's unwelcome accompaniment) encumbers the musical communion of souls Shelley forecasts. If "Nature's art / harmonizes heart to heart," it accomplishes that goal with extraordinary subtlety, promoting Jane's authorship of a "magic circle" that surrounds Shelley in "a thrilling silent life" (*SPP* 44, 46). Shelley intuits that Jane's spirit blankets all creation, and the effect generates a "breath of peace" and "calm" that defuse the "inviolable quietness" (*SPP* 37–40), ostensibly a function of Mary's presence, that otherwise would have stifled communication between Shelley and Jane.

The correspondence Jane's influence makes possible correlates with the mood of peace and tranquility she initiates. In stanza one, Shelley recalls, for example, that

> The lightest wind was in its nest,
> The Tempest in its home;
> The whispering waves were half asleep,
> The clouds were gone to play,
> And on the bosom of the deep
> The smile of Heaven lay. (*SPP* 11–16)

The absence of wind means calm, but in this context the normally charged image of the "nest" suggests security and perhaps fulfillment, rather than abandonment and lacking. Sleeping "waves," playing "clouds" and smiling "Heaven" suggest that Shelley's world is relaxed and not plagued by atmospheric stress. Jane creates for him a world of enchanted harmony; he reads the signs of her influence everywhere he looks. Though Shelley's textual reproduction highlights the effects of Jane's presence, the fact that he must rely on the indirectness of signs establishes, paradoxically, Jane's frustrating inaccessibility.

Almost everywhere in this poem Shelley cloaks candid expression in metaphor. The "pools" from "The Invitation" reappear in stanza four, and in stanza two the pines, under which the party "paused," quickly become a trope for Shelley's life and the wonders of Jane's healing expression. The pines, he recalls, had been

> Tortured by storms to shapes as rude
> As serpents interlaced,
> And soothed by every azure breath
> That under Heaven is blown
> To harmonies and hues beneath,
> As tender as its own;
> Now all the tree-tops lay asleep
> Like green waves on the sea,
> As still as in the silent deep
> The Ocean woods may be. (*SPP* 23–32)

Jane appears in the form of Heavenly breath that breeds calm in the atmosphere and eliminates turmoil from seas of "green waves" and treetops. Heaven's "azure breath" produces calm and vibrant "harmonies" in the same fashion that Jane's voice and Jane's touch settle Shelley's nerves and bring about restorative sleep. Once again, Shelley's association of Jane with air and fluid, here taking the form of breath and sea water, suggests not Jane's direct presence, but Jane's expression of "herself" by way of substitutes for the object voice, a necessity given Mary's censorship of expression on this occasion, but unavoidable nonetheless given the terms of subject formation and fantasy.

The "magic circle" Shelley says Jane "traced" around him, and of which she occupied the "centre" (*SPP* 44, 49), becomes a kind of bubble that contains their two souls within a separate world—evidently a world protected from the onslaughts by the symbolic and the "big Other" of law and custom. The verb "traced" echoes

Shelley's command in the poem's introductory stanza that "Memory" get busy and "trace / The epitaph of glory fled" (*SPP* 5–6). In the context of the introduction, "trace" means "write." The equation doesn't appear to be applicable to stanza three, though, since the "magic circle" Jane traces around Shelley evidently does not consist of words. Nonetheless, what emerges from the comparison is the idea that Jane composes Shelley through some non-linguistic form of communication. Shelley's recollection of having "felt" that "*one* fair form that filled with love / The lifeless atmosphere" (*SPP* 51–2) establishes that the two corresponded with one another somatically, perhaps upon a wavelength approaching the "real." A potential fracture emerges in this construct, however, as a result of Shelley's identification of Jane, ostensibly, as a "fair form." Everything else in the poem suggests that Jane is formless, at best taking shape as "azure breath," or as "a spirit interfused around." Despite the "breath of peace" he draws from her, he evidently remains unsatisfied, desiring a more concrete expression of Jane's influence and some demonstrative contact with her presence. Those elements of her being are necessarily inaccessible. Jane can be no more to him than an abstraction, a "form," or worse, the tracing of a form.

Shelley's narrative suggests that he might have approached a point of traversing his fantasy during the composition of the poem, because the fourth stanza opens with the observation, "We paused beside the pools that *lie* / under the forest bough" (my italics; *SPP* 53–4). Nevertheless, his reproduction of the pool-conceit from "The Invitation" indicates a desire to stave off the "horror of the real." The conceit echoes the arrangement of prototype and antitype Shelley conceives in the essay "On Love," and though it would appear that he again plays the part of the pool and Jane the "world above" reflected on its surface, the roles become interchangeable:

> Each seemed as 'twere, a little sky
> Gulfed in a world below;
> A firmament of purple light
> Which in the dark earth lay
> More boundless than the depth of night
> And purer than the day,
> In which the lovely forests grew
> As in the upper air,
> More perfect, both in shape and hue,
> Than any spreading there ...
> Sweet views which in our world above
> Can never well be seen,
> Were imaged in the water's love
> Of that fair forest green;
> And all was interfused beneath
> With an Elysian glow,
> An atmosphere without a breath,
> A softer day below—. (*SPP* 55–64, 69–76)

Because Shelley and Jane exist in a perfect economy of mutual reflection, each partner playing the role of pool to his or her counterpart's "world above," subjectivity and objectivity appear to be no longer relevant. Their relationship makes them mutually constitutive and therefore present to one another and within one another, as an image contained by the surface of a mirror. The pool represents the prototype, a perfect image of himself the individual conceives, which finds its perfect match in the antitype, a correspondent reflection in the outside world.

Whether the pools represent Jane or Shelley does not matter. What does matter is that the image contained by each is somehow deeper, "purer," "more perfect" and sweeter than the phenomenon it reflects, and this quality indicates that each winter pool constitutes the secret treasure of its other. When the pools and forest come together, the former establishes the subjectivity of the latter by embodying that quality of itself which makes the forest desirable, and in the case of this passage, tranquil and beautiful. The phrase "without a breath" in line 75 conveys both the perfection of the image contained in each pool and its vulnerability. Should a wind pass over its surface, the image becomes disturbed. Shelley underscores the inevitability of such an occurrence when he predicts that at some point "an envious wind" will have "crept by" and "blot" the "dear image out" (*SPP* 81, 84). In this case, the "envious wind" will issue from Mary.

"Without a breath" represents an even more problematical state of affairs, however. If the image reflected in Shelley's pool is Jane's, establishing her as the antitype to his prototype, but also conferring upon her the status of secret treasure that reflects from her back onto him and constitutes him as the perfect subject/object of desire, the phrase "without a breath" indicates the fragility of this erotic arrangement. Jane without her other loses her subjectivity; Shelley without his other loses his. Further, Jane's image without its "breath" would seem to counteract the situation Shelley usually finds himself in, that is, a situation in which he deals with substitutes for Jane's voice, rather than Jane herself. In this context, it seems he has managed to integrate Jane into himself, containing her within the confines of his pool. "Without a breath" in this regard would suggest that he has gained the genuine article, but the construction fails to eliminate the possibility that if Jane is "without a breath," she is also without expression, without a voice. The object voice she represents to him cannot be retrieved. Ultimately, the problematical nature of the phrase "without a breath" introduces an element of instability into the phantasmic matrix of "To Jane. The Recollection."

Shelley presented Jane with the gift of an Italian guitar as well as a poem, "With a Guitar. To Jane," to accompany it, written out in his best copy hand *(SPP* 477, note 1). Evidently, he wanted to represent himself well and hoped Jane would consider the poem a keepsake, recalling it perhaps whenever she played the guitar. The combination of gifts makes sense from a certain metaphysical perspective, because it should create a perfect arrangement in which three media, word, voice and music, would keep one another in check, resulting in perfect harmony.[43] As a collective gesture, though, the gift reaches a point of suspension by virtue of what it represents: an effort by Shelley to offer himself as a set of instruments Jane might play, thereby fulfilling his goals of achieving shared presence with Jane and her music.

A trade-off encumbers the gesture. Shelley risks sacrificing his authority in the sense that he becomes the object of Jane's manipulation; her singing and guitar playing enchant him, and by doing so transport his spirit to levels of emotional pleasure he cannot reach on his own. Placing the poem "With a Guitar" at Jane's disposal surrenders it to her will: she can either read it or let it remain dormant. Viewed from a different perspective, however, Shelley's gesture inverts this possibility, because the gift makes Jane his instrument, subjecting her to his will and his designs. Her voice will necessarily follow the measures of his lyric, and her fingers will sweep the strings of the guitar he gave her, forcing her to channel at least some portion of her expression through the notes of her guitar. In this respect, the gift possesses the capacity to govern her vocality, enabling him to conduct Jane's expression.

Other elements of the gesture contribute to this tendency toward deadlock. For one thing, Shelley's gesture serves as an act of renunciation. Jane might play her guitar when she is alone or for others, and she might read "With a Guitar" when she is by herself, or she might perform a recitation for Edward; perhaps she will listen while he reads the poem to her. All of these scenarios distance Shelley from Jane and stave off the possibility of "'desublimation,'" saving him from having to face what every lover must avoid—the discovery of that "something" beyond expression and realization, that void which the beloved has not the capacity to fill or the capacity to purge from herself or himself.[44] Shelley's adoption of Shakespeare's *The Tempest* as the model for his characterization of the relationship between himself, Jane and Edward contributes to the same goal, designating Shelley's gift as a polite and acceptable matter of convention. Ariel has no choice but to renounce Miranda and to tolerate her preference for Ferdinand.

Shelley refers to the guitar as "this silent token / Of more than ever can be spoken" (*SPP* 10–11). Because he does so in the context of the poem he wrote and then presented to Jane along with the guitar, the image might just as easily refer to the lyric. It serves as a "token," because it substitutes for something, that something being Shelley. The poem is silent, a constellation of words without voice, that will require Jane's vocal skill to bring it to life and to make Shelley present to herself. Her voice, however, would function only as an echo, a reproduction of his—a replica, as opposed to the real thing. The more obvious reference for "silent token" would, of course, be the guitar, an instrument Jane's voice and musical skill will bring to life. The guitar, too, stands in for Shelley in the sense that Jane can use it

---

[43] Mladen Dolar, "The Object Voice," *Gaze and Voice as Love Objects*, ed. Renata Salecl and Slovoj Zizek (Durham and London: Duke UP, 1996) 22–3.

[44] Zizek, "There Is No Sexual Relationship" 211.

to make music, in the same way she can make use of his poem, but without Jane each remains hollow, empty and silent. In the act of constituting him, poem and guitar foreclose on the possibility of shared presence, because neither Jane nor Shelley enters these media in the "kernel" of his or her being. Jane's voice reading Shelley's poem becomes the object Jane is, just as Shelley's presence in the guitar and the poem becomes the object Shelley is, not the "spirit" he believes "inhabits" either one (*SPP* 81). The arrangement Shelley engineers, then, produces its own "'repressed' point of reference."[45]

At some level, Shelley must have appreciated the power of desire. In "With a Guitar" he, in the character of Ariel, bids Jane, in the character of Miranda, to "Take / This slave of music for the sake / Of him who is the slave of thee" (*SPP* 1–3). The locution seems to say that the guitar serves music just as Shelley serves Jane; however, the blurring of identities in the poem extends the range of reference to include the possibility that Shelley is the slave to music. Because he worships music, he finds himself in Jane's service. By presenting Jane with a poem and a guitar, Shelley willingly enters an arrangement that invites domination and qualifies, therefore, as perverse. He makes himself Jane's "slave" in order to steal back from her some of the *jouissance* she, in her representational role, has taken from him. She will reciprocate his gift by providing him with music for his soul and voice to go along with his words, those things he finds lacking in himself. The exchange replicates the relationship formed by master and slave: the slave steals from the master in order to rob him of his joy and thereby secretly dominate him; the master tolerates the action, because it strengthens the slave's servitude, making his life even more sharply oriented toward his master.[46] If Shelley reproduces this arrangement, he creates a situation in which his loss offsets his gain.

The second half of "With a Guitar. To Jane" consists of Shelley's account of the guitar's history. It began life as a tree, sleeping in "repose divine / On the windswept Apennine," but, after an artist "felled" it, the tree found itself reborn as a "loved guitar" capable of echoing "all harmonious thought" and replying "justly ... / To all who question skillfully / In language gentle as thine own" (*SPP* 43–61). The guitar has fared much better than Ariel, who, "poor sprite," currently finds himself "Imprisoned for some fault of his / In a body like a grave (*SPP* 37–9). The substance of each fate suggests that Shelley would rather be the guitar than Ariel. Ariel's imprisonment in Shelley's body cuts him off from Miranda/Jane. The guitar, however, has been cut away from its idyllic existence in the Apennines, but as a result of its metamorphosis has become Jane's intimate correspondent as well as her instrument. Once Shelley identifies himself with Jane's guitar, its story becomes his story. By telling it, he installs himself at a point before the cut of castration, before the point of loss, a maneuver that restores his voice as much as it allows him to access *jouissance* in the form of music.

---

[45] Zizek, *Plague* 7.
[46] Zizek, *Plague* 34.

At least one factor destabilizes Shelley's move, and it involves the fundamental problem with narrative, as Lacan sees it. The subject who engages in narrative often conceives of himself at a point prior to his own subjectivity, a point at which the subject does not exist. In Shelley's case, when he imagines himself as a tree "dreaming" of pleasures, including "songs in July bowers" (49–52), he imagines a time before the onset of subjectivity. The fantasy narrative "occults some original deadlock."[47] Here that deadlock is the subject's perception that he has lost something he never possessed in the first place. Shelley's fabrication of this process compensates for this lacking by portraying the cut, the moment in which he was "felled," as the means to retrieving what he lost. Jane serves not only as the agent of reconnection, but as the repository of the *objet petit a* giving shape to Shelley's desire. In the end, the fable involving the guitar's history does little to resolve the paradoxes that mark Shelley's subject status. As Zizek observes, the price one pays for narrative resolution is that one falls prey to a "temporal loop," because "the narrative silently presupposes as already given what it purports to reproduce."[48]

The protean shifts in identity Shelley executes in the poem seem designed to liberate him from that loop. As much as he is the guitar with its problematical history, he is also the artist who brings it to life and prepares it to communicate with Jane. Associating himself with the artist places Shelley in a position beyond castration and connects him with authorship, the earliest possible origin of the guitar's existence. The arrangement makes Shelley responsible for his own castration as the guitar, and though the act excises him from his blissful state as the dozing tree, it also establishes his subjectivity, suggesting that he is capable of self-creation. The entity he creates and becomes, however, is ultimately as lacking and as silent as a poem. The temporal loop of the guitar's history reasserts its dominion over Shelley.

Shelley emphasizes that the guitar he has given Jane reserves its "highest holiest tone / for our beloved Jane alone" (*SPP* 89–90), and he insists that it will resist the queries of "those who cannot question well / The spirit that inhabits it" (*SPP* 80–1). He implies that the guitar possesses presence and demonstrates a capacity for auto-affection, because its responses reveal to the skilled player who and what the guitar really is. That "kernel" of itself, that "highest holiest tone," that secret treasure at the core of the guitar's being, emerges under Jane's guidance. In this regard, Shelley's fantasy relies on Jane's willingness and ability to constitute him. The reality of substitution, which bears on subject formation, runs counter to this fantasy of presence, however. Consider Shelley's description of the guitar's language:

> Whispering in enamoured tone
> Sweet oracles of woods and dells
> And summer winds in sylvan cells

---

[47] Zizek, *Plague* 10.
[48] Zizek, *Plague* 10–13.

> For it had learnt all harmonies
> Of the plains and of the skies,
> Of the forests and the mountains,
> And the many-voiced fountains,
> The clearest echoes of the hills,
> The softest notes of falling rills,
> The melodies of birds and bees,
> The murmuring of summer seas,
> And pattering rain and breathing dew
> And airs of evening.— (*SPP* 62–74)

The guitar speaks the language of nature's harmonies, the language of music, and by extension, therefore, serves as a countercultural force, a source of *jouissance*. Erotically, it communicates the expressive realities of abstract phenomena that are no less "real."

Yet, those same phenomena speak Shelley's language of substitution. "Fountains" might be "many-voiced," but the substance of their expression consists, ostensibly, of water falling on water. The hills speak in "echoes" and "the softest notes" originate from "falling rills." Water stands in for voice, as does air, imaged here in the form of "summer winds" echoing in "sylvan cells," "breathing dew" and "airs of evening." Offsetting these images that stand in for voice and suggest that the guitar, that Shelley, even coupled with Jane, is as empty as any human subject, are references in the passage to music: the "softest notes, " the "melodies of birds and bees," the "harmonies of the plains," and perhaps even the "airs of evening," if the image alludes obliquely to the musical airs with which a performance by Jane might fill Shelley's evening. Ostensibly, this is what the language of true, or "real," communication would sound like, the means by which the basic elements of nature and, by implication, the basic elements of human nature correspond with one another. The idea that "whispering" serves as the guitar's principal mode of "reply" creates an impression of exclusiveness and of intimacy. It connotes that the guitar has a voice and that it speaks an erotic sublanguage, with all the implications of glossolalia and *jouissance* one might associate with it. Nevertheless, the "tone" it channels remains once removed from presence, as the object voice always does. The fluid and air that accompany that expression generate a suggestion of even greater absence.

Images appearing in the second stanza of "To Jane. 'The keen stars were twinkling'" again raise the possibility that, at certain points in his experience with Jane, Shelley approached the point of traversing his fantasy. On the topic of the "intersubjective encounter," Zizek queries:

> When do I actually encounter the Other "beyond the wall of language", in the real of his or her being? Not when I am able to describe her, not even when I learn her values, dreams and so on, but only when I encounter the Other in her moment of *jouissance*: when I discern in her a tiny detail (a compulsive gesture,

an excessive facial expression, a tic) which signals the intensity of the real of *jouissance*. This encounter with the real is always traumatic; there is something at least minimally obscene about it; I cannot simply integrate it into my universe, there is always a gulf separating me from it.[49]

It is important to emphasize that Shelley's conception of the "real" apparently differs from Lacan's. The conventional notion that two beings have the capacity to communicate with one another in ways more telling than language will allow surfaces throughout Shelley's writing. As Zizek reminds us, however, Lacan's theory of the "real" involves an unwelcome revelation, the horror that fantasy paradoxically means to soften, elide or ignore, but which nonetheless provides fantasy with its distinctive contours. An element of the discernment Zizek mentions enters many of the lyrics Shelley devoted to musically gifted women he knew, but with regard to this "ariette" he wrote for Jane, the moment of recognition reaches a critical level.

Shelley's approach to Jane in "'The keen stars were twinkling,'" replicates the approach he collectively takes in "The Invitation" and "The Recollection." He suspends himself in a moment isolated from time, one caught between a former performance by Jane that altered his world and the prospect of a future performance by Jane, about which he remains ambivalent. The first stanza establishes a parallel between the effect of Jane's voice on guitar "notes" and the moon's influence on "the faint cold starlight of Heaven." One infuses the guitar's otherwise insipid, lifeless guitar notes with sweetness; the other blankets the cold night sky with a gauze of light and, implicitly, warmth:

> The keen stars were twinkling
> And the fair moon was rising among them,
> Dear Jane.
> The guitar was tinkling
> But the notes were not sweet 'till you sung them
> Again.—
> As the moon's soft splendour
> O'er the faint cold starlight of Heaven
> Is thrown—
> So your voice most tender
> To the strings without soul had then given
> Its own. (*SPP* 1–12)

Shelley's recollection elucidates an imbalance in Jane's performance. Specifically, her voice enhances the notes she plays by lending them her "soul." In the process Jane outstrips not so much the guitar's range, but the substance of its expression. The arrangement manifests the long-standing fear in Western metaphysics that

---

[49] Zizek, *Plague* 49.

the unchecked voice channels dangerous emotional energy. Shelley seems to compensate for the guitar's failure by containing Jane within the phonic space of this lyric, particularly by way of rhyme and resonance. The poem's strong element of nasal consonants—for example, "keen," "moon," "among," "Heaven," "throne," "own"—combine with "again," an evocative partner for the word "Jane" that occurs once in each stanza, to evoke the sound of Jane, thereby grounding her to Shelley's own textual world. It is possible, of course, to read the imbalance favorably, seeing in it Shelley's affirmation that Jane's voice transports him from the material and the symbolic world to a realm of the spiritual and the "real;" however, the verbs "shaken," "scatter" and "overpowers" that appear in stanza two (which I will address below) suggest that Shelley finds himself overmatched and uncomfortable.

With respect to the issue of subject formation, the "notes" Jane summons from her guitar and supplements with the sound of her voice constitute her, as much as Shelley's lyric constitutes her, but Shelley's sentiment in the first stanza seems to be that Jane constitutes the notes she plays and sings. She bestows upon them her substance, her presence, her warmth and light, her soul. Apparently, musical "notes" are nothing without the presence of the artist or performer behind them. Shelley's conception of this phenomenon raises the issue of whether or not the same conviction holds for poetry. Is a lyric nothing without the presence of its author? The sounds evoking Jane in "'The keen stars were twinkling'" might just as easily mark her absence in the sense that Shelley tries to summon her, something the note he attached to the poem seems to verify: "'I sate down to write some words for an ariette which might be profane—but it was in vain to struggle with the ruling spirit, who compelled me to speak of things sacred to yours & Wilhelmeister's indulgence—I commit them to your secrecy & your mercy & will try & do better another time'" (*SPP* 479, note 1). Operating on the phantasmic assumption that his lyric already contains him, summoning the sound of Jane would create an open-ended possibility that the two might merge in the text. The idea that the sounds evoking Jane in "'The keen stars were twinkling'" substitute for Jane as much as they constitute her compromises the prospect of such a confluence of souls.

Stanza two of the poem looks toward the future, and it involves Jane's absence as much as Shelley's lacking. He anticipates Jane's "dear voice revealing / A tone / Of some world far from ours" (*SPP* 21–2). Given Shelley's claims about Jane giving out her soul in the first stanza, one might expect him to say that Jane's voice reveals the "kernel" of her being, especially considering that she expresses herself in "a tone" rather than in a word. "Tone" would be the more appropriate medium for spiritual presence, since, at least experientially, it exhibits more fluid boundaries than either the sign or the word, and it carries a connotation of uniqueness. The fact that her "tone" represents something else, specifically "some world far from ours," verifies the object nature of her voice. In addition, it recalls castration. The distant world "far from ours" is a place "where music and moonlight and feeling / Are one" (*SPP* 23–4); it is a world, in other words, of unity and wholeness. As much as Jane's voice will provide warmth, light, a harmony of separate bodies, such as moon and stars, and connection, it will also raise the specter of the "horror of the real." In this poem, Shelley's concept of the "real" remains at odds with Lacan's.

The celestial/atmospheric conceit that supports the poem reveals this disjunction in other places. At the opening of the second stanza Shelley remarks that

> The stars will awaken,
> Though the moon sleep a full hour later,
> Tonight; (*SPP* 13–15)

The observation reveals that the cosmos is, though harmlessly, out of alignment. In musical terms, the cosmos appears to be out of tune, a direct contrast to its symphonic performance under Jane's leadership in stanza one. The image suggests that the lack of alignment or attunement Shelley perceives signals the absence of celestial music, the music of the spheres, a by-product of humanity's fallen condition, a castration that amounts metaphorically to a loss of voice and, therefore, a loss of presence. The condition Shelley notices reverberates in the observations that follow, hinting that he is unsettled by his own forecast:

> No leaf will be shaken
> While the dews of your melody scatter
> Delight.
> Though the sound overpowers
> Sing again, with your dear voice revealing …. (SPP 16–20)

The line "no leaf will be shaken" conveys the delicacy of Jane's touch, a good thing, but equivocation informs the concept of scattered "Delight." Abundant enough to be spread around, the "Delight" Jane sows would be unfocused, perhaps even haphazardly distributed. It might surround Shelley, but it might reach others as well. The verb "scatter" also connotes a lack of discipline, a signal of some aspect of Jane and her treasured mode of expression Shelley finds disturbing. The "intersubjective encounter" with Jane produces a recognition of something "at least minimally obscene," something he realizes he cannot integrate, cannot focus or channel, into his "universe." Perhaps this is what he finds overpowering. Maybe "no leaf will be shaken," but maybe Shelley will be. The possibility of this outcome might be what encourages him to structure this tribute to Jane's music in the way he has, sheltering himself in an atemporal position, between past and future, but also removed from the inertia of the present. The maneuver shows Shelley moving in a direction contrary to what one would expect: by isolating himself within this lyric, with its timeless status, he shields himself from the very thing that has given shape to his fantasy: Jane's voice.

The figurative equation of evening "dews" with Jane's "melody" indicates Shelley's wish to pull back from the overpowering prospect of her influence, inscribing her expression in the form of metonym and thereby removing presence from Jane's performance. However, once one considers that dew occurs when water vapor condenses, the image conveys the suggestion that under certain conditions Jane's voice condenses into a tactile and definable form that is essentially the same as what it was when it existed within Jane's mind and spirit. Jane's voice, in other words, is just a more concentrated form of what Jane is. Susan Wolfson points out that the phrase "Are one," with which Shelley concludes "'The keen stars were twinkling,'" creates the pun, "Are won."[50] The locution prompts one to wonder what has been won, given what seems to be at stake in the poem. Within the scope of Shelley's fantasy, he yearns to be "one" with Jane, a condition that would qualify as a win, should he manage to accomplish it. However, to be "one" with Jane in the only way reality will allow, by listening to her sing and play guitar, means to be plagued by the conditions of one's own subjectivity: lacking, loss and limited authority.

Shelley might have given Jane a copy of "The Indian Girl's Song" and it is possible that Jane performed it to music.[51] Bieri points out, as I already noted, that Shelley might have composed an earlier version for the purpose of hearing Sophia sing it, and the poem bears some of the same elements of the other poems written for Sophia, most notably Shelley's failing heart which yearns for contact with Sophia's. On the strength of manuscript evidence, Reiman and Fraistat assert that the poem is clearly a dramatic lyric. What seems most important about "The Indian Girl's Song," then, is that Shelley wrote it with the idea in mind that it would be sung, most likely by Sophia and then later by Jane. In this case, the poem represents an effort on Shelley's part to control a woman's musical expression by inviting her voice and, therefore, her presence into his lyrics. From this perspective, "The Indian Girl's Song" acts as a medium between Jane or Sophia and Shelley, creating conditions under which either woman's voice might conflate with Shelley's words, eliminating the wound of castration and enlivening his language. The supposed harmony and balance produced by this arrangement belies the same unavoidable power struggle that surfaces in all of the lyrics written for Jane, Sophia and Claire. Shelley desires what a woman's voice represents, but to summon that voice into his poetry makes him vulnerable to colonization by that voice. His words govern it, but it enlivens words that would be dead without it. "The Indian Girl's Song" repeats the same futile maneuver Shelley makes over and over again.

It is possible to read "The Indian Girl's Song" as though it were spoken by its composer, which, technically, it was. In this case, the poem expresses not only a desire for union or reunion, but for the intimacy of shared presence. In this respect, the poem is about the absence of Sophia and or Jane, but also about the absence of voice. The first two stanzas underscore the fallout of shouldering such a burden, specifically that the closest one ever comes to retrieving what one desires takes the form of replacement objects. Here, Shelley represents those objects in the familiar form his fantasy dictated, that is, in images of air and fluid. "Dreams of thee"

---

[50] Wolfson 221.
[51] See Reiman and O'Neill and Chernaik 151.

awaken the poem's speaker and encourage him to "arise" and go to the "chamber window" of his beloved (*SPP* 1, 8). Upon waking he observes that "the winds are breathing low / And the stars are burning bright" (*SPP* 3–4). The decision to seek out his lover is apparently not a conscious one, as the speaker reports that "a spirit in my feet" (*SPP* 6) directs his steps. The lover's calling manifests itself metonymically in the breathing winds, and the fact that it communicates with the "spirit in" the speaker's footsteps suggests that the communion they share represents that which Shelley would have identified as "real."

Stanza two continues the pattern, noting

> The wandering airs they faint
> On the dark silent stream—
> The champak odours fail
> Like sweet thoughts in a dream;
> The nightingale's complaint—
> It dies upon her heart—
> As I must die on thine
> O beloved as thou art! (*SPP* 9–16)

Perhaps dreams often fulfill wishes, but here they draw the speaker into a world of temporal failure where he remains distant not only from the one he seeks, but even from her voice. Echoes and hints of it abound, but these are not enough to fulfill him. The wound of castration here takes the form of a weak heart seeking a life-support system it fails to contact. That connection takes oral form in the poem's third stanza, in which the speaker asks, "Let thy love in kisses rain / On my pale lips and eyelids pale" (*SPP* 19–20). The image establishes the correlation between the speaker's heart condition and the beloved's ministry: shared unspoken correspondence would presumably strengthen the heart's pumping capacity and increase blood flow to "pale lips and eyelids pale." The intimacy of such "real" communication, however, fails to alter "reality." The lovers get no closer to one another than substitutes, as lips and kisses stand in for voice. The erotic construct mirrors the textual. The last lines of the poem reveal that Shelley recognized it would be impossible to accomplish the reintegration of estranged parts. Pressed lips fail to revive him, so he urges his beloved, as his "heart beats loud and fast," to "press it close to thine again / Where it will break at last" (*SPP* 23–4). The result, he knows, will be the same. He will experience a "break" that will never heal.

Shelley gave the poem "Remembrance" to Jane in the hopes that she would set it to music and perhaps sing it. A transcription of the poem, more commonly known as "Swifter far than summers flight," appears in the first edition of *Adonais*, and Donald Reiman speculates that the transcription "seems to have been kept by PBS for his own use," perhaps viewing it as "a kind of coda to the earlier poem, since the lyric employs the imagery of seasonal cycles to argue the negative side of the thesis that was developed in the opening section of his memorial tribute to

Keats."⁵² That same negative imagery involving seasonal cycles suits the poem's phantasmic agenda well, which probably explains why Shelley associated the poem with what Jane meant to him. The note, which appears directly under the text, reads:

> Dear Jane—if this melancholy old song suits any of your tunes or any that humour of the moment may dictate you are welcome to it.—Do not say it is mine to any one even if you think so;—indeed it is from the torn leaf of a book out of date. How are you to day? & how is Williams? Tell him that I dreamed of nothing but sailing & fishing up coral. Your ever affectionate PBS. (*MYR* 359)

Images of passing time open the poem; images of barrenness follow. Jane's swift arrival and swifter departure link the two sets:

> Swifter far than summer's flight,
> Swifter far than happy night,
> Swifter far than youth's delight
> Art thou come & gone—
> As the earth when leaves are dead—
> As the n/Night when sleep is sped—
> As the heart when joy is fled
> I am left alone, — alone— (*MYR* 357:1-10)

Shelley might have sent the poem to Jane because he wanted her to experience, though indirectly, the loss and absence he felt at her departure. The images involving the night speeding away while one sleeps, the earth bearing dead leaves and the heart emptied of joy represent through metaphor what it is like for Shelley to be lacking Jane, his constitutive other. The reference in this stanza to night going so quickly that the sleeper hardly notices implies that the sleeper's experience is vacant, perhaps as absent of life as the earth is absent of "leaves." The revelation counters Shelley's admission in the note that he has been dreaming of "sailing and fishing up coral," something that might dissociate him from the topic of disability featured in the poem. That subject is bereft of his secret treasure, and Jane might get a sense of his condition when she sings the word "alone," placed next to itself and separated by a dash at the stanza's conclusion. The word's phonic signature, a strong nasal quality, might fill Jane's head with the sound of emptiness, thus transmitting Shelley's "real" emotions to her. The transaction would, therefore, provide her with the very thing Shelley finds missing in himself: an echo, or sign, of the constitutive other.

---

⁵² Reiman and O'Neill 360–1. I have chosen to use the version of "Remembrance" in this text, because it contains the note Shelley sent along with it, arguably an integral part of the poem.

The poem's second stanza associates swiftly departing summer with the "swallow," night with the "owlet" and "Youth" with the "wild swan," which he refers to as "false as thou" (*MYR* 357: 11–14). The phrase "false as thou" might refer to the swallow and owlet, or it might refer to Jane. Perhaps true to her husband, she has been false to Shelley by coming and going, rather than remaining by him constantly. The word "false" might also indicate that Jane leaves behind only signs of herself and her former devotion to Shelley as opposed to the real thing. Though he wishes to compensate himself for her absence, he says, he realizes that, "Vainly would my Winter borrow / Sunny leaves from any bough" (*MYR* 357: 17–18). Borrowed "leaves" function as a sign not of presence, but of absence. The rhyming of the final four lines of stanza two, ending with "morrow," "sorrow," "borrow" and "bough" (*MYR* 357: 15–17), underscores the sentiment expressed by the borrowed-leaves trope to the extent that the word "bough" resonates with its three predecessors but fails to replicate their phonic signature exactly. The initial string of sounds departs (it "leaves") and is replaced by the substitute sign "bough," which serves as a vestige of the long *o* from "morrow," "sorrow" and "borrow," but which also creates a rhyme with "thou" from line 14. As in the case of Jane's status, it becomes difficult for Shelley to separate absence from presence.

In stanza three, Shelley refers to himself as a "living grave" (*MYR* 359: 5), observing,

> Lilies for a bridal bed [,]
> Roses for a matron's head,
> Violets for a maiden dead,—
> Sadder flowers find for me (*MYR* 359: 1–4)

He associates flowers with femininity and, as in the poem "On a dead Violet," which Shelley wrote for Sophia, they stand in for what he has lost, in this case Jane Williams. In context, what Shelley lacks is clear: voice and music, which his mind now locates in Jane. When he recommends in line six of the poem that Jane should take the flowers and "scatter them without a tear," however, he seems to renounce the wish for a voice substitute—here taking the form of a "tear." The recommendation implies then that, if he cannot have Jane, he will not satisfy himself with a substitute tear in her stead. Giving up on his constitutive other in the form of Jane and the tear she could supply as a sign of the voice he lacks amounts to a position of strength, because it maintains, paradoxically, Shelley in his subjectivity. By giving "Remembrance" to Jane, though, Shelley weakens his renunciation of her, because, by offering her this "living grave" (*MYR* 357: 5) of himself, he becomes Jane's instrument, something that will become a medium for her voice. The "living grave" of "Remembrance" requires Jane's attention to bring it truly to life.

Shelley's relationship with Claire Clairmont, Mary's stepsister, extended far longer than his relationships with either Sophia or Jane. Ann Wroe believes that Claire "almost certainly" served in the capacity of Shelley's "sometimes mistress" and that, of all the women with whom he became enamored during his Italian exile but could not touch, Claire offered him the opportunity to be with someone "who would love him—perhaps physically, perhaps not—but would not, in any case, possess him."[53] O'Neill, Reiman and Bieri believe the two did in fact have a sexual relationship, Bieri suggesting that it probably took place in 1815.[54] Perhaps because Shelley and Claire so long occupied the same living space, traveled together, shared confidences and often found consolation in each other's company, particularly in the wake of marital or family squabbles, Shelley devoted only one poem, "To Constantia," to the power of Claire's singing voice. Mutual accessibility might have obviated the need for considerable written correspondence between the two (though they did regularly exchange notes and letters), or perhaps there was no need to codify in writing what both already understood so well. Even still, Shelley and Claire must have restrained expressions of their affection for one another for fear of provoking Mary and inciting further scandal, goals they proved to be particularly bad at achieving. According to Judith Chernaik, Claire had "penciled" the notation "wd not let Mary see it" beside a fair-hand copy of "To Constantia" intended for the *Oxford University and City Herald*.[55]

While the extent and duration of Shelley's intimacy with Claire remains as uncertain as Shelley's intimacy with Jane, music, specifically Claire's singing voice, brought them together. Despite an interlude in 1815 during which Shelley reportedly discouraged Claire from studying music[56] (an offshoot perhaps of consummating their relationship, which Bieri, O'Neill and Reiman believe first occurred in the same year), Shelley had otherwise encouraged and supported her study of voice from the beginning. Shelley was not alone his admiration. A singing instructor had once compared Claire's voice to a "chain of pearls." Critics of "To Constantia," most notably O'Neill, Reiman, Chernaik and Ronald Tetreault[57] insist that readers should regard the poem as a philosophical statement, rather than as an erotic confession directed at Claire. The fact that the poem replays fantasy elements we find in the lyrics he composed for Sophia and Jane indicates, however, that the poem carries emotional freight. This reading fails to foreclose on the possibility, though, that Claire became just one more replaceable positive object-other in Shelley's fantasy.

The final stanza of "To Constantia," in which Shelley directs Claire to "cease, cease" (*SPP* 34) her singing, conveys the idea that listening to Claire has taught Shelley the lesson of renunciation. By not renouncing Claire in the past, Shelley subjected himself to the unchecked flood of *jouissance* that flowed through Claire's music, which forced him to confront the instability of his own fantasy

---

[53] Wroe 79, 44.
[54] Bieri 2: 227.
[55] Chernaik 52.
[56] Reiman and O'Neill 277.
[57] Ronald Tetreault, "Shelley at the Opera," *ELH* 48 (1981): 144–71. Tetreault credits Judith Chernaik for being the reader who "finally extricated this poem from its biographical context by reading its obvious eroticism as a metaphor for aesthetic response," 150.

as well as that flaw, or "tic," within Claire that unleashed the "horror of the real" Shelley sought to avoid. The poem demonstrates that the pure heterosexual integration about which Shelley fantasized would result in a loss of subjectivity and, therefore, a loss of desire and poetry. Furthermore, "To Constantia" portrays Claire's music as an overwhelming force that infects Shelley with its own lack of order and definition and ultimately consumes his being. Claire's enchanting voice promotes the formation of a state of afflatus for Shelley, resulting, perhaps, in this lyric; however, her breath, which Shelley mentions at least four times in the poem, emerges as a dominating force that defies relational balance, drawing away Shelley's subjectivity. Claire's voice returns Shelley to a point prior to castration, but in the process swallows up his subjectivity. Only by distancing himself from Claire's influence can he maintain his authority. Paradoxically, then, while it looks as though Shelley's request that Claire "cease" operations amounts to a traversing of his own fantasy, such renunciation protects the integrity of that fantasy by allowing desire to flourish.

In stanza one, Shelley reveals that Claire's "voice, slow rising like a Spirit" (*SPP* 1) creates a pathway for "real" correspondence, a kind of blood communion, between the two. Auto-affectively, her voice embodies the core of who she is; "like a Spirit" it presents itself in essential form, communicating with Shelley through a language of the body:

> The blood and life within thy snowy fingers
> Teach witchcraft to the instrumental strings.
> My brain is wild, my breath comes quick,
> The blood is listening in my frame,
> And thronging shadows fast and thick
> Fall on my overflowing eyes,
> My heart is quivering like a flame. (*SPP* 3–9)

The economy established by her singing and his listening remains unbalanced, however; the confluence of male logos and female *jouissance*, of the male word and the female voice (which represents the object voice) fail to combine harmonically. The observation with which he concludes the stanza, "I am dissolved in these consuming extacies" (*SPP* 11), reveals a stress fracture in the overall arrangement. The word "dissolved" denotes that the whole of his being has fractioned off into particles, spreading beyond his mortal confinement to the universe surrounding it; however, "dissolved" also maintains the possibility that those particles will constellate into their former arrangement once conditions change, in the same way that morning dew dissolves into the sunlit air, only to regroup when the air cools again. The phrase "consuming extacies," though, suggests that the *jouissance* triggered by Claire's voice swallows up Shelley's voice, taking it into itself as an organism takes in nourishment, destroying its former composition and foreclosing, therefore, on the possibility of reconstitution. It would appear that exposure to

Claire's voice breeds linguistic instability; words cannot stand up to the "fast ascending numbers" she "breathest" (*SPP* 26).

Conventional logic suggests that the "instrumental strings" attending Claire's singing should keep her voice in check. However, Shelley's body records nothing but excess. He uses the term "wild" to describe either his reaction or the quality of Claire's voice three times in the poem. In addition to the observation in stanza one that "My brain is wild, my breath comes quick," he notes "Wild, sweet, yet incommunicably strange, / Thou breathest now," and "Cease, cease—for such wild lessons madmen learn" (*SPP* 25, 34). Claire's voice becomes the agent of *jouissance* and, as such, outstrips Shelley's attempt to capture it in language (it remains "incommunicably strange"), or to perceive it as anything but a boundless energy that takes on the properties of shadows, fluid and air. It also adapts itself to "numbers," but the fact that they are "ascending," as Shelley notes, suggests that the range of Claire's voice and the ecstasy he feels are unlimited.

Enveloped by Claire's voice, Shelley confesses, with a hint, perhaps, of distress, in the first line of stanza two that "I have no life, Constantia, but in thee" (*SPP* 12). Her music enslaves him, or did at one point, at least. The poem's formal features—four stanzas of 11 lines each and a regularly irregular rhyme scheme of *ababcdcedee*—indicate that the lesson this particular "madman" has learned, that is, the need for renunciation, has paid off. Within the context of the poem and within the context of the experience it records, though, it is difficult to tell whether Shelley means that he loses his subjectivity when witnessing one of Claire's performances, living, that is, through her, or that he recognizes that Claire and her music become his constitutive other and that without her he would be nothing, a vacancy without definition. Tropes meant to identify the dynamics of their relationship don't eliminate the uncertainty. For example, he claims,

> Now is thy voice a tempest, swift and strong,
> On which, as one in trance upborne,
> Secure o'er woods and waves I sweep
> Rejoicing, like a cloud of morn. (*SPP* 15–18)

If the cloud represents Shelley and the windy tempest Claire, their integration would amount to a natural combination of water vapor and air, two separate elements working in concert. However, when one considers that fluid and air in Shelley's fantasy usually stand in for voice, it becomes clear that the combination of Shelley and Claire is not a combination of the male word working with female music, but qualifies, instead, as an amalgam for voice. Without Claire, Shelley the poet believes he has none. With Claire, Shelley the poet lacks one of his own. In either case, the sexual correspondence of Shelley and Claire produces not a perfect coupling of separate partners, but the constitution/consumption of one partner by its other.

In the final line of stanza two Shelley reports that Claire's song "suspends my soul in its voluptuous flight" (*SPP* 22), indicating that Claire reaches the core part of him and provides it with the buoyancy it otherwise lacks. Though the verb "suspends" connotes support and invests Claire's music with uncommon strength, it also connotes a cessation of activity. Claire's music, in other words, uplifts him, but in doing so keeps it from being productive on its own. Relying on Claire suspends his authority. This paradoxical note of static action continues into the next stanza, where he seems to say that "a deep and breathless awe" filled a void in him in the same way that "dreams unseen" are "felt in youthful slumbers" (*SPP* 23–4). Claire awes Shelley, but because she does so "breathlessly," the suggestion emerges that her influence on him has no life. It might also imply, however, that her song reaches him in some "real" way that goes beyond even the range of voice, serving as a purer form of communion. This possibility gains persuasive force, because it goes along with the observation that Claire's breathing has begun to increase in "fast ascending numbers." Shelley's experience of being captured and then swept away by her song follows the same pattern, suggesting that his body and soul are attuned to the same pattern.

Claire's "strain" breaches "Heaven's" boundary, and it outfits Shelley with the means to migrate to that sphere: "And o'er my shoulders wings are woven / To follow its sublime career" (*SPP* 28, 29–30). Claire's provision of "wings" also represents a restoration of what Shelley believes he has lost. Wings allow him to master the air, the breath of the world, which Claire's song also embodies, and hence make him a master of vocality, the expressive force supporting his lyric. Though he follows the "sublime career" of Claire's music, he is also, in phantasmic terms, following his own sublime career as poet once he recaptures the voice that has evaded him. In this regard, whenever Claire performs, her voice shuttles him back to a point before the moment of castration, a realm "where the world's shadowy walls are past, and disappear" (*SPP* 33). The remedy harbors an additional wound, however; Claire can lift him beyond the "shadowy walls," so that he will see expansive vistas in sharp definition, but the agent of that elevation, Claire's singing voice, itself consists of shadow; specifically, he reports, it is "o'ershadowing me with soft and lulling wings." Restoration becomes deprivation. Claire's music, a presence Shelley evidently cannot reproduce in this poem, ultimately mitigates Shelley's authority at the same time that she constitutes both him and it in her role as other. It should be pointed out, however, that Claire herself remains a muse-like shadow in the poem. "To Constantia" serves as Claire's constitutive other, and this formational dynamic shifts authority back in Shelley's direction.

When Shelley asks Claire to "cease, cease," he reenacts the trauma of castration to stave off the loss of subjectivity that comes with submitting to Claire's dominion, a reading the heavily phallic phrase "Long thus to sink" (*SPP* 35) seems to confirm. He looks next to reconstitute himself:

> Constantia turn!
> Yes! in thine eyes a power like light doth lie,
> Even though the sounds, its voice, that were
> Between thy lips are laid to sleep—

> Within thy breath and on thy hair
> Like odour it is lingering yet—
> And from thy touch like fire doth leap. (*SPP* 36–42)

Because Claire's voice has put his subjectivity in jeopardy, Shelley looks into her eyes, an image of the object gaze, in order to find himself again, the mirror image he sees constituting him. The power that defines Claire, though, lies within her voice and remains a threat, "lingering" all around her. Heterosexual coupling continues to operate as Shelley's fantasy deems, in the sense that it becomes the means to mutual constitution (presumably, when he gazes into Constantia's eyes, she will gaze into his), but voice and music in this instance create an unexpected and unwelcome challenge, because each expresses *jouissance*, a force that resists equilibrium.

"To Constantia" appears to end in defeat, revealing that Shelley has learned a hard lesson: "Even while I write my burning cheeks are wet— / Such things the heart can feel and learn, but not forget!" (*SPP* 43–4). Intimacy with Claire, with her "touch," in the end produces the same result as intimacy with Jane: Shelley finds himself burned. The result of being burned, a wound that marks or scars the recipient, insures Shelley's authority. He might lose voice, that mark of distinction allowing him to present himself to the world, but he gains the ability to "write," to constitute himself over and over again, repetitively, though in myriad forms and formats.

Whether or not Shelley managed to "have," to possess sexually, the three musical women who became objects for his desire and necessary components in his phantasmic schema seems less important overall than what the process of subsuming each of them within his fantasy produced. The process of writing and rewriting the history of these encounters places Shelley, as it does all poets who despair in writing over the loss of the beloved, in the position of the castrato. The negatives of loss and lacking generate the positive of expression. For Shelley, that expression takes the form not of singing (since he has lost not just the masculine quality of voice, but his voice altogether) but the form of inscription, specifically the inscribed lyric, a hybrid form that consists of words but maintains some vestiges of voice in its phonic profile. Whatever Shelley might have fantasized about achieving with regard to correspondence transmitted along channels crisscrossing the "real," what he gained in terms of corresponding with Sophia, Jane and Claire through poetry failed, and continues to fail, at divesting itself of reality.

Chapter 4
Power, Desire and Poetics

In the third chapter of *The Four Fundamental Concepts of Psychoanalysis*, Lacan says, "*man's desire is the desire of the Other*."[1] Shelley's poetics can be approached in these terms. The principal "Other" in Shelley's field of view would be Power, a creative force that finds endless expression in the world and in the human mind. In *A Defence of Poetry*, he refers to Power or its operation, for example, as the poet's apprehension of a "certain rhythm and order," as the poetic faculty, as "eternal music" and as "that imperial faculty, whose throne is curtained within the invisible nature of man" (*SPP* 512, 515, 513). James Chandler raises the notion that the Power to which Shelley refers in *A Defence* amounts to the "spirit of the age," a temporal constellation of creative energy and expression that determines at the same time it is determined by great poets, such as Milton and Dante.[2] In lyrics Shelley devoted to the creative process, Power expresses itself through Mont Blanc and the River Arve, through the West Wind, through the skylark's song, in the form of Intellectual Beauty and, most importantly, through the conceptions and then words of the poet. Shelley's desire to be desired by Power establishes a fantasy formation within his writing that confers upon him the poet's everlasting vision and insight. Coupling with Power during moments of inspiration confirms for Shelley that he possesses a secret treasure, in this case the authority of a poet, and at the core of his fantasy lies the desire to overcome the ephemeral nature of such moments, stretching them out into an endless line, so that he might become, in terms he articulates in the "Hymn to Intellectual Beauty," "immortal, and omnipotent" (*SPP* 39).

As much an erotic as it is an aesthetic arrangement, the relationship with Power Shelley conceptualizes also includes a complexity Lacan regards as typical of the phenomenon consisting of desire for the other's desire, that is, the motivation to experience satisfaction in defying that desire. Shelley contends that Power relies on the human mind to serve as its delivery system to the world of signs we call "reality," and the construct would seem to imply that the artist has the freedom to resist that charge; however, throughout his writing, and in *A Defence* particularly, Shelley argues that the mind has no choice but to submit to Power's capricious, perhaps flirtatious, ministries. No matter how strenuously poets "deny and abjure,

---

[1] Jacques Lacan, *The Four Fundamental Concepts of Psychoanalysis*, ed. Jacques-Alain Miller, trans. Alan Sheridan (New York and London: W. W. Norton & Company, 1981) 38.

[2] James Chandler, *England in 1819: The Politics of Literary Culture and the Case of Romantic Historicism* (Chicago: U of Chicago P, 1998).

they are yet compelled to serve, the Power which is seated upon the throne of their own soul" (*SPP* 535).³ Evidently, the inclination to resist exists, but that inclination rarely materializes into action. Poets end up composing "words which express what they understand not" and performing the role of "trumpets which sing to battle and feel not what they inspire: the influence which is moved not, but moves" (*SPP* 535).

Consistently in his writing, Shelley associates Power with music and with voice. Within the larger frame of his fantasy narrative, therefore, Power becomes implicitly identified with the feminine and with *jouissance*. In addition to functioning as constitutive other, it also represents the object voice, and in this capacity it serves as that missing part of himself the subject poet lacks, making him a creature of desire. Ideally, contact between the human mind and Power during moments of creative inspiration heals the wound of castration, conferring upon its executor extraordinary wholeness that transforms a man of uncommon sensibility into a poet. Throughout *A Defence*, however, Shelley argues that the arrival of Power serves paradoxically as a departure that revisits castration, and the construct is reminiscent of Lacan's description of the operation of the unconscious, which withdraws at the same time it emerges in a manner he calls "pulsative."⁴ Power, too, comes to the poet by way of a rupture in the fabric of the subject's experience, and when it leaves, the poet reverts to his former state no wiser or more eloquent than he was before. It is at the locus of this incision, the place where the subject is cut off from himself, where the unconscious finds expression,⁵ and it is at this same place that Power delivers the poet to poetry.

As soon as the poet expresses through words the rhythm, order and delight to which Power has exposed him, he becomes constituted as a "decentered" subject, and in the process articulates the void of subjectivity, in Shelley's terms, the absence of Power's presence within him. The fantasy informing Shelley's poetics offsets this outcome by suggesting that Power seeks, that it "desires," the poet's words in order to constitute itself within a human reality. Even though Power operates on temporal and cosmic scales well beyond the human mind's capacity to render meaningfully its operation, this "real" aspect of Power's expression remains inherently foreign and outside the bounds of representation. Shelley's conception of the composition process implies that there might have been a time when humans could hear and tolerate what he refers to as "planetary music," an allusion to humanity's inability because of some mythic fall from perfection to monitor the music of the spheres, a time, that is, prior to the moment of castration. However, in *A Defence*, at least, he does not subject himself to the narrative shortcoming of

---

³ William Keach's points out that Shelley's comments in *A Defence* regarding the "arbitrary" (and therefore the potentially tyrannical) conduct of the imaginative mind are at odds with his radical revolutionary politics. See *Arbitrary Power: Romanticism, Language, Politics* (Princeton: Princeton UP, 2004).

⁴ Lacan 43.

⁵ Lacan 43–4.

conceiving of his existence prior to the moment that made his existence possible. Even when he describes the process in which inspiration leads to composition, he maintains the view that prior to the moment of Power's emergence in the poet's mind the poet was not already a poet but merely a man. Nonetheless, he espouses the belief that poets, apparently, experience periodic recovery from castration.

Issues involving loss, absence, emotional injury and ontological inadequacy characterize all of Shelley's writings that concentrate on the mind's creative process and its expression. Shelley knows he lacks voice and Power. To overcome this condition, Shelley characteristically conceives of himself as the instrument of Power. In "Mont Blanc," for example, he sees himself as tributary channel; in the "Hymn" he performs the role of disciple; in the ode "To a Skylark" he yearns to be the bird's protégé; in the "Ode to the West Wind" he prays to serve as the Wind's "lyre" and as its "trumpet" (*SPP* 57, 69), and in *Adonais* he serves as the voice of Keats, whose "being" Power has "withdrawn ... to its own" (*SPP* 375). Shelley's aspirations recall the function of the shofar, a bull's horn that was blown during Jewish rituals in order to provide an official stamp to some decree, making an otherwise mysterious God present to his people.[6] If Shelley were to become the shofar of Power, he and his poetry would become equivalent to the everlasting sound of the law, an immortal and undying expression of authority. As it is in the case of Jewish tradition, however, the construct cannot avoid one crucial shortcoming: though the shofar proclaims God's presence in the law He hands down, it also proclaims His absence from that law, since the language of the law constitutes Him in the mortal world of reality. Though God becomes one with the law, therefore, He is nothing, unconstituted, without it. Correlatively, the shofar becomes the very image of the object voice constituting God's authority at the same time that it establishes Him as a "decentered" subject. It marks the scission, the rupture, pointing toward a void.

Transferred over to the poet and his writing, Shelley suffers the same fate. In enunciating the authority of Power, he only constitutes it as an absence, and the dynamic folds back upon the poet as an authority figure in the world of the symbolic. His words enunciate his absence. An additional problem that bears on this arrangement concerns the substance of the shofar's sound. According to Dolar, because the shofar is split off from language and the law, it falls into the same alternative order as music and *jouissance*, phenomena traditionally associated with the feminine. Consequently, a faultline opens, since the shofar intends to express what Lacan regards as the terrible *jouissance* of the father; neither voice nor shofar can be viewed in sexualized terms. Dolar asks: "Is the voice of the Father an altogether different species from the feminine voice? The secret is maybe that they are both the same; that there are not two voices, but only one object voice, which cleaves and bars the other in an ineradicable 'extimacy.'"[7] This possibility

---

[6] Mladen Dolar, "The Object Voice," *Gaze and Voice as Love Objects*, ed. Renata Salecl and Slovoj Zizek (Durham and London: Duke UP, 1996) 7–31.

[7] Dolar 27.

compromises the integrity of Shelley's fantasy by undercutting the traditional gender-specific conception of power to which Shelley clung.

Shelley's fantasy reveals other elements of this horror. Negotiations with Power in his writing indicate that neither poet nor poetry succeed at closing the gap between absence and presence, between Power and reality. Shelley's West Wind, Skylark, "Spirit of BEAUTY" (*SPP* 13) and Mont Blanc with its River Arve each functions as a sign of Power, no matter how much it conveys the possibility that the two have become consubstantial. In the third section of "Mont Blanc" he insists that the mountain "hast a voice ... which the wise, and great, and good / Interpret, or make felt, or deeply feel" (*SPP* 80–3). Apparently, those possessing the proper gifts have the ability to feel the presence of Power, yet even they confirm that feeling only by means of their perceptions, which rely on outward expression. In the "Hymn to Intellectual Beauty," Power often manifests itself in the Spirit of Beauty, which the poet struggles to feel, to witness in his mind's eye, in an endless variety of natural phenomena. In other poems Shelley defaults to familiar parameters. In the ode "To a Skylark," Power finds expression through the lark's music; in the "Ode to the West Wind" it becomes the Wind's "Spirit fierce" (*SPP* 61); in "Mont Blanc" it primarily takes the form of water, as in the Arve River flowing through a ravine and in the "secret springs" of "human thought" (*SPP* 4), and in *Adonais* it manifests itself indirectly as Nature's music and as Keats's "breath" (*SPP* 487). Fluid and air serve as metaphors of voice throughout Shelley's writing and the idea here seems to be that human perception even under ideal circumstances would be twice removed from the presence of Power. If Power speaks, the human mind gets only as close as stand-in forms. An even more unsettling implication, of course, is that even if one could under ideal conditions hear the voice of Power, one would audit the expression of its absence.

Little of the arrangement between Power and the poet that forms the core of this aesthetic offshoot of Shelley's fantasy seems to favor the poet or the human mind. However, the idea that Power needs the poet's words to deliver its healing and instructive harmonies to the world projects it into an economy of "interpassivity." In the role of instrument, the poet serves as the "interpassive" other. As Shelley acknowledges in *A Defence*, the poet does not have the ability to will himself to write and cannot summon Power to his service whenever he feels the compulsion to write. Into him, therefore, Power discharges its inertia, but Power, as the concept of "interpassivity" dictates, emerges as the genuine passive partner in the arrangement, since it requires the poet to constitute it. The poet's writing reflects the secret treasure which lies phantasmically at the core of Power, but at the same time that treasured image verifies, paradoxically, Power is no more present than the poet.

Symmetry inheres to all aspects of Shelley's formulation of the politics of composition. He conceives a relationship between the poet and Power that reproduces itself in the poet's relationship to the reader. The most obvious difference is that a reader chooses between engaging or ignoring poetic expression altogether, or decides between one author and another. The poet does not possess the capacity to ignore the visitations of Power, nor apparently can he choose to be a poet or not be a poet. This distinction notwithstanding, the poet needs the reader's attention, perhaps even his devotion, if he hopes to enter the world as a living, vocal agent. In this way, those few readers who might admire Shelley function as others who desire him and, as a result, mirror for him the secret treasure that ideally constitutes his purpose. In this respect, the living reader constitutes the poet as a living presence, something words on a page fail to do; textual inscription, Shelley feared, constitutes the artist as a vacancy, perhaps sitting before the reader in the same way Mont Blanc towers before Shelley's "adverting mind," representing itself to him as a "silence," a "solitude" and a "vacancy" (*SPP* 100, 144).

In the same way Mont Blanc, or blank page that nonetheless issues signs of Power, needs Shelley's mind to subject it to the signs of his verse, every poetic text "desires," so to speak, the desire of a living reader to iterate it. And what turns the tables on both the mountain and the poet in this arrangement is that the voice that speaks for Mont Blanc belongs initially to Shelley, as the voice that speaks the words of "Mont Blanc" the poem belongs to the reader. It would appear that the reader, like Shelley looking "on high" (*SPP* 127), serves as the passive partner in the relationship, but it might also be true that what the reader merely reflects back to the poet is the image of his own inertia and ultimately his own vacancy. The image of presence paradoxically registers absence.

Shelley identifies Power in its capitalized form as the cause of poetry only once in *A Defence of Poetry*, though it serves as a spectral presence throughout the essay. In this regard Power qualifies as an aesthetic "big Other," as the "invisible" symbolic Master that must maintain its spectral aura in order to govern.[8] As Zizek illustrates, the father that loses his temper is never as fearsome as the father that does not, but sustains that possibility as an immanent threat.[9] From Shelley's perspective, the threat would be the possibility that Power at some point abandons the poet permanently, in similar fashion to the goddess Astraea, whose "footsteps" departed "from the world," because the evil of men drove her away (*SPP* 522). What makes such a threat all the more unsettling is that poets, according to Shelley, have no choice but to serve as the instruments of Power. Therefore, they can neither be accused of perversely desiring to become the instruments of the other, nor of holding back on Power and showing a lack of respect for its authority.[10] In the final paragraph of the essay, Shelley says,

> The most unfailing herald, companion, and follower of the awakening of a great people to work a beneficial change in opinion or institution, is Poetry ... The persons in whom this power resides, may often, as far as regards many portions of their nature, have little apparent correspondence with that spirit of good of which they are the ministers. But even whilst they deny and abjure, they are yet

---

[8] Slavoj Zizek, *The Plague of Fantasies* (London and New York: Verso, 1997) 63.
[9] Zizek 63.
[10] Zizek 33–4.

compelled to serve, the Power which is seated upon the throne of their own soul. It is impossible to read the compositions of the most celebrated writers of the present day without being startled with the electric life which burns within their words. They measure the circumference and sound the depths of human nature with a comprehensive and all-penetrating spirit, and they are themselves perhaps the most sincerely astonished at its manifestations, for it is less their spirit than the spirit of the age. Poets are the hierophants of an unapprehended inspiration, the mirrors of the gigantic shadows which futurity casts upon the present, the words which express what they understand not, the trumpets which sing to battle and feel not what they inspire. (*SPP* 535)

Though elements of causality and subjugation surface in the interaction between Power and the poet, mutual desire and mutual constitution define their coupling. If Power serves as the master and the poet serves as the slave, each partner needs the other to perform its function. One denotation of the word "hierophant" is interpreter. Shelley's diction implies that the poet translates and in the process unavoidably transfigures the expression of Power for public consumption. Earlier in *A Defence*, Shelley echoes this sentiment, observing that "Few poets of the highest class have chosen to exhibit the beauty of their conceptions in its naked truth and splendour; and it is doubtful whether the alloy of costume, habit, etc., be not necessary to temper this planetary music for mortal ears" (*SPP* 516–17). Evidently, Power fails to make an impression on the world of reality without the poet's good judgment and skill with language. Yet, in this process, the poet still serves as instrument. If he performs the role of "trumpet," he replicates the role of shofar in Hebrew tradition, validating the operative presence and authority of Power in the world. Paradoxically, however, his poems also announce Power's absence, the possibility that nothing lies behind the poet's words. The other metaphors Shelley employs in the passage, that is, "mirrors," "shadows" and "words," convey the same message. All three reflect, or represent, Power, signaling in the process their own distance from it, but in addition all three constitute it, confirming that Power is nothing other than its representation, a troubling reality that folds back on Shelley and his poetry.

In order to illustrate the human mind's relationship to the world, Shelley compares it in the second paragraph of *A Defence* to an "instrument over which a series of external and internal impressions are driven, like the alternations of an ever-changing wind over an Aeolian lyre, which move it by their motion to ever-changing melody" (*SPP* 511). No explicit reference to Power emerges in the conceit; nonetheless it conveys the idea that the engaged mind becomes a kind of sound meter, monitoring influences that otherwise fail to register meaningfully. In this case, the harp registers "internal and external impressions" and various forms of "motion." Shelley insists that the mind is not passive, but active and co-creative, converting the "melody" produced by "impressions" and "motion" into a "harmony" produced by an "internal adjustment" of the human mind. The coupling of partners generates the music of poetry, and it resembles a relationship between equals; however, Shelley's description of the process indicates that some force, internal and/or external is required to set the poetic mind in motion. Moreover, he defines the adjustment made by the human mind as an effort to "accommodate its chords to the motions of that which strikes them, in a determined proportion of sound; even as the musician can accommodate his voice to the sound of the lyre" (*SPP* 511).

It looks as though the mind makes all the concessions, conforming its expression, fitting its words, perhaps, to the phenomena that have excited it. The arrangement empowers the poetic mind, though, in the sense that the shapeless "impressions" and "motions," which fill it with "delight" (*SPP* 511) require order and arrangement to become meaningful. Put another way, these expressions of *jouissance* remain formless unless they register in the human mind. "Ever-changing wind" sets the process in motion, and the metaphor suggests that the force approaching the poet is twice removed from presence, accounting, perhaps, for why Shelley chooses such amorphous terms to identify the agent that inspires the poet and ultimately promotes the mutual composition of harmony. Wind stands in for the object voice, which, like the shofar, would constitute Power. Power lacks that voice, however, and the wind by which it operates becomes a sign of its desire, its need for the accommodations of the poet's voice. The musician who accommodates "his voice to the sound of the lyre" confers language, hence definition, to its music.

Shelley regards the arrangement between the human mind and the forces that excite it not as a specialized activity, but as a fundamental and erotic operation:

> A child at play by itself will express its delight by its voice and motions; and every inflexion of tone and every gesture will bear exact relation to a corresponding antitype in the pleasurable impressions which awakened it; it will be the reflected image of that impression; and as the lyre trembles and sounds after the wind has died away, so the child seeks, by prolonging in its voice and motions the duration of the effect, to prolong also a consciousness of the cause. (*SPP* 511)

Shelley's analogy suggests that the child-like poet operates in a state of innocence. Participating in the poetic process of "accommodation" is not only natural; it is unsullied. Nonetheless, desire apparently motivates the child's activity. It seeks to capture, prolong, and remain faithful to something it has lost. When it responds "to a corresponding antitype in the pleasurable impressions which awakened it," the child's voice and motion become the treasured record of that experience. In the same way that the poet endeavors to prolong through his words the presence of Power and, correlatively, the presence of himself, the antitype of Power, so the child tries to prolong the moment of inspiration and make it lasting. According to its nature, the child, like the poet, tries to leave its mark in the world in order to prolong its constitution. Its actions produce delight, not despondency, because the process produces a mutually constitutive "reflected image." It sees itself and the phenomena that inspired its expression mirrored forth by "its voice and motions."

Expression becomes a process of self- (or more accurately subject-) composition, creating the impression that loss and lacking have been overcome.

Poets become subject to the capricious influx of Power, though notwithstanding Shelley's acknowledgement that occasions might arise when a poet chooses to "abjure or deny" his responsibility to serve, poets accept their calling. The problem is that the agent responsible for composition, what Shelley earlier in *A Defence* refers to as "that imperial faculty, whose throne is curtained within the invisible nature of man" (*SPP* 513), fails to confer upon its "ministers" any lasting benefits. Shelley emphasizes throughout the essay that no amount of experience entitles or enables the poet to compose at will or alters the man that he is:

> Poetry ... is not subject to the controul of the active powers of the mind, and ... its birth and recurrence has no necessary connexion with consciousness or will ... The frequent recurrence of the poetical power, it is obvious to suppose, may produce in the mind an habit of order and harmony correlative with its own nature and with its effects upon other minds. But in the intervals of inspiration, and they may be frequent without being durable, a poet becomes a man, and is abandoned to the sudden reflux of the influences under which others habitually live. (*SPP* 534)

It is possible that, in terms of Shelley's fantasy, the nature of desire informs the poet's acceptance of his role. Desire's "*raison d'etre*," Zizek emphasizes, "is not to realize its goal, to find full satisfaction, but to reproduce itself as desire."[11] When the "poetical power" abandons the poet to ordinary circumstances, in effect it cuts him loose, revokes and nullifies what makes him a poet. This very process of castration, however, constitutes the poet's desire, maintaining him as a desiring subject who nonetheless understands that he serves that "poetical power" as its constitutive other, the object of its desire.

The poet's relationship with Power, the "imperial faculty" seated on a "curtained throne within the invisible nature of man," provides coveted access to "eternal," or "planetary" music, but it also promotes the reproduction of that music through the poet's words and measures (*SPP* 514–15, 517). In fact, throughout *A Defence*, Shelley's rendering of the composition process conveys the idea that the poet, because he "participates in the eternal, the infinite and the one," has been granted privileged access to the presence of beauty and truth not available to other humans or even other artists, such as "sculptors, musicians and painters" (*SPP* 513). The poet, he says, is as superior to the musician as the music of the harp is superior to the music of the guitar (*SPP* 513). The Aeolian lyre conceit suggests that the mind naturally tends to produce "not melody alone, but harmony," and Shelley's comment on art during the youth of the world evinces that men observe a "certain order or rhythm" in "natural objects" and that they endeavor to imitate what they have observed (*SPP* 511–12). Plato and Bacon, according to Shelley, qualified as

---

[11] Zizek 39.

poets because the language of the former is melodious and the prose of the latter "has a sweet and majestic rhythm" (*SPP* 514–15). "All the authors of revolutions in opinion," to Shelley's mind, are poets because "their periods are harmonious and rhythmical and contain in themselves the elements of verse; being the echo of the eternal music" (*SPP* 515).

Echoing his contention that the child endeavors to prolong in its gestures and in its voice the "pleasurable impressions" that excited it, a fundamental version of the way in which a musician "accommodates" his voice to the sound of a lyre, Shelley later in the essay describes the poet as "a nightingale who sits in darkness, and sings to cheer its own solitude with sweet sounds" (*SPP* 516). Shelley's celebration of great poets in Western culture tempers this characterization, though it maintains the emphasis on poetry as something essentially musical and timeless. "The bucolic writers" of Greece wrote poetry that is "intensely melodious," whereas that of "the preceding age was as a meadow-gale of June which mingles the fragrance of all the flowers of the field, and adds a quickening and harmonizing spirit of its own" (*SPP* 521). As for the teachings of Jesus, Shelley encourages the reader to "Listen to the music unheard by outward ears" and, with regard to the topic of love, for which Dante's *The Divine Comedy* serves as a "perpetual hymn," great writers throughout history have embraced it as a topic; the "music" of this chorus, Shelley says, "has penetrated the caverns of society, and its echoes still drown the dissonance of arms and superstition" (*SPP* 524, 526).

Collectively, Shelley's assessment proves problematical. Images consistent with his fantasy of uniting words with voice and music surface throughout his narrative concerning the nature and history of poetry and consequently create a familiar deadlock. Shelley refers to the writings of "the authors of revolutions in opinion" as the collective "echo of eternal music." Furthermore, his admiration for writers devoted to the subject of love reveals that their language inevitably becomes in time an echo that resounds in "the caverns of society." These assessments suggest not only that music produced or channeled by poetry is time-sensitive, but that it is at best a representation of some originary presence. From this perspective, poetry becomes the absence, the void, that needs to be revitalized by each age in order to reiterate truth and beauty with renewed potency. Elsewhere in *A Defence*, he compares poetry in its substance, inception and effect to wind, to the sea and to a fountain, all replicating the implications generated by his use of the word echo.

Shelley's evaluation of the "bucolic writers" and their predecessors, for example, compares the efforts of the latter to "a meadow-gale of June." In speaking of Jesus and the Judeo-Christian prophets, he says the music generated by their teachings gradually emerged in history "as a ceaseless and invisible wind, nourishing its everlasting course with strength and swiftness" (*SPP* 524). He calls Dante's *Vita Nova* "an inexhaustible fountain of purity of sentiment and language" and uses the same metaphor to define "a great Poem" as "a fountain for ever overflowing with the waters of wisdom and delight," its effect a "divine effluence" (*SPP* 525, 528). In the passage referring to poetry devoted to the subject of love as a penetrative force that "echoes" throughout the ages, he emphasizes the capacity of that poetry to "drown the dissonance of arms and superstition" (*SPP* 526). Metaphors such as these, which invest the substance and force of poetry with the qualities of air and fluid, create the impression that poetry is an inexhaustible, boundless resource that promotes and refreshes life. Fountains come ostensibly from a wellspring and winds signal the inevitability of change. As the voice of both poet and Power, poetry extends the authority of these agents into the world.

The same metaphors involving air and fluid also suggest, however, that all great poetry, which serves collectively as the voice of Power finding expression at key moments in human history, is, in fact, a sign of absence, constituting the poet who wrote it and the Power that inspired him, but a void all the same. Poems, in other words, represent the object voice. This consideration runs counter to the idea that poetry delivers the voice of truth, beauty and the inevitability of change to the human world of reality. The great poem remains separate from, lost to, perhaps, the subject that composes it and composes himself through it. Shelley refers to "Poetry" as "the record of the best and happiest moments of the happiest and best minds" (*SPP* 532), associating it, one might infer, with *jouissance*, in the sense that it consists of ecstatic expression exceeding all form and codification. The properties of fluid and air amplify that association. The experience of writing poetry, or reading it for that matter, confirms for its beneficiary that poetry relates to lacking and loss. According to Shelley,

> We are aware of evanescent visitations of thought and feeling sometimes associated with place or person, sometimes regarding our own mind alone, and always arising unforeseen and departing unbidden, but elevating and delightful beyond all expression: so that even in the desire and the regret they leave, there cannot but be pleasure, participating as it does in the nature of its object. It is as it were the interpenetration of a diviner nature through our own; but its footsteps are like those of a wind over a sea, which the coming calm erases, and whose traces remain only as on the wrinkled sand which paves it. (*SPP* 532)

Those exposed to poetry's ministry never find themselves gifted with a presence, only "evanescent visitations of thought and feeling" that create the impression of a "diviner nature" making itself present. The agent at the heart of such an experience leaves no fixed or stable account of itself, though. It makes waves in one's consciousness, so to speak, but the memories, images and feelings it stirs up represent things that are absent.

As they do consistently throughout his writing, images of air and fluid indicate that Shelley's fantasy prohibits escape from the unavoidable deadlocks informing the erotic relationship between Power and the human mind. The creative mind is never more than the instrument of Power and apparently what it comes into contact with during moments of inspiration is not the thing itself, but a metonym (air and fluid) for the object voice that constitutes Power. However, the possibility that Power is not a presence and has no voice, no music, of its own without the poet tilts the balance in the poet's favor, even as the arrangement reveals the poet's disadvantage, that is, that the poet never makes direct contact with the operation of Power through the motions and impressions occurring in the world and within his own consciousness. In perhaps the most famous passage in *A Defence*, Shelley compares the "mind in creation" to a "fading coal which some invisible influence, like an inconstant wind, awakens to transitory brightness: this power arises from within, like the colour of a flower which fades and changes as it is developed, and the conscious portions of our natures are unprophetic either of its approach or its departure" (*SPP* 531). Evidently, the Promethean mind is capable through poetic expression of ascending "to bring light and fire from ... eternal regions" (*SPP* 531), but it fails to capture divinity itself. Instead, a stand in, a substitute for that divine inspiration, breathes within the Aeolian mind. That which constitutes Power for the poet also constitutes its absence.

The inherent instability of Shelley's construction of the composition process and its consequences crystallizes in his assertion that "all high poetry is infinite; it is as the first acorn, which contained all oaks potentially. Veil after veil may be undrawn, and the inmost naked beauty of the meaning never exposed" (*SPP* 528). This coalition of metaphors suggests that poetry, which Shelley later in the same passage compares to "a fountain for ever overflowing with the waters of wisdom and delight," is an inexhaustible resource and that the origin of the "wisdom and delight" it supplies remains a mystery. The abrupt shift from "acorn" to "veil," however, defines poetry as inherently evasive and feminine, a form of expression that teases readers and writers with the promise of consummation, but that in the end resists going all the way and, hence, ultimately fails to satisfy. If poetry serves as the expression of Power in the human realm, it would appear that Power holds some of itself back, resisting the poet's and the reader's desire. Perhaps most unsettling, though, is the implication that a great poem's "inmost beauty" cannot be exposed, because nothing lies underneath all those veils. The trope matches up with Shelley's assertion earlier in the essay that the "imperial faculty" responsible for metrical arrangements of language sits on a "throne ... curtained within the invisible nature of man." Though invisibility does not automatically indicate nonexistence, Shelley's appreciation for the fact that he is dealing with mysteries that exceed the human capacity for perception fails to counteract completely the possibility that invisibility might indicate vacancy. The "imperial faculty," in other words, constitutes itself through poetry and by means of that process also designates that "it" would be a void otherwise.

Despite the proliferation of deadlocks such as these throughout *A Defence*, Shelley invests himself in a fantasy of presence. He consistently describes the aesthetic transmission, both as it affects the poet and the reader, as a process that extends the circle of human consciousness. Poetry unleashes a Big Bang effect on the minds of everyone within its universe. For example, Bacon's language, Shelley writes, "distends, and then bursts the circumference of the hearer's mind, and pours itself forth together with it into the universal element with which it has perpetual sympathy" (*SPP* 515). As opposed to "Ethical science," poetry "acts in another and a diviner manner. It awakens and enlarges the mind itself by rendering it the receptacle of a thousand unapprehended combinations of thought ... Poetry enlarges the circumference of the imagination" (*SPP* 517).

Auditors of Homer, he speculates, must have found their "sentiments ... refined and enlarged by a sympathy" (*SPP* 516) with the characters he created. Those who witnessed the Athenian tragedies experienced a similar effect: "The imagination is enlarged by a sympathy with pains and passions so mighty that they distend in their conception the capacity of that by which they are conceived" (*SPP* 520). In the same passage that describes poetry as "the interpenetration of a diviner nature through our own; but its footsteps are like those of a wind over a sea," Shelley explains that conditions such as these come "principally" to "those of the most delicate sensibility and the most enlarged imagination" (*SPP* 532). Poetry operates in a manner opposite of "those sciences which have enlarged the limits of the empire of man over the external world," because they are not informed by "the poetical faculty" and as a result have "proportionally circumscribed those of the internal world; and man, having enslaved the elements, remains himself a slave" (*SPP* 530).

Shelley's use of words such as "enlarge," "distend" and "circumference" implies that readers and poets have a center and that poetry acts centrifugally as it extends the individual's boundaries out to extraordinary limits, perhaps even to unlimited horizons. At the center of the minds of all great poets lies "Power, which is seated upon the throne of their own soul;" Power, however, fails to find unwavering expression in the poet's mind and when it is absent, the poet, says Shelley, becomes just a man, though "he is more delicately organized than other men, and sensible to pain and pleasure, both his own and that of others, in a degree unknown to them" and, because he is different, "he will avoid the one and pursue the other with an ardour proportioned to this difference" (*SPP* 534). When the "imperial faculty" within becomes active, when Power speaks to the poet, it draws the poet out and away from his parochial center and extends his reach to things, situations, characters and readers before "unapprehended" by him. Power inspires the poet to extend a Power-amplified version of himself through his writing and to make himself and his work the object of a reader's desire. The arrangement replicates itself with regard to the reader in the sense that a great poem enters his or her consciousness and initiates a similar process of expansion. Shelley's discussion of Homer and the Athenian poets illustrates the transaction. "Sympathy" with thoughts and feelings voiced or performed by characters cultivates the auditor's mind and soul.

Evidence that Shelley incorporates a fantasy of centrality, of core presence, into the construction of his poetics abounds in *A Defence of Poetry*. However, what he identifies as a centralized process at the same time emerges paradoxically as a decentralizing process produced by the "decenteredness" required for the formation of subjectivity. Phantasmically, the transactions informing inspiration, writing and reading form a network of constitutional interdependence. Within the temporal space of a poem, the poet serves as the instrument, the mouthpiece, of Power; in this way, the poet's voice establishes Power as a "decentered" phenomenon and in the process marks Power as a void, as something lacking. Reflexively, the poem also speaks for the poet, furthermore, in turn constituting him as a subject. Consequently, the exchange also establishes the poet as absent and as lacking. He becomes just as invisible, just as much a veiled presence, to the reader as Power operating through the poetic faculty is to him. The poet's composition enters the reader's consciousness and perhaps triggers the emergence of Power there. In the process of finding himself mirrored in the characters or in the speaker's thoughts and sentiments, the reader becomes constituted by the textual other, which desires his or her desire. The text speaks not just to the reader, but for the reader. All three subjects, Power, the poet and the reader, join in a mutually defining "'extimacy.'"[12]

Ulmer's contention that poets and readers are lovers in Shelley[13] emphasizes the erotic nature of the exchange between reader and writer in Shelley's aesthetic economy. Shelley conceptualizes the relationship between the two entities, ideally, as a coupling of prototype and antitype. Poetry, he says, "equally creates for us a being within our being" (*SPP* 533); it generates, in other words, the formation within the self of a prototype, an image of itself not disfigured by flaws and shortcomings. In this respect, poetry provides the reader with a model to desire, a part of the reader's self that is missing or lacking, inspiring him or her to seek the antitype, the mirror image, of that conception which might make him or her whole again. In this way the poet and his work provide a larger frame for the reader's consciousness, extending it beyond its former limits. The same sympathetic reader, therefore, mirrors the poet's consciousness, as he or she finds it embodied in the poem.

The problem with this arrangement, however, would be that the reader supplies voice to the poet's otherwise silent words, thereby establishing the poet as a "decentered" subject. The reader's voice introduces the "scission," the rupture, in the middle of full presence that refers to a void.[14] If the poem represents a text handed down by the divine authority of the poet, the reader performs the function of the shofar, ultimately announcing that the poet is absent and exposing in the process the horror of the real Shelley's fantasy aims to avoid. Though the poet composes the words of the text, the self he composes at the same time is not the originary, auto-affective self that Shelley has in mind, but a subject dependent upon the reader's voice—the object voice that iterates the author into the symbolic world.

Shelley's poems focusing on creative processes and transactions usually express a desire for the desire of the other, which finds expression through a variety of representational forms. Inevitably, therefore, poems that fall into this category feature a poet-subject that operates from a position of lacking, implicitly

---

[12] Dolar 27.

[13] William Ulmer, *Shelleyan Eros: The Rhetoric of Romantic Love* (Princeton: Princeton UP, 1990) 19.

[14] Dolar 16.

or explicitly perceiving himself as cut off from the ministries of Power. If the poet-subject places himself within a narrative history, he invariably makes the mistake of installing himself as a subject prior to the moment or event required for subject formation. In *A Defence of Poetry*, Shelley expresses a stoic acceptance of the realities governing composition—the inconstancy of Power; the poet's inability to control the process; the idea that the encounter produces no lasting transformative effects within the poet's makeup—but in such poems as the "Hymn to Intellectual Beauty" and the "Ode to the West Wind," for example, he expresses regret, anxiety and uncertainty in his characterization of the human mind's relationship with Power and with poetry. Lacking generates desire (which cannot be satisfied), and desire encourages Shelley to override those very conditions producing the authority he so desperately seeks.

A fantasy construct, "Mont Blanc" serves as a complex fable of the mind's operation and its relevance to the operations of Power in the perceived world. As all fantasy narratives, however, "Mont Blanc" brings to the surface what it aims to cover up. Specifically, it exposes the void at the root of all expression. Mont Blanc the mountain, the Ravine of Arve and the Arve River are the poem's primary symbols. Mont Blanc represents the ice-engulfed seat of Power, where some "he," evidently, sits poised on "his secret throne" (*SPP* 17). The image resonates with Shelley's description of the positions occupied by Power and the "imperial faculty" responsible for composing metrical arrangements. Recall that the former "is seated upon the throne" of the poet's soul and that the latter's "throne is curtained within the invisible nature of man." Just as Power exists at the center, or core, of the poet's mind, so the Mont Blanc peak forms for Shelley the centerpiece, the hub, of the "Chamouni" valley. Mont Blanc's influence presents Power to the surrounding landscape, replicating the action of great poems and poets on the world—enlarging its circumference by means of its influence. It should be emphasized that, within the overall context of Shelley's fantasy, the same Power that operates from Mont Blanc also emanates from the mind of the poet; this would make Shelley the center of the landscape. In this respect, then, the poem may be viewed as a struggle for centrality and, by extension, for authority, as Shelley's expression competes with, or perhaps seeks harmony with, that of Mont Blanc.

When Shelley addresses the "Ravine of Arve—dark, deep Ravine— / Thou many-coloured, many-voiced vale" (*SPP* 12–13), he addresses the functioning of his own human mind. Power flows from Mont Blanc through the Ravine in the same way that it flows through the human mind and then through the poems that mind generates. The Ravine and the mind serve, therefore, as the instruments of Power, and this construct, so familiar in Shelley's writing, raises the possibility that the passive instrument establishes the true passivity of the so-called agent or author that employs it. "Power in likeness of the Arve" (*SPP* 16) flows through the Ravine and forms a metaphor of Power flowing first through Shelley's "adverting mind" (*SPP* 100) as it observes and then through the text of this poem. The poem "Mont Blanc" becomes, therefore, the mirror image of the Ravine and of Power's action upon it, the antitype to its prototype. Correlatively, the Ravine mirrors the current operation in Shelley's mind as he perceives the Arve's action and composes. The relationship is not only erotic, but incestuous, as the same genetic disposition, in the form of Power, characterizes each partner. The two become mutually constitutive, each performing the role of other to its relative subject, even though in the opening section of the poem Shelley acknowledges that the human mind is but tributary (he uses the word "feeble," *SPP* 7) to the full stream of Power rushing through its channel. By bringing "tribute" to the expression of Power in the form of the Arve, Shelley implies that the human mind recognizes in Power a reflection of the secret treasure it imagines existing at its own center.

Shelley's characterization of the Arve as the direct expression of Power flowing into the world below is compromised by ambiguity. On the one hand, he refers to it as "many-voiced vale" (*SPP* 13); however, the idea that the Arve consists of fluid suggests that it serves as a metonym, therefore a stand in, for the object voice. Shelley's observations involving the river "bursting through these dark mountains like the flame / Of lightning through the tempest" (*SPP* 18–19) associates it with *jouissance*, and its waterfall creating a "veil" that "robes some unsculptured image" connotes the Arve's concealment of something essential, a pure image such as Power, which cannot be rendered. He notices the Ravine's

> ... caverns echoing to the Arve's commotion,
> A loud, lone sound no other sound can tame;
> Thou art pervaded with that ceaseless motion,
> Thou art the path of that unresting sound— (*SPP* 30–3)

Mind and Ravine do no more than "echo" Power's movement through them, and the form of expression emerging from the process is apparently devoid of language, "lone" and "unresting sound" without the support of logos.

Even if the Arve were a representative of the object voice, in other words, that which it constitutes would become something that cannot be represented, or perhaps more accurately, cannot be represented by language—an unknown and within the symbolic realm, therefore, quite possibly a void. The problematical signs of Power's presence paradoxically point to its absence. Shelley's "human mind, which passively / Now renders and receives fast influencings" (*SPP* 37–8) and consequently creates poetry registers this "reality" of the mind's relationship with Power. When Shelley asserts that Mont Blanc, the source behind the process, "art there" (*SPP* 48), he illuminates perhaps the most stubborn deadlock informing his fantasy: if Power is "there," it is there in "art," in this poem, only, and the poem that constitutes it reveals that by being "there" in "art" and in the ravine of Shelley's mind it is equally *not* "there."

Shelley reinforces the substitution angle with respect to the Arve's significance in sections four and five by associating it with air, wind and respiration. He refers to Mont Blanc's destructive force as a "flood of ruin / ... that from the boundaries of the sky / Rolls its perpetual stream" (*SPP* 107–9) and observes that things created by the "race / Of man ... / Vanish, like smoke before the tempest's stream" (*SPP* 117–19). In the valley below,

> ... vast caves
> Shine in the rushing torrents' restless gleam,
> Which from those secret chasms in tumult welling
> Meet in the vale, and one majestic River,
> The breath and blood of distant lands, for ever
> Rolls its loud waters to the ocean waves,
> Breathes its swift vapours to the circling air. (*SPP* 120–6)

As he pans his gaze back toward the frozen wastes of Mont Blanc, he remarks that

> Winds contend
> Silently there, and heap the snow with breath
> Rapid and strong, but silently! Its home
> The voiceless lightning in these solitudes
> Keeps innocently, and like vapour broods
> Over the snow. The secret strength of things
> Which governs thought, and to the infinite dome
> Of heaven is as a law, inhabits thee! (*SPP* 134–41)

If Power emanates through the image of Mont Blanc, the image is forbidding and silent, an image that lacks voice and cloisters the presence it constitutes. As an extension of Mont Blanc, the Arve manifests itself in the forms of breath and moisture, substitutes for voice, which normally represent the subject; additional components of voice ("wind," "air" and "breath") amplify the implication that the Power they express ironically lacks shape and stability. The secrecy and silence of these phenomena would seem to contradict Shelley's assertion that "the power is there" (*SPP* 127), "there" being "high" atop the mountain. These phenomena reveal that Power/power is not there, but *here* in the form of its defining object-others. Silent operations atop the mountain influence the "rushing torrents," "loud waters" and "many sounds" (*SPP* 129) that register below, but its pronouncements become the means by which it enunciates itself into the human world Shelley occupies.

Earlier in the poem Shelley offers a contradictory version of mind's correspondence with Power. He says, "I look on high," (*SPP* 52) and he insists that "the wilderness has a mysterious tongue / Which teaches awful doubt, or faith so mild" and that

> Thou hast a voice, great Mountain, to repeal
> Large codes of fraud and woe; not understood
> By all, but which the wise, and great, and good
> Interpret, or make felt, or deeply feel. (*SPP* 80–3).

If Mont Blanc has a "voice," it refuses to answer the questions he poses prior to this passage regarding the purpose behind the "heaped shapes" informing the "ghastly" scene that stretches out before him. By means of its silence, the "great Mountain" conveys to the poet not only that it does not acknowledge his presence or his questions, but that it does not desire him. Desirous to win that desire, Shelley alters the mode of communication, asserting that he can "feel" the voice of Mont Blanc, that he speaks the same "mysterious tongue" as the "wilderness" and that he can "make" that presence "felt" by others. The problem is that the voice he feels is also the object voice that points back toward absence. The "mysterious tongue" by which the "wilderness" communicates with him, furthermore, signals not that an exclusive intimacy exists between it and the poet, but that two remain distanced from one another. As are fluid and air, tongue is a metonym for voice and for language. The trope paradoxically implies that a sharing of the same tongue relates them beyond language, in some "real," bodily way, perhaps; however, it also connotes that the poet might be twice-removed from Power: he would be once removed if he were able to hear its voice; he would be twice removed if he were to engage a dialogue consisting of tongues, instruments of speech rather than speech "itself."

An additional paradox emerges from the fact that Shelley appears to cast Power in the role of Lacan's "big Other."[15] Ironically, the "big Other" exercises its authority by remaining a spectral presence and by not asserting itself; it must remain an agent or entity that threatens to act. Once it enforces its will, its authority diminishes. Clearly, Mont Blanc exerts its influence on the surrounding landscape, on its "subject mountains" (*SPP* 62) and on subject poet. It becomes the focal point of his landscape, and it subjugates him, in the same way Power subjugates all poets, to its will. To Shelley's mind, Mont Blanc exhibits its capacity to "repeal / Large codes of fraud and woe," a reference, no doubt, to the religious and intellectual systems Shelley associated with the "big Other" of Western cultural history, which were responsible for enslaving men and women to the letter of its law and, therefore, to its language. However, if Power speaks to "the wise, and great, and good," a group in which Shelley implicitly includes himself, it therefore acts, and in the course of acting surrenders its authority to Shelley, who turns it and its phenomenal instruments into his collective subject, that is, the subject of this poem.

The voice one hears in the poem "Mont Blanc" is not that of Power, but Shelley's interpretive reconstitution of its "stillness" (*SPP* 128) in his own voice. The victory that results from this insurrection is short-lived, however, since the words of this poem are, like Mont Blanc and its tributary expressions, signs of Power, substitutes for voice. The reader's voice overthrows the poet's and flows through the words of "Mont Blanc" in the same way that Shelley's voice overthrows the voice of Power and fills in for the "silence, solitude" and "vacancy" established by Mont Blanc. In this regard, then, the music created by Shelley's 10-syllable lines, which bring definition to the sounds and airborne voices flowing through the Vale

---

[15] Zizek 63.

of Chamouni and enunciate human authority, more accurately result from linked interaction, representing "an old and solemn harmony" (*SPP* 24).

Communicating with human intuition, which feels its presence, by means of its "voiceless lightning," its "mysterious tongue" and its "echoing" sounds, Power's most direct expression becomes the equivalent of "planetary music" the human ear has lost the capacity to hear. Shelley's confidence that "the wise, and great, and good" have access to that expression illustrates the narrative shortcoming of placing the subject at a moment prior to its own emergence, a moment that requires loss and other. Shelley's use of the Wordsworthian word "gleam" in each of the final three sections of "Mont Blanc" (*SPP* 49, 121, 127) connotes that vestiges of pre-subjective existence (for Wordsworth that existence consists of the individual's origin as a soul) remain visible to the gifted, "adverting mind." In this regard, the "gleams" Shelley notices in the world surrounding Mont Blanc correlate with the sounds that register within the channel of his own mind, repealing codes of fraud and woe and providing the poet with a faith in presence, no matter how "remote" and "silent" it might seem.

This possibility forecloses on itself, however, if one considers that, if what Shelley sees stretching out before him in the Ravine or Arve and beyond is a metaphor of his mind, the image of this "awful scene" (*SPP* 15) emerges as the object gaze. In section two he observes, "Dizzy Ravine! and when I gaze on thee / I seem as in a trance sublime and strange" (*SPP* 34–5); section four returns to the same thought, noting, "And *this*, the naked countenance of earth / On which I gaze" (*SPP* 98–9). The second locution implies that the earth's "naked" face, like the "blanc" mountain towering in front of him, mirrors his own and by taking on his imprint serves as the scopic extension of the originary self, as it moves out into the world and bestows meaning on everything in it. However, the same ontological maneuver might also be read as an illustration of the loss that leads to subjectivity. Mont Blanc, Shelley's subject mountain, constitutes him and in the process establishes that what lies behind the author and the poem is a blank. In this case, the "naked countenance" Shelley acknowledges lays bare the zero point, the "horror of the real," concerning the nature of poetry and authority.

If Shelley desires Power and its expression in the form of Intellectual Beauty, he desires the desire of this formation even more. His "Hymn to Intellectual Beauty" demonstrates that Beauty appears in myriad visible and elemental forms and visits the poet's heart, but Shelley finds such manifestations in the symbolic unsatisfying, primarily because they confirm the inconstancy of Power. The "extacy" (*SPP* 60) he felt on at least one occasion implies that during moments of fusion between the poet and Beauty, the poet experiences *jouissance*. The "Hymn" presents Shelley's dilemma in such a way as to convey the idea that Power's expressions prove a welcome disturbance of the poet's life-rhythms in the symbolic world. In this regard, then, it is possible to view Shelley as he portrays himself in the "Hymn" as one who remains "hooked on some specific formation ('sinthom') of *jouissance*," someone "ready to put everything at risk rather than renounce *that*."[16] By virtue of this "'sinthom,'" the subject encounters, says Zizek, "the density of his being." This is why he will not give it up, and "when he is deprived of it, his universe is empty."[17] Evidently, though Shelley does not wish to return to the life of the ordinary man unaware of Power's Beauty, the person to whom the poet speaks, he also struggles to tolerate the conditions the great poet finds so burdensome, accepting the fact, that is, that Power subjugates the poet's will and then abandons him without promising to return. An economy such as this stokes desire, though it drives the poet to become as dissatisfied with his "reality" void of Power as he is with his life informed by Power's flirtatious influence.

As its title might indicate, "Hymn to Intellectual Beauty" portrays Shelley as a religious votary, a zealot who refuses to allow doubt to overcome his faith. Though the "extacy" relevant to that faith is private and cannot be directly transferred by such indirect means as poetry, Shelley does not adopt the more typical zealot's attitude, informed by the belief that, because what he experiences goes beyond words, no one outside his belief point has the capacity to experience what the zealot has. Zizek points out that such a person suffers what he calls a perspectival illusion. "The precious *agalma* perceived by him as the ineffable kernel which cannot be shared by others (non-believers)," writes Zizek, "is precisely *jouissance* as that which always remains the same."[18] Shelley's faith rests on the idea that Power and Beauty award the poet privileged access to their mystery and that, if the poet fails at passing that experience on to others, he can at least encourage others to remain open to its presence within them: Power "visits with inconstant glance / Each human heart and countenance" (*SPP* 6–7). As Shelley emphasizes in *A Defence of Poetry*, the poet has no choice but to devote himself to this function. The possibility that his words lack voice, however, jeopardizes his mission in the sense that this condition inhibits his ability to convey the presence of Power to his audience.

The situation generates desire, and desire, in turn, creates space for fantasy to operate. "Hymn to Intellectual Beauty" expresses Shelley's desire for Beauty to "Keep with thy glorious train firm state within his heart" (*SPP* 41); it expresses Shelley's desire for the desire of Power, enabling him to perform confidently as its minister, as one, that is, "who worships thee" (*SPP* 81); furthermore, it expresses his desire to recapture that which he has lost—his voice, the *agalma* that might make him the object desired by potential readers. Section two of the poem directs a series of questions to the "Spirit of BEAUTY," inquiring, for example, "why dost thou pass away and leave our state / This dim vast vale of tears, vacant and desolate?" (*SPP* 13, 16–17). "Vacant" refers to what the human world is like when the "Spirit of BEAUTY" (Beauty in substance, not appearance) remains absent, but "vacant" also represents Shelley's sense of himself as empty, as void of something. His claim in the following section that "No voice from some sublimer

---

[16] Zizek 49.
[17] Zizek 49.
[18] Zizek 50.

world hath ever / To sage or poet these responses given" (*SPP* 25–6), allows for at least three readings: that Beauty does not exist outside the phenomenal world; that Beauty does exist but does not bother to answer: that his voice lacks sufficient potency to summon a response. All three interpretations amplify the anxious notes Shelley sounds in section four when he petitions Beauty to

> Depart not as thy shadow came,
> Depart not—lest the grave should be,
> Like life and fear, a dark reality. (*SPP* 46–8)

A fantasy retrospective, section five and section six of the poem combine to reconstruct a moment from Shelley's past when he evidently made first contact with Power. He recalls,

> While yet a boy I sought for ghosts, and sped
> Through many a listening chamber, cave and ruin,
> And starlight wood, with fearful steps pursuing
> Hopes of high talk with the departed dead.
> I called on poisonous names with which our youth is fed;
> I was not heard—I saw them not—
> When musing deeply on the lot
> Of life, at that sweet time when winds are wooing
> All vital things that wake to bring
> News of buds and blossoming,—
> Sudden, thy shadow fell on me;
> I shrieked, and clasped my hands in extacy! (*SPP* 49–60)

Perhaps because Shelley's experience has taught him that "the awful shadow" of Power "floats though unseen amongst us" (*SPP* 1–2), he endeavors to communicate with it aurally, passing through "many a listening chamber" in the hope of participating in "high talk with the departed dead"—those, evidently, who have access to a world not limited by mortal perception.

In the ignorance of youth, furthermore, he endeavors to summon a response by calling on "the poisonous names with which our youth is fed." Though Power would remain unsullied by such falsehoods, it ignores the youth's entreaties, and if the "Hymn" represents a corrective to these mistakes by aiming Shelley's desire at the proper target, Power continues to remain silent. In reference to his former attempts at contact, he recollects, "I was not heard." No part of the "Hymn" suggests that he is being heard this time, either. In section six, he reveals his frustration over Power's reluctance to grant subsequent moments of intimacy. "I call the phantoms of a thousand hours / Each from his voiceless grave" (*SPP* 63–4), yet no amount of time invested installs him permanently in Power's good graces. His "call" succeeds in summoning up the past, but the past summoned remains "voiceless," therefore lacking in the authority required for successful communication.

The event that forms the focal point of Shelley's reconstruction, the moment, that is, when Power's "shadow fell on me," would seem to confirm Shelley's lack of voice, because Power conveys itself to him on a separate sensory channel, implying that his prayer falls short of its mark. However, the event also suggests that Power itself lacks voice; it shows itself, perhaps, because it lacks the ability to enunciate itself into the symbolic world without the poet's help: Power requires Shelley's "Hymn" to find beautiful expression in the world. The idea that Power reveals only its "shadow" suggests, furthermore, that its Platonic essence—its presence—exists beyond the human world of forms. From a Lacanian perspective, however, Power can become no more than the object constituting it. In this case, Power's expression through "shadow" indicates that "it" is something prone to shifts in appearance as a result of changing light conditions. As the mirror image of Power, "shadow" constitutes it as something not there in any fixed or stable form, but as something that constitutes itself through shifting object-appearances.

Throughout the "Hymn" Shelley's approach to Power and Intellectual Beauty indicates that they communicate themselves through a multiplicity of ephemera. In the poem's opening section, he observes,

> The awful shadow of some unseen Power
> Floats though unseen amongst us,—visiting
> This various world with as inconstant wing
> As summer winds that creep from flower to flower,--
> Like moonbeams that behind some piny mountain shower,
> It visits with inconstant glance
> Each human heart and countenance;
> Like hues and harmonies of evening—
> Like clouds in starlight widely spread,—
> Like memory of music fled ... (*SPP* 1–10)

Addressing the "Spirit of BEAUTY" several lines later, he acknowledges that

> Thy light alone—like mist o'er mountains driven,
> Or music by the night wind sent
> Through strings of some still instrument,
> Or moonlight on a midnight stream,
> Gives grace and truth to life's unquiet dream. (*SPP* 32–6)

Each of these metaphors associates the expression of Power with music, air and fluid, and in doing so Shelley creates a deadlock. Linking Power to music confirms its stature as a missing presence Shelley lacks, the thing that fills his words with life. Playing a familiar role, he becomes the Aeolian harp over which Power sweeps, resulting in music. The idea that the music comes and goes quickly and that it survives in memory emphasizes further that the condition Shelley and all great poets find themselves in is one of lacking.

However, consistent references regarding Power's substance and appearance in the human world to air and fluid counterpoint the fantasy by underscoring the idea that Power expresses itself not through the object voice but through substitutions. Words and phrases from sections one and three such as "Floats," "summer winds," "mountain shower," "mist," "night wind" and "midnight stream" create an undercurrent that reduces Power and Beauty to elemental, that is, to metonymic, levels. Shelley's language implies that, if it is true that the combined expressions of these two related agents can be approached only through objects of their expression, it is also true that Power and Beauty are no more than the objects that represent them. For the poet, unfortunately, Shelley's images suggest that it is impossible to get any closer than the object, or, worse, closer than the substitute. As he says in *A Defence*, veil after veil might be stripped away, but Power never reveals its naked beauty. By way of metaphor, Shelley acknowledges in the final section of "Hymn to Intellectual Beauty" that the mystery of Power and Intellectual Beauty are "not heard or seen" (*SPP* 76) despite their continued presence in the world. Perhaps because the floating "shadow" of Power remains invisible, when Shelley recalls the erotic moment of coupling with it, Power becomes not something he saw but felt, clasping his "hands in extacy!"

In *A Defence of Poetry*, Shelley observes that in "the intervals of inspiration ... a poet becomes a man, and is abandoned to the sudden reflux of the influences under which others habitually live" (*SPP* 534). The poet's internal constitution saves him, says Shelley, because "he is more delicately organized than other men, and sensible to pain and pleasure, both his own and that of others, in a degree unknown to them" (*SPP* 534). This gift equips the poet with the capacity to avoid pain and pursue pleasure. In the "Hymn to Intellectual Beauty," Shelley identifies the human heart as the organ responsible for this capacity. In the opening section of the poem, he claims, for example, that Power, though "unseen," visits "each human heart and countenance." In section three he speculates that "Man" would be "immortal, and omnipotent, / Didst thou ... / Keep with thy glorious train firm state within his heart" (*SPP* 39–41). In section six he reveals his devotion to Power and its expression of Beauty when he confesses that he summons them "With beating heart and streaming eyes ... / ...the phantoms of a thousand hours" (*SPP* 63–4). The heart represents core centrality; it becomes the place from which the poet's efforts originate, and it is an agent of reciprocity. Power contacts the poet's heart, and the poet, following suit, "calls" on Power by means of the same organ.

Implicit in the relationship is the possibility that at the center of Power exists what Shelley in *A Defence* refers to as an "eternal music" and as a "certain rhythm and order." Perhaps Shelley means to imply that communication between Power and the poet consists, therefore, of a shared, unspoken rhythm, a music that can be felt but not heard. Maybe when the "shadow" of Power falls on Shelley, it is responding not to the calls he makes in "many a listening chamber," but to his "beating heart and streaming eyes." When he laments in section four that the "Spirit of BEAUTY" fails or refuses to "Keep with thy glorious train firm state within [man's] heart," the connotative range of the word "firm," viewed in this context, expands to include the idea of strong and steady rhythm, a "glorious train" of beats that synchronize the poet's biorhythms with the eternal rhythms of Power. Correspondence of this kind becomes the aesthetic correlative to the erotic correspondence Shelley's shares phantasmically with Jane, Sophia and Claire. Shelley covets exchanges of this sort, because they gesture in the direction of the "real" and promise therefore a communion not burdened by the conventions of the symbolic.

As in "Mont Blanc," lacking manifests itself in the form of the object gaze. In "Hymn to Intellectual Beauty," however, gaze points back in the direction of Power and Beauty rather than in the direction of Shelley. Throughout the poem, Shelley emphasizes that Power and Beauty remain "unseen," finding indirect expression in the form of "shadow." In section six, Shelley recalls that the "phantoms" of past vigils "have in visioned bowers / Of studious zeal or love's delight / Outwatched with me the envious night" (*SPP* 65–7). Power never revealed itself to Shelley's sight during one of these many moments of watchfulness. He accounts for this failure in the first section of the poem when he claims that Power "visits with inconstant glance / Each human heart and countenance." The statement implies that the gaze of Power shifts constantly, which means that Power constitutes itself through an infinite number of objects. Shelley's phantasmic conception of it, therefore, harbors a fundamental weakness, because it suggests that Power has no center, that it remains a void. Perhaps even more unsettling, though, is that the word "glance" implies that, when Power does bother to "visit ... each human heart and countenance," it does so by way of a glancing blow; Power, in other words, glances in the poet's direction, but never fixes its gaze upon him. Its actions suggest, therefore, that the poet more often than not fails to serve as Power's object of desire. Shelley's experience suggests that he has not succeeded at drawing the desire of this other so crucial to his constitution as a poet.

An additional faultline in Shelley's "Hymn" involves his equivocal use of the words "spell" and "spells," which establishes both the unavoidable necessity of words and the possibility that they constitute absence. In section three, he reasons that, because "No voice from some sublimer world" (*SPP* 25) has ever responded to human queries concerning the inconstancy of the "Spirit of BEAUTY," the "sage" and "poet" (*SPP* 26) have resorted to forging mythic systems as a way of accounting for this mystery. These "records of their vain endeavor," Shelley points out, amount to

> Frail spells—whose uttered charm might not avail to sever,
> From all we hear and all we see,
> Doubt, chance, and mutability. (*SPP* 28–31)

Beauty's evasiveness produces superstition, which, in turn, provokes sages and poets to vocalize "frail," or impotent, "spells." In his own past, Shelley himself might have fallen into this same trap, as his actions in "many a listening chamber," where he "called on poisonous names," suggest. By the time he composed this hymn, however, he had matured. The poem articulates his acceptance of the fact that Power and its "Spirit of BEAUTY," what in the poem he also calls "awful LOVELINESS," provide knowledge that lies beyond language, "whate'er," that is, "these words cannot express" (*SPP* 71–2). Shelley accepts the possibility that all language, including each word comprising this poem, is lacking. Power's refusal to acknowledge the poet's vocal advances narrows that lacking to the absence of voice. Shelley's use of the phrase "frail spells" to refer to chants "uttered" by impotent sages and poets creates a pun suggesting that the root cause of the failure is the sage's and the poet's reliance on words, combinations of letters spelled out into logical units, or signs. Shelley's attempt to formulate a corrective to this frailty in the form of his "Hymn," a devotional utterance meant to be chanted or sung, collapses in on itself because it fails to break the spell of "frail spells."

In the final section of the poem, Shelley implies that the intimate encounter during which the "shadow" of Power "fell on me," so that "I shrieked and clasped my hands in extacy!" qualifies as a "spell." If this is the case, Power's intimate visitations to "the human heart and countenance" devolve into a form of language that is no more capable of issuing presence than Shelley's words are. Shelley closes "Hymn to Intellectual Beauty" by praying that Power will

> to my onward life supply
> Its calm—to one who worships thee,
> And every form containing thee,
> Whom, SPIRIT fair, thy spells did bind
> To fear himself, and love all human kind. (*SPP* 80–4)

Prior to making this request in the poem, Shelley establishes that the poetic mind primarily renders Power's expression through simile and metaphor. Tropes designed to communicate light's multi-sensory emanation from the "Spirit of BEAUTY," such as "mist o'er mountains driven, / Or music by the night wind sent," for example, imply that Power must communicate with the human mind, including the poet's mind, by way of media, by way of observational "records" stored away in memory. Power and its "Spirit of BEAUTY," therefore, rely just as much on "spells" to constitute their expression in the world of signs as poet and reader rely on words to constitute themselves and their experiences. While it might be true that the "Spirit of BEAUTY" confers faith and, therefore, authority upon Shelley by means of its "spells," as he indicates in the final lines of the "Hymn," it is also true that the logos informing Shelley's benediction "binds" that same boundless "SPIRIT" within its constitutive form. Shelley's poem spells out for himself and for his reader what Power is, performing the role of necessary other. Without poetic form, Power's efforts to enter the human world of "reality" would otherwise "Remain the records of … vain endeavor."

The "Hymn to Intellectual Beauty" and "Mont Blanc" illuminate Shelley's fascination with the mind's relationship to Power and its access to presence. The same concerns inhere to the "Ode to the West Wind;" however, Shelley adjusts the poem's emphasis so that it focuses on issues involving the potency of his verse and its capacity to generate presence. The formational dynamic concerning Shelley's desire for the desire of the other emerges in the form of Shelley's quest to become partner to the West Wind, a consolidated stature that would permit him to become, ostensibly, the direct expression of "Autumn's being" (*SPP* 1), Power's manifestation within this fantasy verse narrative. The merger makes sense to Shelley, perhaps, because the West Wind serves as an "unseen presence" (*SPP* 2) and would appear, therefore, to mirror his own stature as the "unseen presence," the respiratory voice at work within his own poems. The phrase echoes Shelley's observation regarding the activity of Power in the world, which also remains "unseen," and the resonance signals an instability in Shelley's portrait of the West Wind.

The Wind becomes the correlative of the "Spirit of Beauty" from the "Hymn to Intellectual Beauty." Ultimately, both serve as constitutive objects, lost objects at that, for Power and Being. By referring to the West Wind as an "unseen presence," however, Shelley links it directly to being, suggesting that the two are consubstantial. The revision communicates the idea that "Autumn's being" has suffered no castration, that it conveys its presence directly through its agent. As an ontological model, therefore, the West Wind presents itself as the perfect constitutive other, since it suggests to Shelley that voice, "*Thy* voice" (*SPP* 41; my italics), can become the auto-affective extension of originary presence, The problem with this model as Shelley conceives it is that it quickly becomes compromised by Shelley's parallel quest to establish himself and his poetry as a continuous, living instrument. In the "Ode to the West Wind" he remains unable to settle upon either of two choices: performing as shofar or performing as Aeolian lyre. Shelley's ambivalence creates a fracture in the partnership fantasy that seeks to forge his words with the Wind's unbridled expression and transformative power. The fracture caused by Shelley's wavering between wind instrument and string instrument widens, moreover, as a result of instabilities inherent to the nature of each instrument. As is so often the case in Shelley's lyrics, the concluding question to the "Ode" ("If Winter comes, can Spring be far behind?" *SPP* 70) signals the persistence of deadlocks that cannot and, considering that fantasy operates by exposing the horror it means to conceal, must not be resolved.

Shelley's entreaty to the Wind to "hear, O hear" (*SPP* 14), which runs throughout the poem, recalls his attempts in the "Hymn to Intellectual Beauty" to summon a response from Power. The desire for partnership with this agent of irresistible influence doubles as a desire that the West Wind will adopt him and his resources. Employing the subjunctive mood in section four, for example, he generates an erotic scenario in which he becomes "A wave to pant beneath thy power, and share / The impulse of thy strength" (*SPP* 45–6). He envisions circumstances under which he might become "a swift cloud to fly with thee" and, apparently provoked by desperation, asks the Wind to "lift me as a wave, a leaf, a cloud!" (*SPP* 44, 53). In section five he requests that the Wind will "Scatter" his "words among mankind!" (*SPP* 66–7). Shelley wants the Wind to "Be thou, Spirit fierce, / My spirit!" (*SPP* 61–2), so that he might express himself with the same force, but also so that "Autumn's being" will find in him an equally indispensable channel. A successful union would insure that his own "breath" (*SPP* 1) would fill his words with life, even though he remains physically absent from them.

Shelley's rolling terza rima, enacting an inevitable process of change as the non-rhyming partner sandwiched in the middle of each stanza burgeons into the dominant rhyming pair in the following stanza, energizes the "Ode to the West Wind;" however, the formula becomes predictable, and it is also limited, because each of the poem's five sections, each consisting of a sonnet, closes with a neatly packaged couplet. No matter how innovative and dynamic it might appear to be, Shelley's expression in the "Ode" can't escape the shadow of Dante, and it cannot escape convention. It lacks *jouissance*, something the Wind expresses in abundance and something that Shelley ardently desires.

He addresses the West Wind as "wild," as "Wild Spirit, which art moving everywhere / Destroyer and Preserver," as "thou, O Uncontroulable!" and as a "Spirit fierce" (*SPP* 1, 13–14, 47). Furthermore, he regards it as a force that he evidently once resembled before life experience wore him down, "tameless and swift, and proud" (*SPP* 56). In his description of its effect on the atmosphere, he observes it herding storm clouds that resemble "the bright hair uplifted from the head / Of some fierce Maenad" that will contribute to a "Vaulted" sky from which "Black rain and fire and hail will burst!" (*SPP* 16, 20–1, 26–8). He notes that, when it blows over the otherwise placid surface of the Atlantic, it forces the ocean's "level powers" to "Cleave themselves into chasms," as its "voice" causes the "sea blooms and the oozy woods" on the ocean floor to "suddenly grow grey with fear, / And tremble and despoil themselves" (*SPP* 37–42). Apparently a direct manifestation of Autumn's law, which in this case serves as the seasonal "big Other," the Wind is dynamic, and its authority is absolute; its manners of expression are unpredictable and ubiquitous. Shelley's terza rima pays tribute to the Wind's action by producing a chain-reaction effect in the poem, each stanza through rhyme burying a seed that sprouts in the next stanza; however, the form represents the epitome of control.

Shelley expresses a fear that his writing has lost its potency, an unavoidable outcome, given the "heavy weight of hours" that "has chained and bowed" him (*SPP* 55). In section four, he looks to a conditional future in which he might become "a dead leaf thou mightest bear" (*SPP* 43) and then several lines later repeats the same trope when pleading for the Wind's uplifting influence, for afflatus. The following section confesses, "What if my leaves are falling" like those of the forest, and he compares his "dead thoughts" to "withered leaves" (*SPP* 58, 63–4). As a metaphor, the word "leaves" ramifies in many directions. Leaves would be the withering pages on which his poems have been written; they are fallen in the sense that they have been severed from him and in the sense that they no longer have life. Even more unsettling, the images of "withered" and fallen "leaves" generate connotations of loss and departure, as in "leaving." His poems cannot escape the reality that life and presence leave them at the moment they blossom. The West Wind becomes a reminder of this inevitability. Perhaps this is why "sea blooms and the oozy woods ... / ... tremble and despoil themselves." The "Uncontroulable" West Wind conducts this process, which explains why Shelley fantasizes about partnering with it. Such a coupling would ensure that his leaves gain a fertile future. By virtue of the possibility that the "Ode to the West Wind" qualifies as one of Shelley's "withered leaves," it would automatically fall within the Wind's purview.[19]

When Shelley mentions that the West Wind's "azure sister of the Spring shall blow / Her clarion," and when he projects that the West Wind will become "the trumpet of a prophecy" (*SPP* 9–10, 69) if his prayers are answered, he logically perceives the Wind as the ideal wind instrument, implicitly identifying it with the shofar. The "voice" that causes the Atlantic seafloor to "tremble" is the voice of "Autumn's being." When voice remains the direct discharge of "being," it remains the perfect instrument, in the sense that instrument and performer are one and the same. The implications of this fantasy construct offer at least one explanation as to why Shelley found female vocalists so attractive. When Shelley writes that the "wild West Wind" is the "breath of Autumn's being," he is asserting that Autumn and the Wind share the same substance and therefore one life. Part of Shelley insists on viewing the West Wind's unbridled expression, its conveyance of *jouissance*, as indicative of a condition prior to castration. As the shofar announces the authority of divine law, the West Wind enunciates the introduction of Autumn's law into the unsuspecting environment, imaged forth in the form of the sleeping Mediterranean in section three of the text.

Metaphysical tradition invests the wind instrument with the capacity to raise the human spirit to the level of divinity. If Shelley were to succeed at making himself the West Wind's partner, his writing would boast the same capacity, affording readers an audience with Power, as it operates through Shelley's consciousness and shapes his locutions. This fantasy prospect hides within its folds, however, the fact that the West Wind, functioning as the "breath of Autumn's being," constitutes not Autumn's presence but its absence by means of its myriad expressions. In this respect, its performance mirrors that of the shofar. Furthermore, the "Ode" desexualizes the West Wind,[20] referring to it as a neutral agent, or "Spirit," creating room for the possibility that its "Uncontroulable" mode of expression might not

---

[19] Of this passage, James Chandler writes, "If we take the account in the *Defence* as understood in this passage, then the simile 'like withered leaves' is problematic in the extreme. For if thought decays as composition begins, then the pages of text, 'withered leaves,' are not so much a metaphor for the dead thoughts as the form that thought takes when it dies. The dead thoughts are driven not like withered leaves, but as withered leaves; they ride the boundary between metaphor and metonymy. Such paronomasia is a function of the textuality to which it playfully alludes" (552). One implication of Chandler's comment is that the reader's engagement in word play provoked by the text sustains the poem's vitality.

[20] See the footnote by Reiman and Fraistat regarding the West Wind's gender (Donald H. Reiman and Neil Fraistat, eds, *Shelley's Poetry and Prose*. A Norton Critical Edition (New York and London: W. W. Norton & Company, 2002) note 3, 298). Despite the fact that

fit into the traditional feminine mold at all. Sexual neutrality, observes Dolar, remains a consistent implication in the tradition involving the shofar's function.[21] This possibility threatens the sexualized concept of authority on which Shelley's fantasy was based.

Shelley's conception of the West Wind is not without its own inherent instability. In section three, he acknowledges the capacity of its "voice" to disrupt the ocean's floor and surface, yet the fundamental trope upon which the "Ode" as a fantasy narrative relies identifies the "breath of Autumn's being" as a movement of air. Throughout Shelley's writing, air and wind serve as a metonyms for voice, a connection made explicit in this context by the opening reference to the West Wind as "breath." Shelley's twofold desire that the West Wind will mirror him as he reflects it ultimately results in Shelley becoming, as is the Wind, a substitute for the voice which has been cut away from "Autumn's being." If the Wind were to answer his prayer and become "Spirit fierce, / My spirit," it would move him and his poetry further away from presence, not closer to it. To become a wind instrument evidently means gaining the capacity to convey *jouissance* to a trembling world, but it also apparently means becoming cut off from the source of that *jouissance* in a process that instantly forecloses upon itself.

If Shelley comes close to a point of "traversing the fantasy" in the "Ode to the West Wind," he attempts to revise the components of the narrative in order to protect the integrity of that fantasy. In the final section, for example, he assigns the West Wind the role of "The trumpet of a prophecy" and announces that the Wind will operate "through my lips," suggesting that he will become the musical performer and the Wind will serve as his instrument. Shelley's choice of the noun "lips" as opposed to "mouth" generates implications of volition and manipulation in the sense that moving lips form words. The entire trope, therefore, images forth the ideal partnership between his words and the Wind's energy Shelley has had in mind all along. A shift in metaphors earlier in the same section elucidates Shelley's misgivings about the arrangement he desires, though. When he summons the Wind to

> Make me thy lyre, even as the forest is:
> What if my leaves are falling like its own!
> The tumult of thy mighty harmonies
>
> Will take from both a deep, autumnal tone,
> Sweet though in sadness. (*SPP* 57–61)

Shelley anticipates that the merger will produce transformative music, in the form of "mighty harmonies," to which both partners make equal contributions.

---

tradition entitled Shelley to conceive of the West Wind as feminine, in my estimation the poem understates that sexual orientation. See also Chandler's discussion of the issue.

[21] Dolar 28.

The Wind would grant him the gift of afflatus, filling his words and poems with its spirit, but allowing him at the same time the opportunity, in terms he uses in *A Defence*, to "temper" the Wind's eternal music for mortal ears. In keeping with metaphysical tradition, Shelley's string instrumentality would maintain the Wind's tendency to "lift" its auditors, but would also inhibit its capacity to outstrip the symbolic realm completely and approach the dangerous realm of unchecked desire. The maneuver parallels his initiative in giving a guitar to Jane as a way of conducting the range of her music. In addition, it resets character roles within this narrative so that they remain predictably complementary. Shelley performs the role of masculine composer-conductor and the West Wind performs the role of feminine inspiration—words and structure combining with "voice" or "breath."

As part of the conclusion to the "Ode to the West Wind," Shelley looks forward to the possibility that successful contact with the West Wind will produce a chain reaction in which "the incantation of this verse," will "Scatter, as from an unextinguished hearth / Ashes and sparks, my words among mankind!" (*SPP* 65–7). The forecast reveals the core component of his fantasy: the capacity to vocalize himself eternally through his words. Early in the poem he compares the West Wind's ability to drive dead leaves to an "enchanter's" ability to drive away ghosts. The Wind's status as "the breath of Autumn's being" suggests, however, that, as Autumn's expression, the Wind would have more in common with the chant than with the "enchanter." This faultline in Shelley's construct indicates what is important to Shelley: he wants to be the enchanter, not the chant; he desires, that is, to become a living voice, rather than the record of that voice in action.

If the West Wind responded to Shelley's entreaties when he was composing the "incantation" which is the "Ode to the West Wind," what remains now is the poetic record of that transaction. After the fact, the true "enchanter" of the "Ode" would be the reader, who invests Shelley's words with his or her own voice. This condition, perhaps, is what lies at the root of Shelley's dramatic pronouncement that "I fall upon the thorns of life! I bleed!" (*SPP* 54). In his "sore need," Shelley confronts the mortality of his present voice; once it vocalizes this poem, it flees like so many "ghosts." The reader who picks up the "Ode to the West Wind" and fills it with the breath of his or her being chases away the ghostly presence of Shelley haunting, but not inhabiting, these words.[22] In a compelling way, every poem, because it constitutes the writer who composed it, serves as the ghost of that writer. Poems become spectral presences that represent a void. Though the reader, summoning the poet's presence, replicates Shelley's action when Shelley summons the West Wind's influence, the voice that constitutes that presence is not the auto-affective extension of the poet, but a disembodied voice separate from his own. Perhaps what Shelley fears most is that the act of reading reenacts the reality of castration.

---

[22] See Andrew Bennett's helpful discussion of Shelley's belief that the best poets haunt their poems and their future readers. *Romantic Poets and the Culture of Posterity* (Cambridge: Cambridge UP, 1999).

At several points in the "Ode to the West Wind" Shelley exhorts the Wind to "hear!" him. In light of the conditions governing the relationship between poet and reader with regard to subjectivity, the request might just as easily apply to the reader, whom, Shelley hopes, will hear him through the magic of this "incantation." To "hear" Shelley would be to place him "here," in this poem, making him present in his own creation. The poem's structure sends a message that would appear to dampen Shelley's fantasy, however. Each section halts the rolling progress of its terza rima stanzas, Shelley's words swirling forward in the fashion of wind-blown leaves, with a couplet that brings the chain reaction of rhyme to a close. This feature of the "Ode" pronounces a death sentence of sorts, articulating the fact that all writing, just as all writers, must eventually end. Each successive section of the poem renews the pattern established by the section that precedes it. In doing so, however, it revises the phonic signature. The process speaks to the nature of poetry. Successive generations of voices trigger the "incantation of this verse," but they fail to restore the vocal signature of the writer who conceived and then composed that verse. Though it might be argued that the reader becomes the poet's instrument of resurrection, the claim fails to eliminate the undesirable possibility that the poem becomes the reader's instrument, an "interpassive" object that reveals the true inertia, the emptiness, of both reader and writer.

The ode "To a Skylark" tackles the same issues involving voice and presence, except that in this poem a skylark becomes the vehicle for powerful, unseen authority representing the ideal poet as well as the object voice. The skylark expresses itself directly through its beautiful music. Shelley admires its capacity to "Pourest thy full heart / In profuse strains of unpremeditated art" (*SPP* 5), and he accepts the fact that, in addition to announcing its presence by means of its singing voice, the skylark can be "felt" ("we feel that it is there," *SPP* 25) by means of signs that point in its direction. In this respect, the skylark is no different than Power's "Spirit of BEAUTY," which shows itself through media that directly reflect its sublime substance. Stanzas three and four exemplify the skylark's relationship to the moral world:

> In the golden lightning
> Of the sunken Sun—
> O'er which clouds are brightening,
> Thou doest float and run:
> Like an unbodied joy whose race is just begun.
>
> The pale purple even
> Melts around thy flight,
> Like a star of Heaven
> In the broad day-light
> Thou art unseen,—but yet I hear thy shrill delight. (*SPP* 11–20)

Shelley's language conveys the idea that a "blithe Spirit" (*SPP* 1) forms what he takes to be the skylark's core, or originary, essence. That "Spirit" finds expression through images of boundless light, which reflects directly what the skylark is.

Shelley's observation that the skylark pours forth its "full heart" suggests that its "profuse strain" becomes the inexhaustible extension of the skylark's being, coming as it does from its center. The skylark sings not through the instrumental accompaniment of its throat, but directly from its heart, the organ of truth and the origin of its rhythm. Furthermore, emphasis on the fact that the skylark's heart is "full" implies that no part of the bird's being is empty; it exists, apparently, in a pre-subjective state, a state where the loss of castration has no place. These assertions fail to counteract completely, however, that Shelley, in auditing the skylark's song, detects not presence, but absence. When he asserts, in the opening stanza, "Bird thou never wert" (*SPP* 2), he acknowledges the skylark's status as an abstraction, but the statement also implies that the lark, because it remains in a pre-subjective state, has never registered in the symbolic. Though Shelley judges that "from thy presence showers a rain of melody" (*SPP* 35), he also understands that "In broad day-light / Thou art unseen."

Throughout the poem, Shelley consistently chooses images to represent the skylark that involve an absent or hidden agent. Not only is the bird an "unbodied joy" and "a star of Heaven" invisible during the day; it is also "Like a Poet hidden / in the light of thought;" "Like a high-born maiden" singing far up in her "palace tower;" "like a glow-worm ... / Scattering unbeholden / Its aerial hue" (*SPP* 36–7, 41–2, 46, 48–9). And though the lark's spirit of joy evidently flows without risk of running out, its song reminds Shelley of emptiness. An entire "Chorus" of songs celebrating "the praises of love or wine" would be "But an empty vaunt, / A thing wherein we feel there is some hidden want" (*SPP* 64, 69–70). Shelley's assessment of the distinction between the skylark's "strain" and any human facsimile only reminds him that "We look before and after, / And pine for what is not" (*SPP* 86–7). Furthermore, his representation of the lark's expression illustrates that the listener approaches the bird's presence through its voice and music only. In this regard, then, the skylark is no different than the mortal subject-poet who, ideally, the reader approaches by way of voice and music. In its elusiveness, however, the skylark comes to represent the lost object voice, the "thing" fuelling Shelley's desire; it becomes the "thing" he cannot recapture—something he can only approximate in the form of similes and metaphors that, in turn, only confirm his lacking and the vacancy of his language.

What on the one hand function as images conveying the life-giving ministry of the skylark's musical outpourings on the other hand function as images suggesting its voice can be approached through metonyms. Whereas the "Ode to the West Wind" is rich in images involving moving air, the ode "To a Skylark" is replete with images involving moving water. The skylark's song "pourest" from its heart. It inhabits the "golden lighting / Of the sunken sun" where it "floats" and "runs." Shelley observes that "The pale purple even / Melts around thy flight" and that its "voice" fills the night air in the same way that "From one lonely cloud / The moon rains out her beams—and Heaven is overflowed" (*SPP* 27–30). It outperforms "rainbow clouds" from which "there flow not / Drops so bright to see / As from thy presence showers a rain of melody" (*SPP* 33–5), and it ranks above the

> Sound of vernal showers
> On the twinkling grass,
> Rain-awakened flowers,
> All that ever was
> Joyous, and clear and fresh, thy music doth surpass. (*SPP* 56–60)

Shelley also refers to its song as a "flood of rapture" and as a "chrystal stream," and he wonders "What objects are the fountains / Of thy happy strain? (*SPP* 65, 85, 71–2).

This pattern of imagery undercuts the implication running throughout the poem that the skylark's spirit inhabits its song and that Shelley has direct access to the bird's spirit by means of its singing. A more disturbing byproduct of the pattern concerns the skylark's stature as a metaphor of the poet, however. Shelley recognizes the lark's voice only in terms of its ostensibly fluid properties, meaning he comes no closer than a substitute for voice, which, in Lacanian terms, constitutes the bird. Just as the skylark can only be known through its constitutive or, worse, its substitutive forms, so the poet can be known only through his words—signs and tropes that stand in for the voice that is not there. The text of the ode "To a Skylark" becomes a graphic metaphor of this possibility, in the sense that it consists of a profusion of metaphors. Shelley generates the "overflow" as a way of vocalizing what the skylark is fundamentally, but in the end he manages to leave the reader with a string of silent metaphors that fail to present the bird or Shelley in "unpremeditated art." Herein lies the paradox of Shelley's success in failure: he and the skylark *are* what Shelley's language makes them out to be.

Shelley petitions the skylark to "Teach us, Sprite or Bird, / What sweet thoughts are thine" and then narrows the field to, "Teach me half the gladness / that thy brain must know" (*SPP* 61–2, 101–2). These requests reveal Shelley's awareness of his own lacking as a poet. The skylark possesses a quality of thought and feeling that escapes the orientation of the mortal auditor. They also reveal, though, the possibility that, in keeping with Shelley's fantasy, the skylark desires the mortal poet. Correspondence between the two authors, Shelley implies, would produce a union of consciousness that in turn would result in the harmonic marriage of music with word. The skylark's expression extends beyond all conventional "measures / Of delightful sound" and is "Better than all treasures / That in books are found," yet as a "Scorner of the ground" (*SPP* 96–100) the skylark needs others through which to constitute itself in the mortal world of "reality." As an unstructured "overflow," a "flood," of music, it must rely on words and signs to inscribe it, so that it becomes more than a profusion of "unbodied joy."

Shelley's language invests the skylark's music with qualities of *jouissance*. Images throughout the poem identify its song as a perpetual overflow of delight ("a flood of rapture so divine," *SPP* 65); moreover, they suggest that it overmatches all forms of containment and portray its presence as ubiquitous. "All the earth and air / With thy voice is loud," Shelley notes (*SPP* 26–7). He observes, "The blue deep thou wingest, / And singing still dost soar, and soaring ever singest" (*SPP* 9–10). The lark initiates a perpetual cycle of expressive activity. In this regard, it also becomes an image of desire, which knows no end; it "ne'er knew love's sad satiety" (*SPP* 80). Shelley's assessment exposes a paradox that serves his phantasmic vision and closes the gap opened elsewhere in the poem when he says, for example, "I know not how thy joy we ever should come near" (*SPP* 95). Despite the skylark's access to endless "fountains" of joy, its inability to find containment for its expression and thereby find reciprocation for its expression of pure love of existence ironically links it to the poet, for endless desire also characterizes his composing efforts. Knowing "love's sad satiety" confirms the poet's mortality and distinguishes him from the skylark; however, the idea that he finds himself caught in a process of singing that never satisfies establishes his kinship with the immortal skylark.

The affiliation no doubt empowers Shelley to speculate that, if the skylark were to mentor him,

> Such harmonious madness
> From my lips would flow,
> The world should listen then—as I am listening now. (*SPP* 103–5)

In the form of "harmonious madness," his verse would become a perfect blend of concord and discord, of order and disorder, of logos and *jouissance*. In addition, it would assume the same generosity and constancy of the skylark's strain, flowing ostensibly from his heart and mouth to the ears of captive auditors. Moreover, the prospect that he stands to learn "half the gladness" known to the skylark indicates that his "lips" will facilitate the output of two authors. Everything Shelley has said about the nature of the skylark's song and about the distinction between it and mortal expression, however, makes one wonder whether or not such an arrangement would serve well those who would be listening, since the two strains, Shelley's and the skylark's, remain at least partially ("half") foreign to one another.

By claiming that the skylark expresses its "full heart," Shelley implies that the lark lacks nothing. Once Shelley's "lips" temper the lark's music for mortal ears, cutting its delight, it stands to reason that little, if any, of its divine rapture would survive. Either Shelley's "lips" would filter out the lark's boundless joy, with which no mortal reader can identify, or they would serve as the "interpassive" instrument of the skylark's gladness. In that capacity they would ultimately reveal the inertness, the groundlessness, of the lark's unbridled joy. However, by reducing the quantity of the lark's delight by roughly one half, Shelley's lips would become the locus of castration, in that they would announce what the mortal poet does not understand or has not experienced as much as they would articulate what he does know. Perhaps worse, only half of what they say would represent Shelley.

The arrangement would reduce Shelley's presence by 50 percent, making him absent to his own expression at least one half of the time. Shelley's equation of his newfound voice with water by means of the word "flow" widens the faultline even further, since running water serves as a metonym of verbal communication: the flow of moisture accompanies but is not equivalent to the flow of words. Correlative to Shelley's experience that the lark's expression conveys its absence, whatever emerges from Shelley's "lips" will likely lead a "world" of listeners to the same conclusion.

If absence and loss become a focal point in the ode "To a Skylark," castration becomes the most notable phantasmic concern in Shelley's lament over the loss of Keats's voice in the elegy *Adonais*. In Keats's death Shelley finds a mirror image of his own loss of voice, and in demonstrating that the voice of Keats survives in its fundamental, spiritual form, he hopes to construct a fantasy of his own voice surviving. The most striking aspect of Shelley's treatment is that it says almost nothing about the quality or enduring effect of Adonais's, that is, of Keats's, poetry. A steadily fading memory of vocality alone survives Adonais, and Shelley's construction of that vocal potency throughout the poem indicates that Adonais left no indelible record of himself. In stanza two, Shelley claims that one of many "listening Echoes ... / ...with soft enamoured breath, / Rekindled all the fading melodies" (*SPP* 14–16) Adonais had evidently composed. An additional reference to the impact of Adonais's death within the ranks of Echo indicates that one "Lost Echo sits amid the voiceless mountains, / And feeds her grief with his remembered lay" (*SPP* 127–8). Shelley's language, employing terms such as "melodies" and "lay," shifts emphasis away from the realm of inscription and toward the realm of iteration. The Echoes pay homage to Adonais by vocalizing his compositions. Potentially misrepresentative, Shelley's diction creates the impression that Adonais will be known now for his ability as a composer, or songwriter.

Shelley's tribute to the life and accomplishments of Adonais consistently concentrates on the impression left by his voice. In stanza 12, for example, he records,

> Another Splendour on his mouth alit,
> That mouth, whence it was wont to draw the breath
> Which gave it strength to pierce the guarded wit,
> And pass into the panting heart beneath
> With lightning and with music ... (*SPP* 100–4)

The passage suggests that the "breath" of Adonais rather than the words he spoke managed to "pierce" the breast of the reluctant auditor and thereby gain entrance to that person's core. His breath served as the vehicle for "lightning" and "music," media that evidently operate outside the realm of logos. A manifestation of pure thought, lightning strikes, unlike language, suddenly and unexpectedly. A manifestation of pure feeling, music enters the heart and either amplifies or restores its natural rhythm. Adonais's expression provides illumination and supplies vivacity, but as "breath" it emerges as the accompaniment of voice, not voice itself. The image, therefore, chafes against Shelley's implication that the compositions of Adonais consisted of direct emanations from his spirit, the only aspect of him that will survive eternally.

After a brief period of mourning during which Nature grieves the lack of Adonais, a loss that leaves the bucolic world silent and void of echoes, Nature becomes the receptive resting place of Adonais's essence. In grief her mountains become "voiceless" and without the Echoes "a drear / Murmur, between their songs, is all the woodmen hear" (*SPP* 134–5). In her care,

> He is made one with Nature: there is heard
> His voice in all her music, from the moan
> Of thunder, to the song of night's sweet bird;
> He is a presence to be felt and known
> In darkness and in light, from herb and stone,
> Spreading itself where'er that Power may move
> Which has withdrawn his being to its own. (*SPP* 370–6)

As the voice of Adonais blends with Nature's music, with "the moan / Of thunder" and "the song of the night's sweet bird," it increases in range, becoming ubiquitous and renewable, and it gains potency; however, his voice loses its individuality as Power withdraws his presence into "its own." Under these conditions, Adonais no longer qualifies as a poet because he no longer speaks his mind or does so with distinction. Once he becomes indistinguishable from the natural signs that constitute him, he will cease to be a subject poet, a presence that ideally can be reached through the medium of words.

Shelley compromises his fantasy of the poet's immortality at several points in *Adonais*, but perhaps no more decisively than in the elegy's closing stanzas, which formulaically celebrate the triumph of Adonais over life and his critics. Shelley consoles the survivors of Adonais, including those reading the poem dedicated to his memory, with such assertions as, "He has outsoared the shadow of our night" (*SPP* 352); "He lives, he wakes—'tis death is dead, not he" (*SPP* 361); "The One remains, the many change and pass" (*SPP* 460). Shelley heartens himself by claiming that "the low wind whispers near: / 'Tis Adonais calls!" and asserting that "The breath whose might I have invoked in song / Descends on me" (*SPP* 475–6, 487–8). By invoking the "breath" of Adonais, Shelley calls upon a substitute for the voice of Adonais. Though "breath" accompanies voice, as Urania learns in stanzas 25 and 26, voice does not always accompany breath. What "descends" on Shelley fills him with Adonais's influence, but it does not enable the recovery of this lost voice. Shelley's earlier remark that "Adonais calls" in the form of a "low wind" that "whispers near," conveys the same reality. The call takes the substitute form of the wind whispering, becoming the equivalent of "drear murmur" heard by "woodmen" once Adonais's death causes Echo to remove her substitute voice from the world. Both forms of communication signal absence rather than presence.

The arrival of Urania intimidates Death and temporarily restores life to the body of Adonais. According to Shelley, "breath / Revisited those lips, and life's pale light / Flashed through those limbs, so late her dear delight" (*SPP* 219–21). As a representative of poetry and inspiration, Urania nurtured Adonais's gift when he was alive, yet not even she can resurrect his voice. Death leaves and "breath" returns to the "lips" of Adonais, but his voice and his music remain absent. Urania evidently understands that "breath" signals the absence, rather than the presence, of Adonais, for in her despair she exclaims, "'Leave me not wild and drear and comfortless, / As silent lightning leaves the starless night!'" (*SPP* 222–3). Urania recognizes that her existence now becomes the mirror image of Adonais's, in that it lacks sonic accompaniment (ostensibly thunder to go along with lightning) and illumination. She begs him to

> "Stay yet awhile! speak to me once again;
> Kiss me, so long but as a kiss may live;
> And in my heartless breast and burning brain
> That word, that kiss shall all thoughts else survive...." (*SPP* 226–30)

Her statement implies that poetry cannot survive without voice. Adonais's inability to "speak to [her] once again" places her at a loss and relegates her to an endless cycle of desire. Urania's desperation evidently causes her to confuse a kiss with a word, though in the end the error makes no difference, since neither will embody the presence of Adonais.

The loss of Adonais becomes a metaphor of castration. By cutting Adonais from the world, death has removed his distinctive voice from the universal phonic field. To Shelley's mind the stroke impoverishes the mortal world, leaving it lacking, even if in ways noticeable only to Shelley and his fellow poets who come to mourn Adonais. The poem *Adonais* portrays a world that wounds all mortals and especially all poets. In the case of poets, the literary establishment performs the role of "big Other," except that in the case of Keats, Shelley, Byron and Moore its authority is apparently neither spectral nor diminished as a result of its action. In stanza 17 Shelley observes that "Albion wails" its loss in the fashion of an "eagle" circling its "empty nest" (*SPP* 147–50), both suffering from privation. He then curses with the mark of "Cain" the reviewer "who pierced thy innocent breast, / And scared the angel soul that was its earthly guest!" (*SPP* 152–3). The song of Adonais exhibited similar penetrative properties, but its ability to disarm "the guarded wit" and "pass into the panting heart beneath" represents an act of addition rather than subtraction.

Poetry's representatives in *Adonais* all bear wounds. The implication is that they continue to function as writers despite them. The irony is that these wounds enable them to function as language producing subjects. Shelley records, for example, that Urania rushed from her "secret Paradise" when she finally acknowledged the death of Adonais, and that

> she sped,
> Through camps and cities rough with stone, and steel,
> And human hearts, which to her aery tread
> Yielding not, wounded the invisible
> Palms of her tender feet where'er they fell:
> And barbed tongues, and thoughts more sharp than they
> Rent the soft Form they never could repel .... (*SPP* 208–14)

Unaccompanied by the voice of Adonais, Urania finds herself unwelcome in the world, unable to penetrate hard "human hearts" and to place her feet on the ground of mortal reality.

The more notable mourners of Adonais have fared little better. "Fame" wounds Byron, to whom Shelley refers as the "Pilgrim of Eternity," forcing him to suppress the full force of his language—"veiling all the lightnings of his song / In sorrow" (*SPP* 264, 267). Thomas Moore bears the scars of the Irish people. Shelley calls him "The sweetest lyrist of her saddest wrong, / And love taught grief to fall like music from his tongue" (*SPP* 269–70). Finally, Shelley portrays himself as the proud, world-weary martyr whose potent language (troped as the phallic "light spear topped with a cypress cone" from Dionysian tradition) "Vibrated, as the ever-beating heart" (*SPP* 291, 294). Of himself, Shelley recalls that "He came the last, neglected and apart; / A herd-abandoned deer struck by the hunter's dart" (*SPP* 296–7). Though hounded by literary critics and merciless public opinion, Shelley stays true to his mission and maintains his core values and his integrity. As a metaphor of poetry, the image of the vibrating spear suggests that Shelley's writings emerge directly from his heart, delivering that which is most valuable in him, his secret treasure, his presence, to the world. As a constituent image in Shelley's fantasy, the wound left by castration in the form of the "hunter's dart" enables Shelley to speak the penetrating truth to a hostile world, though all it has done is strip away affectation. A paradox, Shelley's self-portrait demonstrates his desire to have it both ways.

The narrative Shelley devotes to the demise of Adonais constructs the poet's death as a loss of vocal presence. By silencing the voice of Adonais, fiendish critics have struck a blow against all poetry. When Shelley advises Urania to "let thy loud heart keep / Like his, a mute and uncomplaining sleep" (*SPP* 22–3), he implies that Adonais has lost his voice in death. Subsequent references to the reactions of Dreams and Echoes depict their futile effort to recall and then preserve that voice. Suitably, Shelley describes the mourning of Adonais as a wet, tear-filled event. One particular Dream "faded, like a cloud which had outwept its rain," while other remnants of Adonais's noble mind "Came in slow pomp;—the moving pomp might seem / Like pageantry of mist on an autumnal stream" (*SPP* 90, 116–7). Even "Pale Ocean," says Shelley, "in unquiet slumber lay, / And the wild winds flew round, sobbing in their dismay" (*SPP* 125–6). Wind and water images connote the outpouring of emotion experienced by all who knew Adonais, but they also italicize the reality that metonyms are all that remains of his marvelous voice. Combining this pattern of images with Shelley's appraisal of Adonais's vocal power—that his breath could penetrate the ears of even the most skeptical auditor—exposes a seam in the narrative fabric; the pattern reveals the unsettling possibility that the powerful utterance of Adonais was produced by castration, the "death" that made Adonais a subject. Shelley's story fails to overcome the typical narrative deadlock of installing Adonais at a point before his own formation as a subject. Such is the way of desire.

Shelley desires the vocal potency with which his imagination invests Adonais, and he desires the desire of such contemporary poets as Byron and Moore, who mourn the loss of a fellow "shepherd." Furthermore, if Urania represents inspiration and poetry, he desires to serve as medium, and, finally, he desires the desire of the reader, whom he implicitly addresses each time he announces the exhortation "O Weep for Adaonais" (*SPP* 19) or reaches out rhetorically in dialogic statement: "What softer voice is hushed over the dead?;" "Our Adonais has drunk poison—oh!;" "Peace, peace! he is not dead, he doth not sleep;" "Who mourns for Adonais? oh come forth / Fond wretch! and know thyself and him aright" (*SPP* 307, 316, 343, 415–16). Shelley would have been aware of the specular aspects of his elegy. He writes in honor of the departed Keats, but the reader of *Adonais* regards the poem as a record left by the deceased Percy Shelley. Personal experience would have exposed Shelley to the intimacies of reading and would have exposed him to the idea that reading a poem, as Andrew Bennett points out, is equivalent to listening to a ghost. Engaged readers search for the originary presence, for the secret treasure, of an author. Elegiac laments that formulaically aim at placing someone's death within a communal context also perform the function of creating a bond between the elegist and the elegist's readers.

The elegy provides a perfect fantasy vehicle for Shelley, because it creates a situation in which the voice of the elegist now speaks for the deceased, effectively overcoming the wound of castration. Memorialized in Shelley's words, the voice of Adonais survives Keats in mythic form. The union produces a marriage of Adonais's musical breath with Shelley's words. Keats became a "presence to be felt and known," like Power's "Spirit of BEAUTY," the Autumn's breath in the form of the West Wind or the heavenly raptures announced by Shelley's skylark, and that "presence" spreads "itself where'er that Power may move / Which has withdrawn his being to its own." Though an abstraction, a ghost, Keats re-enters the world in Shelley's *Adonais*. Shelley's elegy, in turn, maintains the "presence" of that "Power" for all eternity, theoretically, or at least as long as poets and readers exist. The death of Keats results, therefore, in the return of Shelley's lost object voice, but not without a reminder that Shelley gets no closer to Keats's presence than Keats's "breath," which in this context confirms Shelley's substitute role.

Shelley sings in the absence of Adonais and the song he composes is all that remains of Shelley; it serves as his expressive substitute. The last few lines of the poem reinforce this possibility by implicitly comparing Shelley to Dante's Ulysses setting out on his final voyage. What Shelley observes, "The massy earth and sphered skies are riven! / I am borne darkly, fearfully, afar" (*SPP* 491–2), his use of the word "borne" reveals the deadlock he cannot escape. Finding the "presence" of Adonais has given him new life, but it has also implicated him in the cycle of death necessary for authorship. Even if Shelley risks perversity by adopting the death of Keats as an occasion for installing himself in the position of the instrument which speaks in Keats's stead for all the ages, the maneuver cannot foreclose on its undesirable opposite, in which Keats's death provides the opportunity to compose a poem that becomes the "interpassive" instrument speaking in Shelley's stead. Within this scenario, the apparently active Shelley becomes the absent author constituting himself in the form of *Adonais*.

Though soberly portrayed in *A Defence of Poetry*, Shelley's relationship with Power in many of his poems exhibits an emotional charge and range of instability similar to what appears in the poems he composed for musically talented women. In both cases one finds a desire for the desire of the other. Jane, Claire and Sophia could evidently be just as flirtatious as Power and it might have been their independence as much as the prospect of retrieving something lost that motivated Shelley to write so many poems for them. If Shelley's accounts of his relationship with Power are reliable, it would appear that Power might have proved more worthy of his devotion than any woman, and even though he must have known early that the two would never converge permanently, he also must have known that it regularly provided him with the magic required for composition. It provided him with a prospect to recover from loss no woman could match.

Though Shelley's poems concerned with the operations of Power pronounce various degrees of desperation, the existence of those poems testifies to Shelley's faith that Power operated through him, as it had through the minds of Dante, Milton and others, and that the existence of a secret treasure within him went, therefore, without question. At most, the "chasm of an insufficient void" of which he complains in the essay "On Love" would have been the source of periodic suffering. Without it, Shelley no doubt recognized, there would be no desire, and without desire there would be no poetry. In this regard, it would seem that Shelley's statement in *A Defence of Poetry*, that even when poets wish to "deny or abjure, they are yet compelled to serve, the Power which is seated upon the throne of their own soul," he has come to terms with the fact that Power's behavior is both necessary and desirable.

Conclusion
Fantasy and Renunciation

In this book I have tried to establish that a large portion of Shelley's writing consists of a fantasy in which Shelley seeks the unification of language, or the word, with voice and its correlative form of expression, vocal music. Achievement of this goal would grant the poet immortality in the sense that his poems would sustain his voice for all time, granting him eternal authority. The problem with Shelley's project is that it consistently winds up in a state of suspension, as anything he gains is almost simultaneously offset by a loss. Deadlock and instability plague his fantasy at every turn. Zizek reminds us that the very nature of fantasy involves exposing the horror it means to conceal, and in Shelley's case that horror might involve something far more disturbing than just the loss of masculine authority.

Zizek's application of Kierkegaard's triad to Wagner provides a useful model for summarizing the function of fantasy in Shelley's writing. According to Zizek, the triad consists of three versions of the impossible sexual relationship. In the "aesthetic" mode, the subject indulges passion in the hope of attaining the pure, "incestuous" relationship; in the "ethical" mode, the subject channels drives into acceptable avenues, such as marriage; in the "religious" mode, the subject renounces fulfillment completely and translates the pursuit of fulfillment into a spiritual quest.[1] If one were to conceive of this model as a progression, it would appear that as one climbed the ladder, so to speak, "the pressure of prohibition and/or impossibility gets stronger;" however, those elements "*loosen*," says Zizek, because the "religious" mode permits total enjoyment outside the law, with love and lover maintained in an inviolable state of suspension—unchanged by act and firmly masked, because consummation remains unreachable and in actuality undesirable.[2] Zizek observes, "If an aesthetical endeavor to seize the full moment ends in fiasco and utter loss, paradoxically, religious renunciation, the elevation of the lady into an untouchable and unattainable object, leads to the trance of enjoyment that transgresses the limits of the Law."[3]

The deadlocks that emerge throughout Shelley's fantasy qualify as moments of suspension that ultimately produce just such a "trance of enjoyment," because they function collectively as a safety feature designed to keep Power, voice, and the music of feminine expression at a safe distance. Whereas Kierkegaard's "triad," according to Zizek, consists of a progression that leads ironically to enjoyment,

---

[1] Slavoj Zizek, "There is No Sexual Relationship," *Gaze and Voice as Love Objects*, ed. Renata Salecl and Slavoj Zizek (Durham and London: Duke UP, 1996) 209.

[2] Zizek 211; 212.

[3] Zizek 212.

the progression flattens out in Shelley's writing so that the operation of each mode ultimately produces one uniform effect. By facilitating renunciation, each mode protects Shelley from the horrors his fantasy aims to conceal. Without renunciation Shelley would have had to confront these unsettling prospects: that the recovery of voice annihilates subjectivity; that correspondence with Power jeopardizes personal initiative and volition; that immersion in currents of feminine expression threatens the integrity of the word.

Shelley defends against liabilities such as these and thereby maintains his status and function as a poet by creating conditions under which it appears that Power, voice and woman are unattainable or in some situations that they have renounced him. Throughout his writing, Power and its various agents of expression ignore Shelley's entreaties. Voice tantalizes him by appearing in substitute forms, and musical women remain behind social and institutional barriers. Frustrations such as these shield Shelley from the possibility of full confrontation (which would expose him to the vulgar aspects of each object, that zero point of being which shatters all desire) at the same time that they force him to consider the potential impossibility of his ultimate goal.

In narrative and dramatic poems focused on heterosexual couplings, Shelley, through his characters, operates in the "aesthetic" mode. Prometheus and Asia, Lionel and Helen, Laon and Cythna, the Poet and veiled maid and, to a certain extent, Shelley and Emily succeed at achieving the ideal of incestuous consummation, though genre provides Shelley with a ready-made fantasy framework that allows him to distance himself from the disastrous fallout of such relationships. The third act of *Prometheus Unbound*, for example, suggests that once Prometheus and Asia reunite their lives devolve to a state of suspended animation, a life in death. Laon and Cythna experience a parallel fate. Immolation ushers them to a subliminal realm in which they exist primarily in a storied past. Helen's devotion to Lionel delivers her to the static life of an exile, haunted by the past and pining for home. Similarly, the Poet's visionary consummation with the veiled maid empties his mind and his world of all mortal hope and passion, the very things that make us human. And finally, the prospect of sexual union with Emily enables Shelley to escape the stultifying laws of his community, yet the island paradise to which he brings her subjects them both to a non-historical life of forced isolation.

As a metaphor, each of these outcomes suggests that consummating the fantasy of fusing word with voice and music fails to produce either endlessly expressive life, or endlessly living expression. Shelley's fantasy delivers these results by way of narrative poetry, the form of which counteracts and, therefore, paradoxically facilitates renunciation of the success it seems to promote. To function as the uninvolved author of a poem's storyline is to give fictional expression to desire without running the risk of suffering its social and philosophical pitfalls. Narrative permits indulgence, in other words, without forcing the narrator to suffer the "aesthetic" consequences of indulgence.

The lyrics Shelley composed for Jane, Sophia and Claire illustrate Kierkegaard's concept of operating in the "ethical" mode, whereas Shelley's poems devoted to the mind's relationship with Power and the essay *A Defence of Poetry* exemplify Kierkegaard's notion of operating in the "religious" mode. In many of the lyrics, Shelley characteristically portrays his wife, Mary, his friend Edward Williams, and various iterations of social protocol and legal restraint as inconvenient or unwanted impediments. However, marriage, family bonds and generic conventions relevant to lyric expression provide distance from the desired object and preserve the integrity of Shelley's goal, allowing him to spiritualize his relationship with the three women whose music attracted him while paradoxically disclosing his desire for corporeal intimacies. The strategy performs two functions: it preserves the alluring magic of each woman's music, and it releases each correspondent from the responsibility of having to terminate their relationship. Both elements sustain desire.

Elements of the "religious" mode inform *A Defence of Poetry* and poems focusing on the creative process, but not as one would expect. In these writings, it would appear that Power renounces the poet, stringing him along in order to ensure his loyal service. The poet, according to Shelley, has no choice but to comply, no matter diligently he commits himself to renounce it, to "deny and abjure" his calling. The arrangement ultimately serves Shelley's purposes, however, because it ensures the enduring necessity of language. If Power were to become a steady expressive force in human experience, mediation might become unnecessary. Because each person would have direct access to its presence, no one would require the poet's intervention.

Regarding the application of Kierkegaard's triad to sexual relations, Zizek notes that the adulterous relationship, which promises access to an ideal union forbidden within the symbolic world of monogamous marriage and sexual fidelity, offers a false escape that in the end winds up supporting the symbolic construct. When the adulterous relationship fails, the adulterers are forced to fall back on their marriages, having learned that there is nothing beyond them, the alternatives amounting to empty promises. According to Zizek, the attempt to escape the emptiness of marriage forces one up against the possibility that all options create the same vacuum. Applying the triad to Shelley's writing reveals the operation of a similar current of recognition, or borderline recognition, running across the landscape of Shelley's fantasy. Without the commitment to renunciation, the confluence of word, voice and music remains an apparently reachable possibility; if these modes of expression were somehow to merge, however, the need for meaning, and maybe even meaning itself, might vanish.

Shelley's writing conveys the idea that Power ignores his advances; however, once one recognizes that the dynamic is a product of Shelley's fantasy, the possibility arises that this is what Shelley truly desires. In the "Hymn to Intellectual Beauty" he speculates that "Man" would be "immortal and omnipotent" should the "Spirit of BEAUTY" become the mind's constant companion. Perhaps Shelley desires that Power should remain inconstant as a way of protecting himself from the possibility that the marriage of Power and the poet's mind would erase, or void, the poet's humanity, eliminating all desire and aspiration in the process of transforming "Man" into a divine creature. The fate of Prometheus and Asia in Act 3 of *Prometheus Unbound* becomes a metaphor of this horror. The couple has earned immortality and eternal companionship, but they have lost all touch with humanity and its unlimited potential for suffering, which requires constant vigilance and proactive initiative to keep in check. The union of Prometheus and Asia appears to have lost this capacity and in many ways their coupling epitomizes what Shelley recognized as the great flaw in the domestic union: it limits love (which cannot survive without desire) and, therefore, produces a life of suspension. This explains why the heterosexual and heteroerotic models informing Shelley's fantasy of ideal expression and immortal authority are fundamentally flawed.

The unification of word with voice and music, as illustrated by the union of Prometheus and Asia, forecloses on desire and on subjectivity, or on what is commonly regarded as identity. Just as the recovery of the lost object voice would cancel out subjectivity altogether, so the confluence of language and vocal expression would eliminate the possibility of meaningful expression as Shelley knew it, and, perhaps even more alarming, the need for expression at all. Again, whether or not Shelley recognized in full the implications of his fantasy does not appear to matter. The subject's awareness of his or her "factor" fails to benefit the subject. To reiterate a powerful comment from Zizek I quoted earlier, such awareness "somehow 'depossesses' the subject, reducing her or him to a puppet-like level 'beyond dignity and freedom.'"[4] The deadlocks and inconsistencies characterizing Shelley's fantasy of becoming the eternally vocal poet in the end insure that his desire to unite word, voice and music by means of heterosexual and heteroerotic union does not succeed. Only through failure and renunciation can Shelley maintain his identity, his authority, his subjectivity and, perhaps most importantly, his humanity.

---

[4] Slavoj Zizek, *The Plague of Fantasies* (London and New York: Verso, 1997) 8.

Bibliography

Anderson, Erland. *Harmonious Madness: A Study of Musical Metaphors in the Poetry of Coleridge, Shelley and Keats*. Salzburg: Institut fur Sprache und Literatur, U of Salzburg, 1975.

Bennett, Andrew. *Romantic Poets and the Culture of Posterity*. Cambridge: Cambridge UP, 1999.

Bieri, James. *Percy Bysshe Shelley: A Biography*. 2 vols. Newark: U of Delaware P, 2004.

Bonca, Teddi Chichester. *Shelley's Mirrors of Love: Narcissism, Sacrifice, and Sorority*. Albany: State U of New York P, 1999.

Brisman, Susan Hawk. "'Unsaying His High Language': The Problem of Voice in *Prometheus Unbound*." *Studies in Romanticism* 16 (Winter 1977): 51–86.

Brown, Nathaniel. *Sexuality and Feminism in Shelley*. Cambridge: Harvard UP, 1979.

Brown, Richard E. "The Role of Dante in *Epipsychidion*." *Comparative Literature* 30 (1978): 223–35.

Chandler, James. *England in 1819: The Politics of Literary Culture and the Case of Romantic Historicism*. Chicago and London: The U of Chicago P, 1998.

Chernaik, Judith. *The Lyrics of Shelley*. Cleveland and London: Case Western Reserve UP, 1972.

Claridge, Laura. *Romantic Potency: The Paradox of Desire*. Ithaca and London: Cornell UP, 1992.

Clarke, George Elliott. "Racing Shelley, or Reading *The Cenci* as a Gothic Slave Narrative." *European Romantic Review* 11 (Spring 2000): 168–85.

Colbert, Benjamin. *Shelley's Eye: Travel Writing and Aesthetic Vision*. Aldershot: Ashgate, 2005.

Cronin, Richard. "Shelleyan Incest and the Romantic Legacy." *Keats–Shelley Journal* 45 (1996): 61–76.

De Palacio, Jean L. "Music and Musical Themes in Shelley's Poetry." *Modern Language Review* 59 (1964): 345–59.

Dolar, Mladen. "The Object Voice." *Gaze and Voice as Love Objects*. Ed. Renata Salecl and Slavoj Zizek. Durham and London: Duke UP, 1996: 7–31.

Duffy, Cian. "'The Child of the Fierce Hour.' Shelley and Napolean Bonaparte." *Studies in Romanticism* 43 (Fall 2004): 399–416.

———. *Shelley and the Revolutionary Sublime*. Cambridge: Cambridge UP, 2005.

Fenner, Theodore. *Leigh Hunt and Opera Criticism: The "Examiner" Years, 1808–1821*. Lawrence: UP of Kansas, 1972.

Ferber, Michael. "Shelley and 'the Disastrous Fame of Conquerors.'" *Keats–Shelley Journal* 51 (2002): 145–73.

Fischman, Susan. "'Like the Sound of His Own Voice': Gender, Audition and Echo in *Alastor*." *Keats–Shelley Journal* 43 (1994): 141–69.

Foss, Chris. "Shelley's Revolution in Poetic Language." *European Romantic Review* 9 (Fall 1998): 501–18.

Fraistat, Neil. "The Material Shelley: Who Gets the Finger in *Queen Mab*?" *The Wordsworth Circle* 33 (Winter 2002): 33–6.

Fulford, Tim. "Conducting the Vital Fluid: The Politics and Poetics of Mesmerism in the 1790's." *Studies in Romanticism* 43 (Spring 2004): 57–78.

Gallant, Christine. *Shelley's Ambivalence*. New York: St. Martin's P, 1989.

Gelpi, Barbara Charlesworth. *Shelley's Goddess: Maternity, Language, Subjectivity*. New York and Oxford: Oxford UP, 1992.

———. "Keeping Faith with Desire: A Reading of *Epipsychidion*." *Evaluating Shelley*. Ed. Timothy Clark and Jerrold Hogle. Edinburgh: Edinburgh UP, 1996: 180–96.

Goslee, Nancy. "Depersoning Emily: Drafting as Plot in *Epipsychidion*." *Keats–Shelley Journal* 42 (1993): 104–19.

———. "Shelley's Cosmopolitan 'Discourse': Ancient Greek Manners and Modern Liberty." *The Wordsworth Circle* 36 (Winter 2005): 2–5.

Harrison, Margot. "No Way for a Victim to Act? Beatrice Cenci and the Dilemma of Romantic Performance." *Studies in Romanticism* 39 (Summer 2000): 187–211.

Hazlitt, William. *The Complete Works of William Hazlitt*. Ed. P. P. Howe. 21 vols. New York: AMS P, 1967.

Hildebrand, William. "Naming Day in Asia's Vale." *Keats–Shelley Journal* 32 (1983): 190–203.

Hoagwood, Terence. "Rev. of *Shelley's Eye: Travel Writing and Aesthetic Vision*, by Benjamin Colbert; *Shelley and the Revolutionary Sublime*, by Cian Duffy; *Shelley and Vitality*, by Sharon Ruston." *The Wordsworth Circle* 37 (Autumn 2006): 249–52.

Holmes, Richard. *Shelley: The Pursuit*. Elisabeth Sifton Books, 1974.

Homans, Margaret. *Women Writers and Poetic Identity*. Princeton: Princeton UP, 1980.

Hubbell, Andrew J. "Laon and Cythna: A Vision of Regency Romanticism." *Keats–Shelley Journal* 51 (2002): 174–97.

Hughes, D. J. "Coherence and Collapse in Shelley, with Particular Reference to *Epipsychidion*." *ELH* 28 (1961): 260–83

Hunt, Leigh. *The Autobiography of Leigh Hunt*. Oxford: Oxford UP, 1928.

Johnson, Samuel. *A Dictionary of the English Language*. 2 vols. London, 1755.

Keach, William. *Shelley's Style*. New York and London: Methuen, 1984.

———. *Arbitrary Power: Romanticism, Language, Politics*. Princeton: Princeton UP, 2004.

Kirchoff, Frederick. "Shelley's *Alastor*." *Keats–Shelley Journal* 32 (1983): 108–22.
Kramer, Lawrence. *Music and Poetry: The Nineteenth Century and After*. Berkeley: U of California P, 1984.
Lacan, Jacques. *The Four Fundamental Concepts of Psychoanalysis*. Ed. Jacques-Alain Miller. Trans. Alan Sheridan. New York and London: W. W. Norton & Company, 1981.
Leask, Nigel. "Shelley's Magnetic Ladies." *Beyond Romanticism*. Ed. Stephen Copley and John Whale. London and New York: Routledge, 1992: 52–78.
——. *British Romantic Writers and the East: Anxieties of Empire*. Cambridge: Cambridge UP, 1992.
Leighton, Angela. "Love, Writing and Scepticism in *Epipsychidion*." *The New Shelley: Later Twentieth-Century Views*. Ed. G. Kim Blank. New York: St. Martin's, 1991: 220–41.
Linkin, Harriet Kramer. "Shelley's Power as Perceiver." *European Romantic Review* 4 (Winter 1994): 151–62.
McConnell, Frank. "Shelleyan 'Allegory': *Epipsychidion*." *Keats–Shelley Journal* 20 (1971): 100–12.
McDayter, Ghislaine. "'O'er Leaping the Bounds': The Sexing of the Creative Soul in Shelley's *Epipsychidion*." *Keats–Shelley Journal* 52 (2003): 21–49.
McGann, Jerome. "The Secrets of an Elder Day: Shelley after *Hellas*." *Keats–Shelley Journal* 15 (1966): 25–41.
Mellor, Anne K. ed. *Romanticism and Feminism*. Bloomington: Indiana UP, 1988.
——. *Romanticism and Gender*. New York: Routledge, 1993.
Molinari, Lori. "Revising the Revolution: The Festival of Unity and Shelley's Beau Ideal." *Keats–Shelley Journal* 53 (2004): 97–126.
O'Neill, Michael. "*Adonais* and Poetic Power." *The Wordsworth Circle* 35 (Spring 2004): 50–7.
Peterfreund, Stuart. "Shelley, Monboddo, Vico, and the Language of Poetry." *Style* 15 (1981): 382–400.
——. *Shelley among Others: The Play of the Intertext and the Idea of Language*. Baltimore and London: The Johns Hopkins UP, 2002.
Potkay, Monica Brzezinsky. "Incest as Theology in Shelley's *The Cenci*." *The Wordsworth Circle* 35 (Spring 2004): 57–65.
Quillin, Jessica K. "'An Assiduous Frequenter of the Italian Opera': Shelley's *Prometheus Unbound* and the Opera Buffa." Opera and Romanticism-Praxis Series. Romantic Circles, www.re.umd.edu/praxis/opera/quillin/quillin.html#top.
——. "Shelleyan Lyricism and the Romantic Historicization of Musical Aesthetics." *Keats–Shelley Journal* 54 (2005): 133–47.
Randel, Fred V. "Shelley's Revision of Coleridgean Traditionalism in *Lines Written among the Euganean Hills*." *Keats–Shelley Journal* 51 (2002): 145–73.

Reiman, Donald H. and Michael O'Neill, eds. *The Manuscripts of the Younger Romantics. Percy Bysshe Shelley. Fair-Copy Manuscripts of Shelley's Poems in European and American Libraries*. Vol. 8. New York and London: Garland Publishing, 1997.

Richardson, Alan. "Romanticism and the Colonization of the Feminine." *Romanticism and Feminism*. Ed. Anne K. Mellor. Bloomington: Indiana UP, 1988: 13–25.

Rogers, Neville. "More Music at Marlow." *Keats–Shelley Memorial Bulletin* 5 (1953): 20–5.

Roussetzki, Remy. "Aggravating Shakespeare: Endless Violence in Shelley's and in Musset's Theater of Anxiety." *European Romantic Review* 15 (December 2004): 493–510.

Ruston, Sharon. *Shelley and Vitality*. Basingstoke: Palgrave Macmillan, 2005.

Schapiro, Barbara. *The Romantic Mother: Narcissistic Patterns in Romantic Poetry*. Baltimore and London: The Johns Hopkins UP, 1983.

Schmid, Thomas. "'England Yet Sleeps': Intertextuality, Nationalism, and Risorgimento in Percy Bysshe Shelley's *Swellfoot the Tyrant*." *Keats–Shelley Journal* 53 (2004): 61–84.

Schulze, Earl. "The Dantean Quest of *Epipsychidion*." *Studies in Romanticism* 21 (Summer 1982): 191–216.

Steinman, Lisa. "Shelley's Scepticism." *ELH* 45 (1978): 255–69.

Stouffer, Andrew M. "Celestial Temper: Shelley and the Masks of Anger." *Keats–Shelley Journal* 49 (2000): 138–61.

Shelley, Mary. *The Letters of Mary Wollstonecraft Shelley*. Ed. Betty T. Bennett. 3 vols. Baltimore and London: The Johns Hopkins UP, 1980–8.

———. *The Journals of Mary Shelley: 1814–1844*. Ed. Paula R. Feldman and Diana Scott-Kilvert. Baltimore and London: The Johns Hopkins UP, 1987.

Shelley, Percy. *The Letters of Percy Bysshe Shelley*. Ed. Frederick L. Jones. 2 vols. Oxford: Clarendon P, 1964.

———. *Shelley: Poetical Works*. Ed. Thomas Hutchinson. Corr. G. M. Mathews. Oxford and New York: Oxford UP, 1970.

———. *Shelley's Poetry and Prose*. Ed. Donald H. Reiman and Neil Fraistat. New York and London: W. W. Norton & Company, 2002.

Tetreault, Ronald. "Shelley at the Opera." *ELH* 48 (1981): 144–71.

Thurston, Norman. "Author, Narrator and Hero in Shelley's *Alastor*." *Studies in Romanticism* 14 (Spring 1975): 119–31.

Ulmer, William. *Shelleyan Eros: The Rhetoric of Romantic Love*. Princeton: Princeton UP, 1990.

Wasserman, Earl. *Shelley: A Critical Reading*. Baltimore: The Johns Hopkins UP, 1971.

White, Newman I. *Shelley*. 2 vols. New York: Alfred A. Knopf, 1940.

Wilson, Eric Glenn. "Shelley and the Poetics of Glaciers." *The Wordsworth Circle* 36 (Spring 2005): 53–6.

Wolfson, Susan. *Formal Charges: The Shaping of Poetry in British Romanticism*. Stanford: Stanford UP, 1997.

Wood, Gillen D'Arcy. "Cockney Mozart: The Hunt Circle, the King's Theater and *Don Giovanni*." *Studies in Romanticism* 44 (Fall 2005): 367–97.

Wroe, Ann. *Being Shelley: The Poet's Search for Himself*. New York: Pantheon Books, 2007.

Zizek, Slavoj. "There Is No Sexual Relationship." *Gaze and Voice as Love Objects*. Ed. Renata Salecl and Slavoj Zizek. Durham and London: Duke UP, 1996: 208–49.

———. *The Plague of Fantasies*. London and New York: Verso, 1997.

Index

Note: numbers in brackets preceded by *n* refer to footnotes.

acting 13
Adonais 13, 149, 180–5
   castration in 180, 182, 184
   death in 182–5
   immortality fantasy in 181–182
   Nature in 181
   poets in 182–3
   Shelley's self-portrait in 183, 184
   voice/breath in 180–1, 183–4
   void in 181
adultery 14, 25–6, 189
"Aeolian Harp, The" (Coleridge) 13
aesthetics 2–3, 4, 8, 12–14, 45(*n*3), 188
   and erotic fantasy 169, 187, 188
   and power 147, 150, 151
   and self-presence 157–8, 159
afflatus 142, 172, 175
agalma 96, 124, 165
air/fluid imagery 27–8, 30–1, 137–8, 143, 150, 155–6, 162, 163, 167–8, 172–5, 180–2, 185
   and desire 31, 88–9
   and feminine expression 35, 38, 47, 57–8, 60, 91, 127
   and music/poetry 3
   and void 62, 115, 121–2, 124–5, 133
   see also breath; wind
Alastor 1, 7, 10, 38, 39
   Arab maiden in 45–6
   interpassivity in 43, 45–51
   jouissance in 46–7, 50–1
   music in 45(*n*2), 46–9
   Nature in 49–50
   objet petit a in 48–9
   poet-narrator relation in 45–7, 45(*n*3), 48–9, 50–1
   veiled maid in 46–9, 50, 51, 62

Anderson, Erland 2–3, 32–3, 45(*n*2)
anti-Mozart "cabal" 16–17
antitype/prototype 28–9, 35–6, 59, 83, 129, 153, 160–1
Arnold, Matthew 13
Arve River 147, 160
Asia (*Prometheus Unbound*) 44, 70, 72, 73–7, 188
   and conch shell 77, 78
authorship 69

Bacon, Francis 154, 157
Beauty 164–6, 167–70, 176, 189
Bennett, Andrew 7–8, 175(*n*22), 184
Bible 12
Bieri, James 83, 100, 101, 110, 114, 137, 141
"big Other" 36, 127, 151, 182
   law as 25, 92, 95, 96, 127, 163, 172
Billington, Mrs 33
Bonca, Teddi Chichester 19(*n*59), 52
breath 47–50, 53, 57–8, 78, 113, 124, 127–9, 142–4, 174, 175
   and absence/loss 104–5, 133
   as erotic image 89–90, 138
   see also air/fluid imagery
Brisman, Susan Hawk 67(*n*15)
Brown, Nathaniel 101(*n*18)
Brown, Richard E. 88
Brzezinski Potkay, Monica 12
Byron, Lord 13, 83, 182, 183

Caroline of Brunswick 14
castration 43, 46, 50, 69, 71, 76(*n*24), 81, 99, 104–5, 106, 180
   pre-castration fantasy 90–1, 142, 144, 173
   and reading 175
castrato 116, 145
Cenci, The 12–14, 16

Chandler, James 14, 16, 147, 173(*n*19)
Chernaik, Judith 111(*n*33), 141
Childe Harold's Pilgrimage (Byron) 13
Christianity 12
Clairmont, Claire 2, 29, 31, 32, 33, 40, 83, 92, 95, 96, 100, 140–5
   musical ability of 141
   Shelley's poem to *see* "To Constantia"
   Shelley's relationship with 140–1
Claridge, Laura 6–7, 8, 67(*n*15), 76(*n*24)
Clarke, George Elliott 12
class 16–17
Colbert, Benjamin 12
Coleridge, Samuel Taylor 13
conch shell metaphor 77–8
Cronin, Richard 51(*n*6)
Cythna (*Revolt of Islam*) 17–18, 44, 51–2, 54, 55–6, 61

Dante 12, 88, 147, 155, 172
De Palacio, Jean L. 2, 45(*n*2)
dead flower imagery 87–8
deadlock 9, 19, 50–1, 95, 97, 114, 123, 132, 161, 187, 190
decenterment 21, 23, 37, 39, 41, 86, 123
   and Power 148, 149, 158–9
Defence of Poetry, A 5, 16, 41, 64, 175
   poetic composition in 154–5, 157, 165
   Power in 147–9, 151–2
   "religious" mode in 189
desire 10, 23–5, 28, 30–1, 55, 70, 95–7, 160, 185, 190
   and air/fluid imagery 31, 88–9
   competing 99
   for desire of other 147
   and power 147–8, 154
   as secret treasure 24, 28, 30, 38, 44, 46, 79, 86, 97
   Shelley's, of musical women 95, 96–7, 189
   and subjectivity 23
despotism 13, 15, 16
desublimation 25–6, 28, 40, 89–90, 106, 123, 130
Diderot, Denis 13
divine law 37–8, 76(*n*24), 107–8, 149, 173
Dolar, Mladen 18, 23–4, 25, 36–8, 41, 149
Don Juan (Mozart) 34
doubleness/doublespeak 118
Duffy, Cian 12, 53(*n*11)

Emily (*Epipsychidion*) 10, 17, 82–92
   as ideal 88, 90
   inspiration for 82–3
   and interpassivity 44
   and loss 90–1
   and music 88–90
   and poet 84–92, 188
England, political reform in 13–14
Epipsychidion 10–11, 17, 39, 82–92
   dead flower image 87–8
   Emily *see* Emily
   interpassivity in 43–4, 84
   jouissance in 88, 89–90
   masculine authority of 85, 87
   metaphors in 84–5, 86–7
   metonyms in 88–9
   mirror trope in 86, 90
   music in 83–84, 88–90, 91–2
   pre-castration fantasy in 90–1
   sex in 83, 88–9
   subjectivity in 92
   and Teresa Viviani 82–3, 86–7(*n*29)
Examiner reviews 33, 34
Excursion, The (Wordsworth) 13
extimacy 159

Faerie Queen (Spencer) 34–5
fantasy
   and desire *see* desire
   and poetry 39–41
   and power 40–1
   void in *see* void
fantasy, Shelley's poetic 9–11, 17, 21, 24–7, 187–190
   deadlocks in *see* deadlock
   and desire *see* desire
   desublimation in 25–6, 27, 28
   and female singers 33, 38–40, 95–9
   feminine expression in 25–7, 35, 38, 51–2, 65–7, 73–4
   flaws in 41–2, 52, 62–3, 67, 73–8, 92–3, 99, 142, 144, 175–6
      see also under Williams, Jane
   and interpassivity 43, 51–2, 63
   jouissance in *see jouissance*

metaphor and 86–87
poet as immortal 8, 51, 57, 69, 76, 78–9, 147, 181–2, 187
"Real" in *see* "Real"
subjectivity and 21, 23
and three elements of voice 27–31, 60
Feldman, Paula 100
feminine expression 63, 65–7, 187–8
as true expression 51–2
feminist perspective 6–7, 8
Fenner, Theodore 3, 32
Ferber, Michael 13, 14
Fischman, Susan 7, 8
fluid *see* air/fluid imagery
Fodor, Madame 34
Foss, Chris 5, 67(*n*15), 72(*n*23)
Fraistat, Neil 14, 15, 116, 119, 137
French Reunion festival 15
French Revolution 18, 37, 53
Fulford, Tim 53(*n*10), 112

Gallant, Christine 19(*n*59)
Gelpi, Barbara 5(*n*12), 10, 67(*n*15), 71, 76(*n*24), 87–8(*n*29)
gender politics 6, 7, 8, 149–50
Gisborne, John 110
Godwin, William 13
"Good-Night" 106–7
Goslee, Nancy 14(*n*46), 87(*n*29)
Great Marlow period 2, 4, 31–2
Greek poetry 155, 158
Grove, Harriet 19(*n*59)
guitar 88, 110, 114, 129–35, 137, 154, 175

harmony 12, 34, 84, 92, 130, 152–5, 164
cosmic/heavenly 44, 60, 135–6
illusion of 137
phonic 72
and union 83–4, 121
harp 1, 27, 47, 63, 65–6, 81, 100, 102–3, 152, 154, 167
Harrison, Margot 12, 13
Hazlitt, William 33–4, 35
Helen (*Rosalind and Helen*) 44, 63–7, 188
Hildebrand, William 67(*n*17)
historist accounts 11–17
Hitchener, Elizabeth 101
Hoagwood, Terence 11

Holmes, Richard 100
Homans, Margaret 6(*n*17)
Homer 158
Hubbell, Andrew J. 13
Hughes, D. J. 86(*n*29)
Hunt Circle 2, 14–17, 32
Hunt, Leigh 2, 31–2, 33, 109
"Hymn to Intellectual Beauty" 147, 149, 160, 164–70
jouissance in 164–5
loss/void in 1, 165–7, 169
Power-Beauty in 167–70, 189–90
use of "spells" in 170

identity 3, 7–8
immortality fantasy 8, 51, 57, 69, 76, 78–9, 147, 181–2, 187
incest 188
"Indian Girl's Song, The" 111, 137–8
interpassivity 38–9, 43–93, 176
in *Alastor* 45–51
and *jouissance* 44–7, 50–1, 56–7
and music 46–9
and poet–narrator relations 45–7, 45(*n*3), 48–9, 50–1
and Power 150
in *The Revolt of Islam* 43, 51–63
and subjectivity 43

Jesus 155
Jewish tradition 37, 41, 149
Johnson, Samuel 34–5
Jones, Miss 100
jouissance 18–19, 25, 27, 36–8, 40, 41, 133–4
and interpassivity 44–7, 50–1, 56–7
and logos 58, 63, 64, 66–7
Judeo-Christian tradition 37–8

Kant, Immanuel 12
Keach, William 14, 15–18, 51(*n*7), 45(*n*3), 95, 96, 97, 110–11, 116, 118, 148(*n*3)
Keats, John 138–9, 150
see also Adonais
Kierkegaard's triad 187–9
Kirchoff, Frederick 45(*n*3)
kissing *see* lips/kissing

Kramer, Lawrence 2–3

La Scala 32
Lacan, Jacques/Lacanian perspective 9–11, 17, 132
   "big Other" 36, 92, 95, 163
   on desire 23, 28, 30–1, 147
   jouissance 18–19, 25, 27, 36–7
   objet petit a 22, 23, 27, 28, 30, 31
   "Real" 6, 33, 40, 42, 97, 134, 136
   horror of 52
   subjectivity 21–3
language
   limits of 41, 96, 97
   metonyms for 163
   and power 15–18
language theory 12
Laon and Cythna 13, 15
Laon (*Revolt of Islam*) 1, 51–4
   and Cythna 51–2, 55–6, 58–9, 188
   and Hermit 54–5, 60–1
   language/metaphors of 52–5, 56
   and Laone 56–8
   passivity/male identity of 53–5, 56, 61
law 9, 36–8, 76(*n*24), 78, 119, 187, 188
   divine 37–8, 76(*n*24), 107–8, 149, 173
   and Other 25, 92, 95, 96, 127, 163, 172
Lawrence, David 15
Leask, Nigel 51–2(*n*7), 112(*n*34)
Leighton, Angela 86(*n*29)
light imagery 53, 88
likeness, search for 28
Lines written among the Euganean Hills 13
"Lines written in the Bay of Lerici" 119–22
Linkin, Harriet 45(*n*3)
lips/kissing 30, 49–50, 66, 78–9, 101–2, 104–5, 107–8, 124–6, 138, 179–80
literary establishment 182, 183
literature canon 8
logos 9, 25, 37, 41, 58
London, operas in 3, 14–15, 26, 32, 96
London Philharmonic Society 2
loss 90–1, 102–5, 107, 109, 114–22, 133, 135–40
   breath metaphor 104–5, 133
   music and 1, 88, 98
   and poetry 156–157
   see also void

love 2, 4, 28–31
   and antitype *see* antitype/prototype
   ice metaphor 31
   and poetry 155–56
   and thirst 28, 30, 34
"Love's Philosophy" 107–9
Lussier, Mark 14(*n*46)
lyre imagery 29, 30, 35, 49, 59, 149, 152–3, 154, 155

McDayter, Ghislaine 10–11, 17, 91(*n*33)
McGann, Jerome 109–10(*n*26)
"Magnetic Lady to Her Patient, The" 112–14
male poet 28, 35, 38, 39, 44
   and desire 99
   and feminine expression 51–2
   and narrator 45, 45–7, 45(*n*3), 48–9, 50–1
marginalia 15
marriage 110, 114, 120, 189–90
masculine poetic authority 8, 18, 21, 68, 76, 77, 85, 87, 99, 142–3, 145
   and fantasy flaw 52, 62–3
   and feminine expression 25, 26–7, 39
maternal breast 28, 30
McConnell, Frank 86(*n*29)
Mellor, Anne K. 6(*n*17)
mesmerism 53, 110, 112, 113, 118, 121
metonyms 12, 70, 74, 88–9, 113, 163, 168, 174, 183–4
Milton, John 12, 147, 185
mirror trope 22, 26, 28, 39, 44, 71, 74, 86, 107, 128–9
Molinari, Lori 14, 15
Monboddo, James 4
"Mont Blanc" 147, 148, 151, 160–4
   "horror of the Real" in 164
   jouissance in 161
   Mont Blanc/Arve symbols 147, 160, 162
Moore, Thomas 182, 183
Mozart, Wolfgang Amadeus 2, 3, 15, 16–17, 32
music
   and identity 3
   and interpassivity 46–9
   and intimacy 1

in Johnson's *Dictionary* 34–5
and *jouissance* 36–7
and loss/lacking 1, 88, 98
and Nature 29–30
and "Real" 98–9
as sexual expression 8–9, 57–9, 61–3
as structural/stylistic feature 4, 5–6
transcendent qualities of 2–3
transformative qualities of 3–4, 174–5
music and poetry 2, 3, 4–5
musical instruments 26–7, 49, 173, 174, 175
see also guitar; harp; lyre imagery
musical women 1–3, 9, 44, 173, 188–9
effect on Shelley 96
poems for 95–145
castration metaphor in 99, 104–5
fantasy flawed in 99
jouissance in 98–9
language devices in 96, 98, 103
limits of language in 96, 97
masculine/feminine in 98–9, 108–9
poet's vacancy in 99, 104–5
power struggle in 137
"Real" in 97–9, 104, 108, 145, 169
self-presence in 98, 103, 109, 137
Shelley's desire in 96–7
and Power 137, 169, 185
prima donnas 3, 26, 32–4
in Shelley's fantasy 95, 96–7
Shelley's love of 29, 31, 35, 95
Shelley's phonic manipulation of 96, 97–8

Naples 14
Narcissus/Echo myth 7
narrative problem 132, 148
Nature 1, 7, 25, 29–30, 49–50, 125, 150, 181
nesting bird image 116–17, 127
New Philology 12
Nicene Creed 12
Novello, Vincent 2, 32

object voice 44
object-relations theory 30(*n*32)
objet petit a 22, 23, 27, 28, 30, 31, 36, 38, 40, 41, 132
and interpassivity 48–9, 62
"Ode to Liberty" 14

"Ode to Naples" 14
"Ode to the West Wind" 16, 35, 41, 149, 160, 170–6
Autumn in 172, 173, 175
fantasy flaw in 175–6
formal structure of 172
music in 173, 174–5
Power/presence in 171
West Wind symbol 147, 171, 172, 173–5
"On a dead/Faded Violet" 87–88, 103–6
absence/loss in 104–5
"On Life" 5
"On Love" 1, 28–31, 34, 35, 58, 83, 92, 128, 185
"One Word is Too Often Profaned" 122–3
O'Neill, Michael 13, 33, 95, 96, 100, 110, 111(*n*33) 116, 118, 141
opera 3–4, 16–17, 32–3
prima donnas 3, 26, 32–4
and Shelley's style 4
opera buffa 4
other 43, 98–9, 133–4, 139
and desire 70, 97
female 44
Power as 147
and subjectivity 81, 86
text and *see* interpassivity
see also "big Other"
Ovid 7

Parker, Robert 99
Pasta, Madame 33
pathological situations 43
pathology 11, 19
Peacock, Thomas Love 2
Peterfreund, Stuart 12
Peterloo massacre 16
philology *see* New Philology
phonic fields 96
phonological analysis 5, 6
Plato 12, 154–5
poetic genius 8, 44
poetry
and absence/loss 156–7
bound to language 6–7, 10
and fantasy 39–41
and music 2, 3, 4–6

and poet's identity 3, 7–8, 9
and posterity 8
and Power 154–8
and reader 36, 150–1, 157–9, 175–6
transformative effect of 5
and voice/word 5–8, 21, 26, 36, 96–7
writer–text relationship *see*
  interpassivity
political reform 13–14, 17–18, 148(*n*3)
  conflict with language theory 15–16
  symbolized by women 18, 51–2(*n*7), 61
post-structuralism 12
Power 40–1, 147–85, 187–8, 189
  and air/fluid imagery 155–6, 168
  and Beauty 165–70, 176
  as "big Other" 151, 163
  and castration 148–9
  and composition process 154–5
  and decenterment 148, 149, 158–9
  and desire 147–8, 154
  despotism 13, 15, 16
  and gender 149–50
  and *jouissance* 148, 153
  and language 15–16
  and mind 161–3, 170
  and music/voice 148, 152–5
  poet as instrument of 149, 150–80
  and poet–reader relations 150–1,
    157–9, 175–6
  and poet's partnership fantasy 171–2
  shofar and 37, 41, 78, 149, 153
  and void/absence 148–9, 150, 151,
    152, 156–7, 159
  wind metaphor for 153
presence 170–1
prima donnas 3, 26, 32–4
  effect on Shelley 96
Prometheus Unbound 5, 38, 39, 67–82,
    188, 190
  Asia's transformation 75–6
  conch shell metaphor 77–8
  critical approaches to 67(*n*15)
  Demogorgon 74, 76, 81–2
  desire in 70, 74–6
  Earth
    and Moon 79–82
    and Prometheus 70–1, 78–9
  fantasy flawed in 67, 73–8, 190

feminine expression in 70
influence of Claire on 2
interpassivity in 43, 70, 72, 73–4
Ione/Panthea 71–5, 77–8, 79, 81
jouissance in 74–5, 79, 81
Jupiter's Phantasm 67–70, 72
language of 67, 72(*n*23), 74, 80
male authority in 68, 72, 74, 76, 77, 81
metonymy in 70, 74, 76
music in 73–4
Oceanides 72, 76
Panthea's dream 74–5, 76–7
phantasmic narrative of 67–8
poetry's transformative effect in 5
Power in 82
Prometheus's curse 68–9, 70–1
Prometheus's kiss 78–9
sexual imagery in 78–80
subjectivity in 68–9
voice in 70–2, 73, 76, 77, 82
prototype *see* antitype/prototype
proxy 69, 70
pseudo-historical account 4
psychoanalytic approach 8–11, 17–18, 97,
    116
pulsation 17

Queen Mab 15
Quillin, Jessica 3, 4, 10

Randel, Fred V. 13
"Real" 6, 33, 40, 42, 97, 134, 136
  communication 144
  horror of *see* void
  and music 98–9
    see also under musical women,
      poems for
rebirth imagery 126
Reiman, Donald 95(*n*1), 100, 110, 116,
    119, 137, 138–9, 141
"Remembrance" 111, 138–40
renunciation 106–7, 116–17, 123, 188
repetition 98
Reunion festival 15
Revolt of Islam, The 38
  Cythna *see* Cythna
  Hermit/male poet in 54–5, 60–1
  interpassivity in 43, 51–63

jouissance in 56–7
Laon *see* Laon
music/sexual expression in 57–9, 61–3
narrator/Woman in 61–3, 79
Tyrant in 59, 60
void in 62
women's power in 17–18
rhetoric 12
Richardson, Alan 51–2(*n*7)
Rime of the Ancient Mariner (Coleridge) 13
Rogers, Neville 2, 33(*n*45)
Romantic hero 13–14
Romantic poets 4
and culture of posterity 7–8, 35
and identity 6–8
Rosalind and Helen 38, 188
interpassivity in 43, 63–7
jouissance/logos in 63, 64, 66–7
Lionel's death 65
music in 65–7
poet/narrator in 63–4, 67
poetic authority in 63, 64, 65–6, 67
Rossini, Gioacchino 3
Rousseau, Jean Jacques 4
Roussetzki, Remy 13–14
Ruston, Sharon 14, 15

Salecl, Renata 26(*n*26), 106(*n*24)
Schapiro, Barbara 19(*n*59)
Schmid, Thomas 13, 14
"Scholar Gypsy, The" (Arnold) 13
Schulze, Earl 86(*n*29)
Schumann, Franz 11
Scott-Kilvert, Diana 100
seasonal cycles 138–9
secret treasure 23, 69, 71
desire as 24, 28, 30, 38, 44, 46, 79, 86, 97
poet's authority as 40–1, 50–1, 52, 147, 183, 185
and Power 150–1, 161
and void 56, 90, 122, 125, 129, 139
self-construction 6–7, 9
self-construction/-presence 6–7, 9, 38, 51, 57, 69, 76, 96, 111, 187
"Serpent is Shut Out from Paradise, The" 116–19

sexual expression in Shelley 8–10, 17, 18, 25, 37–42, 188, 189–90
and interpassivity 43–4, 51–2, 63, 66
in orchestral arrangement 27
in three elements of voice 27–31
in women's singing 27, 29
Shelley, Mary 2, 31–2, 33, 83, 101, 117, 189
and Jane Williams 120, 123–4
marriage 110, 114, 120
and Sophia Stacey 100
Shelley, Percy Bysshe
marriage 110, 114, 120
and mesmerism *see* mesmerism
musical life of 2–3, 14–15, 31–3, 100
and other poets 13
and posterity 8
scholarship review 1–19
and vitality debate 15
Shelley, William (son) 109
Sheridan, Alan 97
shofar 37, 41, 78, 149, 153, 173–4
Sicily 14
slave narratives 12–13
somatic movement/effect 1, 26, 40, 58–9, 93, 96, 98–9, 101, 111–12, 128
Southey, Robert 18, 51(*n*7)
Spain 14
Stacey, Sophia 29, 40, 87, 92, 95, 96, 99–109
poems to
erotic imagery in 101, 105–6, 107–9
"Good-Night" 106–7
harp-playing in 103
jouissance in 102–3, 105, 106
loss in 102–3, 104–5, 107, 109, 137
"Love's Philosophy" 107–9
masculine/feminine in 108–9
music in 100–1, 102
"On a dead/Faded Violet" 103–6
poet's vacancy in 104–5
renunciation in 106–7
rhythmic devices in 103, 105, 109
"Time Long Past" 109
"To—(I fear thy kisses, gentle maiden')" 105–6

"To Sophia" 102–3
  Shelley's relationship with 100–1
Steinman, Lisa 45(*n*3)
Stephens, Miss 34
Stouffer, Andrew M. 14(*n*46)
stringed instruments 26–7, 49, 175
subjectivity 21–3, 68–9, 81, 176
  Cartesian 22
  and desire 23
  and interpassivity 43, 48, 63, 84
  jouissance and 36–7
  and love 30
  and voice 22–3
sublime 12
Swellfoot the Tyrant 14
synesthesia *see* metonyms

Tempest, The (Shakespeare) 130
Tetreault, Ronald 3–4, 32, 67(*n*15), 141
text 84
  and Prometheus's curse 69
textual other 43
thirst 28, 30, 34
Thurston, Norman 45(*n*3)
"To—('I fear thy kisses, gentle maiden')" 105–6
"To Constantia" 3, 33, 141–5
  breath in 143
  fantasy flaw in 142
  formal structure of 143
  jouissance in 141–3
  poet's authority in 142–3, 145
  power of music in 143–4
  pre–castration fantasy in 142, 144
  "real" communication in 144
  subjectivity in 143, 145
  word–voice in 142–3
"To Jane. The Invitation" 123–6
"To Jane. 'The keen stars were twinkling'" 133–7
"To Jane. The Recollection" 123–4, 126–9
"To a Skylark" 41, 149, 176–80
  jouissance in 178–9
  metaphor for poet in 178, 179–80
  voice/presence in 176
  void in 177, 178, 180
"To Sophia" 102–3
tragedy, Elizabethan 13–14
transitivity 3
travel writing 12
typesetting 15

Ulmer, William 35–6(*n*51), 159

"veiled maid" 44, 46
Villa Magni 110
vitality debate 15
Viviani, Emilia (Teresa) 82–3, 86–7(*n*29), 95(*n*1), 101
vocal authority 6–7, 8, 26
  see also masculine poetic authority
voice 5–8
  and divine law 37–8
  elusiveness of 24–5
  and fantasy 23–5, 187
  and *jouissance* 36–7
  management 6–7
  poet's 45
  and string music 27–8, 29
  subject formation and 21–42
  three elements of 27–31, 60, 77, 88–9, 162
  and void 23–4, 26, 88–9
  women's 25, 26, 27–8
  women's singing *see* musical women
  and word 5–8, 21, 25–7, 36, 41–2, 96–7, 142–3, 190
    see also under Williams, Jane, Shelley's poems to
void 23–4, 26, 28, 36, 39–41, 52, 92, 99, 125–6, 127, 135–6, 181
  and air/fluid imagery 62, 115, 121–2, 124–5, 133
  and interpassivity 43–4, 49, 62, 78, 88–9
  and power 148–9
  and secret treasure 56, 90, 122, 125, 129, 139
  see also under "Hymn to Intellectual Beauty"; "To a Skylark"

Wasserman, Earl 45(*n*3)
water metaphor 124–6, 127, 129, 133
West Wind symbol 147, 171
Western metaphysical tradition 24, 26, 134–5

"When the Lamp is Shattered" 114–16, 117
White, Newman Ivey 100–1
Williams, Edward 111, 116–17, 120, 130, 189
Williams, Jane 29
   and Mary Shelley 120, 123–4
   and mesmerism 110, 112, 113, 118, 121
   musical abitities of 110, 129–30
   Shelley's poems to 3, 6, 11, 17, 40, 88, 92, 95–6, 98, 101, 109–40
      air/fluid imagery in 137–8
      castration in 114–15, 119, 120, 132, 137, 138
      enchantment in 111, 112, 114, 124
      fantasy flawed in 114, 123, 125–6, 129
      "Indian Girl's Song" 111, 137–8
      Jane unattainable in 116–19, 122–3, 126
      Jane's breath in 127–9
      Jane's voice in 111, 112–13, 120–1, 130–1, 140
      jouissance in 116, 123, 125, 131
      language of 122–3, 135, 139, 140
      "Lines written in the Bay of Lerici" 119–22
      loss/absence in 114–19, 120–2, 137–40
      "Magnetic Lady to Her Patient" 112–14
      mirror/echo in 124, 125–6, 128–9
      nesting bird image 116–17
      "One Word is Too Often Profaned" 122–3
      "Real" in 111–12, 113, 123, 128, 133, 138
      "Remembrance" 111, 138–40
      seasonal cycles in 138–9
      self–presence in 111, 112, 114, 130
      separation/union in 113–14, 124–9
      "Serpent is Shut Out from Paradise, The" 116–19
      "To Jane. The Invitation" 123–6
      "To Jane. 'The keen stars were twinkling'" 133–7
      "To Jane. The Recollection" 123–4, 126–9
      voice/word in 111, 116, 120–1, 124–5, 129–31, 134–5, 137, 142–3
      "When the Lamp is Shattered" 114–16, 117
      "With a Guitar. To Jane" 88, 129–37
   Shelley's relationship with 110, 123–4
Wilson, Eric Glenn 14(*n*46)
wind instruments 26–7, 173, 174
wind metaphor 153, 156, 172
"With a Guitar. To Jane" 88, 129–37
   celestial imagery of 134–5, 136–7
   erotic expression in 133
   guitar image in 130–1, 132–3, 134–5
   Jane's voice overpowering in 135, 136–7
   jouissance in 133
   loss/absence in 133, 135–6
   narrative deadlock in 132
   phonic devices in 135
   "Real" in 133–4
   subjectivity in 132
   word-voice-music in 129–31, 134–5
Wolfson, Susan 5–6, 17, 95–6, 98, 110, 111, 116, 118, 137
Wollstonecraft, Mary 18, 51(*n*7),
women
   and interpassivity 43–4
   and male poet 39–40, 44–6
   and music *see* musical women
   and power 7, 17–18, 25, 137, 169, 185
   slave narratives 12–13
   symbolise political reform 18, 51–2(*n*7), 61
   unattainable 116–19, 122–3, 126, 188
Wood, Gillen D'Arcy 14–15, 16–17, 26(*n*27)
word *see* logos; *and see under* voice
Wordsworth, William 13, 45(*n*3)
writer–text relationship 43–4, 50–1
Wroe, Ann 83, 96, 140–1

Zizek, Slavoj 9, 11, 15, 18–19, 70, 85, 98–9, 105, 106, 151, 165, 189, 190
   on desire 154
   on fantasy 23, 24, 25, 39, 41–2, 187
   on narrative 132
   on "Real" 133–4

For Product Safety Concerns and Information please contact our EU
representative GPSR@taylorandfrancis.com
Taylor & Francis Verlag GmbH, Kaufingerstraße 24, 80331 München, Germany

www.ingramcontent.com/pod-product-compliance
Lightning Source LLC
Chambersburg PA
CBHW052340230426
43664CB00041B/2570